127 Reasons Why You Are An Idiot

And how to be less...idiotic

YANN SOMOU

a moany prick of an author

127 Reasons Why You Are An Idiot / Yann Somou - 1st ed.

Dedication

For my friends, family and all the world's idiots who provide limitless inspiration on a daily fucking basis

Contents

Introduction

First of all, it's worth remembering that '127 Reasons Why You Are An Idiot' is just one person's opinion. It's a collection of one hundred and twenty-seven things that bother me, and potentially me alone. So, there is no need to take whatever you read to heart; since when do you give a shit about what some anonymous prick has written… *cough* social media comments *cough*

Having said that, everyone and I mean *everyone*, even the most stalwart defenders of common courtesy and social niceties will recognise themselves in at least one or two of these chapters – which is kind of the point. We are all fallible, we all have flaws, we are all human. Seeing something you do regularly, written down and shamed, in black and white, is meant to be a reminder of that fact. The important thing is being cognisant of your inadequacies and working to eradi-cate them day by day.

If you feel attacked at any point while reading this book – good. Kudos to you my friend, it appears that you might be one of the few who possess some semblance of self-awareness. If, on the other hand, you finish the last page thinking that none of the rants within applies to you, that's incredible news. We've finally stumbled upon the non-existent perfect person! Are you the Messiah we've all been waiting for? Or are you simply lying to yourself? Maybe even blissfully unaware of the twat that other people see in you?

I can only hope that you find it within yourself to read '127 Reasons Why You Are An Idiot' in the manner with which it was written. There is a lot of swearing and, yes, it's pretty harsh in places. But it is mostly written in jest, poking fun at every single one of us, in a way that hopefully allows you to get your self-deprecation on.

However, I didn't write this book just so you could chuckle and pass on certain chapters to the worst offenders. By all means, be entertained. But, there *is* a serious element to the book and an underlying message that will hopefully become clear.

The world we live in is going to shit. Yes, our actual physical planet is fucked, whether it be through climate change, overpopulation, deforestation, pollution, overuse of natural resources, overfishing, de-sertification, fresh water scarcity, soil erosion, or a thousand and one other environmentally catastrophic problems. But, I'm more focused on the deteriora-tion of the community aspect of our world. There is no doubt that we are gradually losing touch with our humanity.

Technology is one of the biggest culprits. We are starting to rely on our devices more than our social support networks. We expect most things to be resolved at the click of a button. More time spent around technology, instead of cultivating our real-life relationships, is making us generally less intelligent, less empathetic, less sympathetic and less caring.

Another big culprit is capitalism. Capitalism means that companies value profit over everything, even peo-ple. In such a system, it's no surprise that money has become the most important thing. People do not neces-sarily keep a company going, revenue does. If a compa-ny could generate revenue without people, it wouldn't hesitate. This is all well and good if it's just the attitude of a non-living legal entity. But this thought process has filtered down to us human beings. We have been indoctrinated to believe that money is the be-all and end-all. That life is about getting more and more and more of it. That we are constantly in direct com-petition with each other. Consequently, we have become greedy, we vote for policies that benefit our monetary interests instead of our collective societal well-being and, again, we are caring less about each other.

Our losing touch with humanity isn't easy to notice. It is happening so slowly that it's almost imperceptible. But it is happening. And one way in which it is discernible is in our daily interactions. How we treat others in the street, how we talk to each other, how we treat our friends, how we act in certain situations. Manners are being thrown out of the window. Common courtesy is becoming uncommon. We're starting to ignore the unwritten rules that hold society together. We've stopped doing the small things for each other that used to make daily life a bit more bearable.

I, for one, have accepted this state of affairs for what it is. Technology, capitalism, how far our humanity has slipped – it's already happened, and there's nothing we can do about the past. But that doesn't mean we have to accept it as our future. '127 Reasons Why You Are An Idiot' is an attempt on my part to bring us back to basics, to realise all the little ways in which we have started to not give a shit about each other. If we can all make this first step, while recti-fying the way we act around each other, thinking kind-ness and compassion first, then maybe, just maybe, we can build a future where our humanity remains intact. Because one thing is for sure – without our humanity, there is no way in hell we can possibly work together effectively, for long enough, with enough compassion and without greed, to solve any of the big, calami-tous, earth-shattering issues that are already wiping their feet on our collective doormat.

In any case, I've been droning on for quite a bit now. A little secret: the original title of the book was 'don't be stupid, idiot' – fairly self-explanatory advice. You could probably just read that and become a slightly better, more caring person as a result. At least for the ten minutes that follow – I know how forgetful a wanker you can be.

Manners & common courtesy

Holding the door open

When polite people open a swinging door, they automatically look behind to see if someone is close to following them in. If so, they stand there and hold the door open for them. This is an example of a wonderful thing called common courtesy and is just one of the many little things that make for a civilised world.

Impolite wankers like you, on the other hand, are more than happy to open a door, walk straight through it and let it swing shut in the face of the person following you in.

People could be forgiven for thinking that maybe you just aren't aware that holding the door open for people is the right thing to do. And to be fair, this would be plausible, because you are that stupid.

However, most of the time you *do* look behind, yet let the door go anyway! The mere fact that you check behind you proves that you do, in fact, know that you should hold the door open if someone is approaching. Why would you check otherwise? For some reason though, you just can't bring yourself to be nice. Almost as if you feel embarrassed to be doing the right thing. Or maybe you look at the person and decide they aren't worth it. Maybe it's an old lady, maybe it's someone not that good-looking. Or perhaps you feel you just don't have the time to wait.

Whatever the reason, you don't realise what you've done to that person. You've essentially just told them that you couldn't give a flying shit about them. And I'm not saying you *should* care about this stranger, you don't know them, nor do you owe them anything in particular. But you have an obligation to your fellow humans to do the little things that make life bearable, like holding the door open for them. That's why common courtesy is a fucking thing.

While we're at it, it's pretty much universally understood that, when someone holds a door open for you, you express gratitude. We're not asking for a fucking wrapped gift. A simple, "Thank you", or, "Cheers, mate", would suffice. Alas, you are apparently not privy to this universal understanding. It would appear that saying thank you to someone who does something nice for you is just too much to bear. It's beyond a joke how often I've seen you walk straight through a door, that a polite person has held open for you, without even a glance in their direction, let alone any appreciation. And then when they tut or loudly say, "HOW ABOUT A THANK YOU!?", you look back at them all bewildered and sheepish as if you don't understand what they've just said and why they said it. You know full well why you arsehole.

Do you have some kind of deluded assumption that it's that person's job to hold the door open for you or something? Are you that stupid and unaware of your surroundings that you didn't even realise someone held the door for you? Or is it that you just genuinely don't appreciate the kind act, your thought process being that you never asked them to do it, so you consider this person to be a complete mug, knowing full well you would never do the same for them?

In any case, what an entitled prick you are. Your parents obviously didn't raise you right, that's the sad truth. Common courtesy, good deeds, spreading a little niceness, these things are not embarrassing. You are never too busy to hold a door open for someone, no matter what they look like. And you are never too big or important to thank people for it. As far as the rest of us are concerned, you're a menace to society and a waste of fucking air.

- [Pointless] Exercise -

The next time you open a door and someone is approaching behind you, fucking stand there and hold it for them - humble yourself and do the right thing for once. It costs you nothing, you will spread a little positivity in the world and you'll feel good about it when they say thank you. I promise your street cred won't be harmed, you muppet. While we're at it, let's also practise what you should do when someone holds a door open for you in the future. Say, "Thank you". Say it with me. "Thank you". Once more. "Thank you". Wasn't that easy? Now let's practise for when someone doesn't hold the door for you. Say, "Fucking prick". With a bit more gusto, come on. "Fucking priiiiick!!!" Well done. Idiot.

Know an idiot who needs to read this chapter?

- Scan the QR code
- Click the link
- Send it their way!

Continuously interrupting

There are three types of people in the world. Those who don't like speaking. Those who like to have proper conversations - you know, those things where one person listens while the other speaks, then vice versa. And then there's you - the wanker who thinks that a conversation consists solely of you giving your opinion, then another one, and another one, without leaving any space for the other person to chime in.

What I will say is at least you don't discriminate when it comes to setting - you'll interrupt people wherever you can. Down the pub. In business meetings during presentations, even after the presenter has specifically asked for everyone to please save questions for the end. I've even seen you ask people questions and interrupt to answer them yourself!

The Dalai Lama once said: "When you talk, you are only repeating what you already know. But if you listen, you may learn something new".

This quote really gets to the crux of what conversations should be about. We give our opinion on a particular topic, then someone else gives their own point of view while we listen, affording us the opportunity to think about the topic from a different perspective. It's impossible to benefit from a conversation in which only we are speaking. Logically, we literally can *only* repeat what we already know. We can only profit from a conversation and learn something new if we are listening to others, who may or may not know something that we don't.

The point of a conversation is *not* to constantly interrupt with your own opinion. You are supposed to let the other person speak. And you are supposed to actually listen to them. Yes, even if they're talking shit.

Knowing all of this, why do you have such an issue with not listening to your conversation partners? Why do you always feel the need to jump in and prevent them from finishing their points? In my experience, the answer is always one of the following.

1 – You don't even realise you constantly interrupt. You actually enjoy talking. You just love the sound of your own voice. You think that you're taking on an unnecessary role of keeping the conversation dynamic and flowing. Fine. But how do you not see the eyeballs rolling when you do it?! Do you not see people constantly breaking eye contact, fed up with the constant barrage that is your voice? Read the bloody room, mate.

From time to time, people point it out and you act shocked. "Like OMG, that's not me!?" Well, it is you. You're the only one who's been speaking for the last fucking three hours, in what is supposed to be a conversation, not a shit lecture.

The next conversation you have after you've been called out is pretty hilarious. As usual, it takes you less than a minute to start cutting off the speaker. The difference now though is that you're suddenly, magically aware of the rolling eyeballs. So you pipe down. However, when someone else then takes over, it's all you can do to refrain from jumping in. You're literally itching to say your piece. Putting your hand over your mouth to shut yourself up. Incessantly opening your mouth like a fish to indicate you've got something to say. Waving your hands about with a complete lack of self-control. Embarrassing, but at least you're trying.

2 – You actually believe your opinion is always more valid than whoever is speaking. You genuinely think that what you have to say is more important.

Don't get me wrong, sometimes it's true. There are a lot of muppets in the world, you're bound to have more valid opinions than one, max two, of them.

The problem is that you think your opinion and what you have to say *always* takes precedence. Any logical person knows that can't possibly be the case. Nevertheless, you cannot help it, because you hold yourself in way too high regard. You're a twat who thinks they're better than the rest of us. You feel there is no point wasting time, waiting for others to finish their point, because what you have lined up will inevitably be more valuable to the conversation.

3 – You interrupt people as a sign of strength. You want them to feel inferior to you. Interrupting people is an alpha tactic that you employ, to simultaneously take control over the discourse and portray your lack of interest in the original speaker's opinion. The problem here is, while you think you've succeeded in your bully's mission, no one is thinking, "What a powerful person". They're simply thinking, "Fuck this, let the prick speak, I can't be bothered". No wonder everyone at work hates your guts and you've got no mates.

Whatever the reason for your constant interruptions, one thing seems certain. You obviously prefer the alternate version of the Dalai Lama's quote: "When you listen, I am talking. But when you talk, I also talk." What a wanker.

– [Pointless] Exercise –

If you really want to better yourself and stop interrupting people, why not appoint a designated slapper? Get your mind out of the gutter, you dirty bastard, we're not talking about a scantily clad female. Rather a specific person who has the power to slap you in the face every time you interrupt someone. Your mates and colleagues will fucking love this – they'll be chomping at the bit for the extra responsibility. Idiot.

Know an idiot who needs to read this chapter?

- Scan the QR code
- Click the link
- Send it their way!

Queue cutting

Cutting shapes? Dance, my friend.

Cutting remarks? Get harsh with it.

Cutting queues? Fuck right off.

Oi! Oiiii! Dickhead who can't wait for anything! Yes, you! Do you see that mysterious line of people apparently waiting for something? Do you know what it's called? Of course you do, it's a fucking queue! It's common knowledge that you're supposed to join the end of it and wait for whatever it is you're waiting for, just like everyone else.

So, what the fuck makes you think you can just jump in at the middle, or worse still, brazenly walk all the way to the front?

Is it that you simply don't give a shit about the people in the queue or their time? Maybe you just don't want to wait? Well, I've got news for you wank-stain, no one wants to wait. But we do it because it's fair – you get what you're waiting for in order of when you arrived. I don't think I can make it any fucking simpler. I mean, when kids run to the front of a queue because they don't know any better, parents say, "Don't do that, there's a queue!" Most people take that learning experience with them as they become adults. You, however, seem to have forgotten that particular lesson.

I wonder whether you just don't think *you* should need to wait in line. Maybe you think you're better than everyone else in the queue. Maybe you think that we're all mugs for waiting. One thing's for sure, I can't wait for you to try explaining that to the one nutter in the queue who will happily punch your fucking lights out.

At the end of the day, it's the pure arrogance of cutting queues that irks. You're trying to get away with not doing something that no one wants to do, but everyone does anyway. Most people see a queue, accept it and go to the back of the line. But not you. You've got the gall to try and skip it altogether. It'd be fine if you saw the queue, thought "Fuck that", and then went elsewhere. Instead, you think "Fuck that", and then try to further mess with other people's valuable time.

Does this scene sound familiar, knobhead? There's a huge queue at the poorly managed Asda self-checkout, as fucking usual. You bypass the whole thing and walk straight up to a checkout machine, pretending you somehow haven't seen the monstrosity going all the way up to the fucking bakery section at the back of the shop. You hope that no one says anything. When someone tells you there is a queue, you act all shocked and apologetic. Are you really trying to tell us that you didn't see this one hundred and forty-eight person long queue? Piss off, you're not fooling anyone, you twat. To the back of the line with you.

Sometimes you decide not to respond to those who challenge your imaginary right to cut the queue. You'll simply ignore them, like the prick you are. We have a trick for that though, one you are probably already familiar with. We'll keep challenging you, keep pointing you out and embarrassing you. After a few rounds, inevitably, you won't be able to take the shame of it anymore. Eventually, you'll turn around, point at yourself and say "Me?" Yes, mate. Who do you think we're talking to? You're the only one around here who just did something wrong, you prat. Then you'll walk sheepishly to the end of the line, accompanied by jeers and cheers reminiscent of getting kicked out of a nightclub queue.

Other times you stay in the line after cutting in no matter what, deflecting all awkwardness like water off a duck's back. That's where we just have to chuck you the fuck out. Or at least slowly edge you out with consistent little shoulder barges. Physical passive aggression is the key in this situation.

The worst example of queue cutting, however, is using fast-track tickets at amusement parks. This is probably your queue-cutting wet dream, considering no one really has the right to admonish you. Here, you've actually paid for the queue-cutting privilege. The rest of us just have to stand there, armpit to armpit in the baking sun, watching you walk straight past us in a separate line, without a care in the world. These tickets are an evil invention; they go against all the values we hold dear in a courteous society and should be banned outright. No one should get away with not having to queue, I don't care how much of an embarrassment-proof arsehole you are or how much money you have.

- [Pointless] Exercise -

The next time you see a queue, feel free to think, "Fuck that", and then actually fuck off. Do not try to cut the queue. The mere contemplation of it makes you a total twat. Otherwise, prepare for several hundred passive-aggressive shoulder barges within the next two minutes. No football referee is going to save your pussy arse from these broad motherfuckers. Idiot.

Know an idiot who needs to read this chapter?

- Scan the QR code
- Click the link
- Send it their way!

Manspreading

You've got some fucking balls. Great big boulders sitting between your legs. At least, I'm assuming you do. That's the only reason I can think of that would explain your exaggerated manspreading and apparent need to take up so much space while sitting down.

But you don't, do you? Men generally do not have balls so big that they require the leg space of three people. Yes, there are some blokes with abnormally gigantic bollocks. But these blokes are few and far between, and you're probably not one of them.

So the question remains, why do you feel the need to spread your legs like this, especially on public transport?

Maybe you just really want to display your bulge as prominently as possible, without being arrested? If that was the case, it's a damn shame your bulge is the opposite of impressive. I'd actually be ashamed to showcase something so, well, small.

Maybe you think it makes you look hard – some kind of gangster, alpha bullshit? I refer you again to the lack of bulge, which kind of destroys that facade.

Maybe you are crying out for some human contact in your life, just trying to touch the people next to you? Well, in that case, what you need is a proper, romantic relationship – not the touch of some annoyed rando's legs, you muppet.

No, the real reason is you are an arsehole with no consideration for anyone else. It is, admittedly, much more comfortable to sit like this, with your legs spread out. There is even physiological evidence to show that it can be difficult for some men to sit straight-legged. But, if everyone spread their legs for maximum comfort, there'd be a bloody riot every day on the tube. Sometimes you have to forego comfort for the satisfaction of being a considerate person.

In truth, nothing gives you the right to spread your legs so wide. Causing major discomfort to those on either side of you, while everyone else sits with straight legs, is just not fair – even if it is a little more difficult for you to do. Unfortunately, you just don't give a shit. If it really was so difficult to sit straight-legged and you had at least one considerate bone in your body, you'd remain standing instead. But you don't. *You* want to be comfortable, so you *make* yourself comfortable. Fuck everyone else.

- [Pointless] Exercise -

You're obviously a knobhead, so I don't hold much hope that you'll change your behaviour when it comes to manspreading. So instead, here's some advice for those who find themselves having to deal with you. You have knees, use them; this might well be the true reason why God gave them to you. You need to dig the side of your knees into the manspreader's legs, pushing just enough to cause him a little pain. But not so much that he'll cause a scene and start moaning like a little bitch. When he whips his head round to look at you in astonishment that you would dare to try to regain your space, just smile at him like nothing's happening. Show no exertion. It will drive him nuts. He'll push back for a bit, sure. But be stubborn. Do not give up. Continue pushing. I guarantee he isn't used to this – normally people just accept the manspreading. The standoff will end with him finally realising that it's actually more comfortable to sit properly than deal with this nutter. You will regain your space. Idiot.

Know an idiot who needs to read this chapter?

- Scan the QR code
- Click the link
- Send it their way!

Responding to, "How are you?"

What do you think people mean when they ask, "How are you?", "How are you doing?" or "How's it going?". As those who have an ounce of social awareness are all mostly aware, the answer is very much dependent on the context and who is asking.

For instance, when your mum asks you how you are, she probably actually wants to know how you are. She cares about you and is genuinely interested and invested in your wellbeing. Here, you can drone on about your current first-world predicaments to your heart's content. The same goes for family, good friends, in fact anyone with whom you share a genuine, caring relationship with a bit of depth.

In the context above, you are free, if not expected, to answer, "How are you?", with the truth of how you are. It's good for your mental health and it's normally safe to open up to these people.

You in particular, however, seem to think the same applies when *anyone* asks, "How are you?". I hate to break it to you, you gullible muppet, but not everyone cares about you. Not everyone is a nice person, happy to talk about your feelings. People, in general, aren't so friendly that they'd ask this question to relative strangers if they expected an outpouring of truth in response. It's unfortunate, but the world is what it is and people are who they are.

This leads us perfectly to another context for this type of question. Nowhere is there a better example of it being asked, and the answer expected to be short and sweet, than the workplace. When your boss arrives in the morning and asks how everyone is doing, do you hear anyone giving them their life story? Do you hear anyone mentioning their problems and feelings? No. Why? Because the workplace is for work. It's why bereavement leave is a thing. When your colleague asks you how it's going, they are neither expecting nor asking for you to break down and commence a communal deep dive into your fucked up state of mind.

The question, “How are you”, in certain contexts like work, is a courtesy. A social norm if you will. It’s just what people say. It’s a precursor to getting down to the business of working. The workplace is not a safe space, no matter what your company says to the contrary. Much more often than not, your colleagues are not your true friends. Your boss doesn’t truly care about you or your personal problems. It’s not the place to talk freely.

But you just don’t get this. I’ve seen people like you, being asked how you are at 8 AM during the morning coffee meeting, and then proceeding to monologue for twenty-five minutes about all of your personal issues, none of which are at all related to work. No one else gets a chance to speak during that time and the meeting only lasts half an hour!! Even worse, people have no idea how to respond, because they don’t know you well enough to comment or give proper advice. So there’s an inevitable awkward silence, after which everyone just moves on to talk business, leaving you feeling a little naked for saying how you actually felt, yet getting zilch in return.

Maybe it’s better explained in this way: if you were introduced to someone for the first time and they asked you how it’s going, would you start opening up to them about your issues and how you actually felt? When you go to a shop and the till operator asks you how your day is today, would you take that as an invitation to reveal everything that you’re currently worried about? No, of course bloody not. They’d think you were a right weirdo. The correct answer to, “How are you?”, “How are you doing?” or “How’s it going?”, in almost every case other than when you’re talking to your mum or your close friends, is any variation of, “Not too bad, how are you?”. Nothing more, nothing less.

- [Pointless] Exercise -

Stop thinking solely about the words within this question. Also, consider the context in which the question is asked. More often than not, it is asked with the best of intentions but is really just a courtesy. Not everyone is prepared and willing to receive your barrage of woes and worries. If your family and friends ask how you are, that's the time to be honest! It might feel bizarre to open up to them after telling colleagues and everyone else that you're "not too bad". But this is your chance for some free therapy and you most definitely should take it. We all need to talk things through and let our emotions out sometimes, but we need to make sure to do it at the right times. Idiot.

Know an idiot who needs to read this chapter?

- Scan the QR code
- Click the link
- Send it their way!

Littering

There is nothing worse than watching someone throw rubbish on the floor. For nice people, it's their horrible, daily reminder that yes, wankers like you exist and are wanky enough to just lazily throw their shit wherever they want.

I'm not even coming at this from an environmental, let's save the world, green warrior perspective. I'm coming at it from an it's fucking disgusting perspective. It's like, do you think bins are on the streets for a fucking laugh or something? What possesses you to care so little about the environment you live in, that you would actively contribute to it looking shitter?

What is so frustrating is that you know it's wrong. It's pretty bloody obvious from that guilty look around to see if anyone is watching, prior to slyly dropping the rubbish. But unfortunately, that guilt is never enough to stop you from fucking doing it anyway.

Other times, you couldn't give a shit who sees you. You let your rubbish fall to the floor as soon as you've finished with it, without a care in the world.

Quite simply, you have been brought up wrong. No doubt in my mind. No self-respecting parent would bring up their kids to just throw rubbish to the floor. But shit parenting is no excuse for shit behaviour.

I've even seen you throw rubbish at a bin from a distance, hoping to make the shot. You go, "Oooooooooohh" with your mates if it was close, but then you laugh and walk away! What the fuck, mate!! I'm all good with you shooting your shot, but go pick the fucking thing up if you miss. You are obviously aware that's where the rubbish is supposed to go!

The respect people would have for you if you could humble yourself and retrieve your litter… You might think your mates think it's cool to litter, but to "debase" yourself in front of them and show a bit of moral fortitude goes much further, trust me.

Personally, I think it all comes down to one of two things.

Sometimes it's an issue of convenience. When there are no bins around, you feel guilty about dropping litter to the floor, but not guilty enough to hold onto it until you find one. This is bad enough.

But most of the time, you really are stupid enough to think that littering makes you look hard. You think that other people actually respect you for your lack of fucks to give. Well, I've got news for you. They don't. All you're doing is reaffirming the notion that you're a twat who doesn't deserve nice things. You're a rebel, rebelling against fuck all. It might seem a harsh conclusion to form based on just throwing rubbish to the floor but, in my opinion, you're a no one with no morals.

- [Pointless] Exercise -

Just because there's no bin in sight, that doesn't mean it's fair game to throw your rubbish on the floor then blame it on the council for not providing enough bins. Hold onto it until you do find one, you lazy prick. As I've said many, many times, you need to think: "What if everyone did what I am doing". If everyone littered and refused to use bins, what do you think the world would look like? Take London for example, there are millions of people milling about every day. If everyone threw their rubbish on the floor, the streets would be an absolute fucking mess, overflowing with shit everywhere. It wouldn't be a nice place to walk about, would it? And you would probably be the first to moan about how grim the place looked, you moany bitch. So take your rubbish and throw it in the fucking bin. Better still, stick it up your arse. Even better still, piss off and take a dip in the Great Pacific Garbage Patch, like the grimy prick you are. Idiot.

Know an idiot who needs to read this chapter?

- Scan the QR code
- Click the link
- Send it their way!

Using initiative

It does strike me sometimes how you seem so incapable of using that blobby thing, hidden beneath your thick skull.

Now, this inability to use your noggin presents itself in a wide array of situations. But when it comes to you needing to use your own initiative, it really does become unavoidably fucking clear.

For some reason, as soon as you are asked to think for yourself or delve one step further down a logical thought process without being led, your brain turns to complete and utter, shitty mush. Maybe that is actually what happens? I don't know, I'm not a doctor.

I doubt it though. You're just a lazy bastard, aren't you? If you aren't spoon-fed everything, told exactly what to think, what to do next, step by step, then you just won't do it. God forbid you ever take action based on the fact that it's the next obvious, logical step, and not just because someone told you to. You're basically still a child.

The biggest issue I have with this is that it portrays a lack of consideration on your part for your fellow human, for what might make their experience that little bit better. You seem unable to think ahead, even for the sake of common decency.

Let's throw some examples at you - see if any of them stick in that otherwise useless head of yours.

- When the bin is full - decent people would empty it and insert a new bin bag. But no, not you. You just balance more rubbish on top.
- When there is washing up to be done in the sink - decent people would add their own washing up to the pile and then proceed to actually do the washing up, making those utensils fucking shine. But no, not you. You just pile on more and more plates without a second thought.

- When you make dinner for yourself and someone else – decent people bring the food in *with* the required cutlery, bearing in mind it's only you and one other person. But no, not you. You can't make that quantum leap of thought and work out that two sets of cutlery might be needed.
- And my personal favourite: when someone at home says, "Put the kettle on would you" – decent people would take that to mean, "You couldn't make me a cup of tea could you?". But no, not you. You will walk into the kitchen, turn on the kettle, normally without even checking to see if there's enough water, then come and sit straight back down. I mean, what the fuck, mate. Make the fucking tea, you lazy prick!!

Do any of those remind you of someone? Yeah, I thought so. And don't you dare temper your apology with the bullshit excuse that you just don't think. That's not an excuse as a fucking adult, mate. You don't think because you can't be *bothered* to think. Just because no one tells you precisely what you need to do, doesn't mean that you don't need to do it.

We're all painfully aware that you think about yourself, and yourself only. You have obviously never trained that muscle in your brain that allows you to use your initiative, to think through what more you *could* do to help other people or to consider what your next step *should* be in any given situation. But know this, your lack of initiative is really fucking irritating. It's the absolute height of laziness and will bite you in the arse at some point.

- [Pointless] Exercise -

Start going about your daily life thinking about what else you could possibly do. Maybe there's something you can do to make something easier for the next person. Maybe there's something you can do just so that someone else doesn't have to. Maybe there's something you can do that your boss or parents forgot to ask you to do, but they assumed/hoped that you would have the wherewithal to realise it needs to get done anyway. When someone says, "Can you pass the salt?", give them the fucking pepper too. When someone says, "Have you got a pen?", also bring them some fucking paper. Thinking they've probably already got paper is a twatty excuse - use your initiative and bring it just in case. And for the love of fuck, make the tea when you're asked to put the kettle on - don't just boil some fucking water. Idiot.

Know an idiot who needs to read this chapter?

- Scan the QR code
- Click the link
- Send it their way!

Accepting you're wrong

Disagreements, arguments, disputes, whatever the fuck we want to call them, are inevitable. There will always be someone who disagrees with us at one point or another. It could be about something trivial or something a little more serious. However, I don't really give a shit what it's about – the actual argument doesn't matter. What does matter is what we do when we realise we're wrong. There is only one correct response: acceptance.

But, correct or not, accepting that you're wrong is beyond you, isn't it? You don't care that the true aim of an argument should be to actually get to the crux of the matter and work out the truth. In fact, arguing with you is an absolute fucking nightmare because, for you, the aim of an argument is seemingly just to argue. You are never willing to concede anyone else's point of view or accept irrefutable evidence, especially when it detracts from the validity of your points. As a result, every argument with you stays unresolved. You argue for the sake of arguing and turn the sacred argument into a complete waste of fucking time.

Your twattish tactics include amnesia, brazen denial of points you previously made and shouting progressively louder and louder just to make it seem as though you are winning. This is despite the fact that anyone with half a brain cell can tell you're talking utter shite.

The worst part of arguing with you pricks is when you actually *win* an argument. You make damn sure the whole world and its fucking mother knows. You take the piss out of us for days, and never, ever let us forget the one time you caught us out. That's all well and good, my wanky friend. But at least we accepted we were wrong. As someone who could never do that, there is no way in hell you should feel entitled to dish it out when you're right for the first time in twenty years.

I get the impression sometimes that it is down to shame. As if you feel that, by accepting you are wrong, you are debasing yourself – bringing shame to your household or some other stupid shit like that. You know you *should* accept you were wrong, but your ego just won't allow you to.

I also think you might feel that at a certain point, you have argued your point of view so ferociously and passionately that backing down now, even though it is only after having been proved wrong, seems like the most embarrassing thing you could possibly do.

But the truth is, there is no shame in accepting you were wrong. In every dispute, there is almost always someone who is right and someone who is wrong. We have all been wrong in our lives and, with us being the fallible human muppets that we all are, I guarantee we will all be wrong again.

Admittedly, sometimes it's not actually a case of you refusing to accept you were wrong. It's more that you simply *can't* accept you were wrong because you're too stupid to even realise it. I have some sympathy here – it's not entirely your fault that your genes don't allow for a brain capacity that has the ability to reach simple logical conclusions. But the question does then arise, what the fuck do you think you're doing arguing with anyone about anything?!

– [Pointless] Exercise –

The next time you realise you were wrong, just hold your fucking hands up and accept it, you absolute waste of ego-centric space. You are nothing special, you are not God's gift to logic, everyone is wrong sometimes – get over it. Whether the realisation that you were wrong comes during the argument, or after you've been provided with proof, means nothing compared to the fact that you do the decent thing and accept it. Yes, it's preferable if your stupid fucking brain could work out the logic of why you're wrong *before* the argument. But we all understand that, for you, that's not always feasible. Try to also remember that, despite the fact you refused to accept it, you *did* realise you were wrong in the end. And if your humble intelligence sufficed to finally work it out, then everyone else listening to the argument undoubtedly also realised it. This means that even though you think you are saving face by denying you are wrong, everyone around you already knows you're wrong, and either thinks you're utterly dense or just a complete prick who can't accept it. So logically, the only way for you to truly save any face whatsoever in this situation *is* to accept you were wrong. So fucking do it from now on. Idiot.

Know an idiot who needs to read this chapter?

- Scan the QR code
- Click the link
- Send it their way!

Weak handshakes

In many cultures, the primary way people greet others, especially when meeting for the first time, is the humble handshake. So it's pretty important to have a good one, wouldn't you say? We all want to make a good first impression.

Even more important considering there are plenty of people who believe that they can tell a lot from a handshake, down to what kind of person someone really is.

Handshakes are even sometimes considered an imperative soft skill. Many hiring employers make up their minds about whether the subsequent interview is even worth having in the first five seconds, based solely on the handshake!

Now, this is all common knowledge, even for thickos. So why do you still insist on shit, weak handshakes? Seriously, what the fuck are you doing with your hands!!

Unfortunately, there are a number of ways in which you perform these shite handshakes.

Sometimes, you make me feel like I'm shaking hands with a fucking baby! Where are the bones in your wrist, mate?! Why am I having to move your hand up and down while you just let it hang there like a weak, floppy fish?

You're the type of person who would avoid eye contact while shaking hands, which, in my book, is basically tantamount to treason. Averting your eyes while shaking someone's hand gives the impression that they don't deserve your full attention. It comes across like you were done with this person before you even shook hands, and can't wait to move on to the next one.

Other times, you don't even offer your *hands* for shaking. You prefer a fucking *finger* shake, not letting the opposing palm get anywhere near your own. I'm not going to hurt you, you big pussy. It can't be a weird hygiene thing either, I actually washed my hands after my last shit!

Maybe you didn't think it was going to be a handshake, and instead thought you were simply holding out your fingers to one of your subjects for a cheeky kiss on the ring? Entitled prick.

Whatever the chosen awful handshaking method, the main issue is that you don't truly comprehend how bad an impression you're making. Those with whom you are shaking hands are constantly assuming that you'd rather not be greeting them at all, that you're disgusted by the thought of shaking their hand, that you're only doing it because it's "what you do". Your handshakes are also causing people to feel like they've unknowingly done something wrong or that they are somehow not worthy of holding your grimy hand. The upshot is the semblance of a distinct lack of respect on your part.

- [Pointless] Exercise -

Shaking hands in a respectful way isn't that fucking difficult. But if you really are that awful at it and just didn't realise, here are some helpful pointers. Make sure you offer your full hand and keep your wrist strong, do not let your hand just hang there. And for fuck's sake, maintain eye contact, you rude bastard. If you truly do harbour resentment to the person with whom you are about to shake hands, or you just would rather not shake hands with anyone, then don't fucking do it, you prick. Better that, than the other person having to go through the ordeal, and I mean *ordeal*, of your shit, weak, pointless handshake. Idiot.

Know an idiot who needs to read this chapter?

- Scan the QR code
- Click the link
- Send it their way!

Personal space invasion

Talking and being around people is, unfortunately, pretty much necessary in social situations and at work. Which is normally fine, especially if those we need to mix with are to our liking and not complete arseholes.

However, what makes these situations really fucking awkward, is when you decide that you can't properly mix with other people unless you are right on top of them. It's like, we *can* flick noses if you want mate, but I'd rather we just talk.

You are what I refer to as a personal space invader. No, not a shitty interpretation of an archaic arcade game. Rather, I'm just saying that you are a twat who does not appreciate that there is an invisible bubble of space around everyone that should not be encroached upon unless you have a certain relationship.

Think about it. The distance from another person to our face that we feel comfortable with, is very much dependent on the level of familiarity we have with that person. The amount of space we want between ourselves and strangers we have just met is maybe more than that between ourselves and colleagues we have known for two years. And equally the space we desire between ourselves and said colleagues is probably more than that between ourselves and close friends. Another level again when it comes to romantic partners.

Admittedly, the amount of personal space desired by someone is subjective and depends entirely on that person. But, it is universally accepted that there is at least a minimum requirement to ensure that most people do not feel uncomfortable. Nevertheless, there are always those socially challenged muppets like you who just don't seem to get it.

In the office, you encroach on others' personal space all the fucking time. A pretty common example is when we show you something on our computers, while we are sitting down, and you decide to hover right behind us, with your chin just above our heads. Sometimes you even then take control of the mouse and put your other hand on the table, meaning you're all over us. Or you move your chair so close to us, while also leaning forward, that if we were to turn and look in your direction, we'd smash our heads together or be staring into each other's fucking souls. Often you're the manager with no sense of personal space. You'll arrive at our side, with no prior warning, demanding answers to your questions, and either sit on our desk right next to us or stand with your crotch in our faces.

In a social setting, you're the stranger we've just met, touching us when we don't want you to. Or sidling onto the bench beside us for a more intimate conversation, but sitting way too close. Even as a good friend, you are guilty of personal space invasion. Sometimes you get way above your station and stand mere millimetres in front of us for a chat. Look, we're friends, yes. But, that doesn't mean I want to be able to clearly see your nose hairs or the retina inside your eyeballs.

As I said, it can be a little difficult to judge the amount of space you *should* provide, since everyone has a different preference. Well, I mean, it's not that hard really, I'm just trying to make you feel better, you thicko. But if you genuinely can't work out how much space to provide, simply from having been around other people throughout your entire life, the least you can do is take one of the many hints provided. For example, when you're too close, most people will either lean away or actually take a step or two back to reestablish a comfortable gap.

This is a sign for you to back the fuck up. If you take the hint, your personal space invasion will be forgotten, as quickly as it happened. But not taking the hint and continuing to do it… that shines a huge fucking spotlight on your inability to read social cues. I've even seen you act so dense that, upon someone leaning away or taking a step back, you compensate by leaning further in or even taking a step forward yourself! Absolute numpty.

- [Pointless] Exercise -

You're a lost cause, so here's some advice for those who need to deal with personal space invaders like you. If someone is invading your personal space, play 'personal space chicken' with them. Do not move away, in fact, move in closer yourself. Hold unwavering eye contact. Make the original invader feel so uncomfortable, that they just *have* to move away. Teach those fuckers that your space is not to be messed with. If they do not waver, a swift headbutt normally does the trick. Idiot.

Know an idiot who needs to read this chapter?

- Scan the QR code
- Click the link
- Send it their way!

Pushing in your chair

There is a lot to be said about someone's manners, their respect for their fellow human and their consideration for their immediate surroundings, through the simple observation of whether or not they push their chair in. So you must be a right arsehole.

The first and most obvious reason why this is the case is that you inherently know that it is something you *should* do. Don't lie to yourself. You may not know where this subconscious understanding comes from, but you best believe it's there. So, for you to ignore it means you're happy to disregard your own conscience. And anyone who is happy to take no notice of their own conscience is probably a serial killer in the making. But there are other, more tangible reasons why pushing your chair in is important.

No one wants to sit at a table in a space with chairs sprawled all over the gaff. It makes the place look untidy and leaves a poor impression on anyone who enters the room. Things that look untidy, are very rarely worth spending time on or in. This goes for restaurants, conference rooms, lecture halls, libraries and pretty much anywhere else with unfixed seating. Unorganised chairs are no good for custom, winning over potential clients or team morale.

So it stands to reason that pushing your chair in, on the other hand, actually helps businesses succeed. It means your favourite restaurants will stay open because customers want to be there. It means colleagues and service workers, such as waiters, do not have to dash about resetting everything after you. It means you might keep your job, at a company that potential clients actually want to work with. So have a bit of respect for your own and others' livelihoods, and what consequences your actions can have, you massive prick.

Furthermore, despite what your excuse of a mind might think, there *is* a thought process behind placing tables where they are. They are situated strategically to allow people the space, and an adequate gangway, to move between them. But, this is only possible when the chairs are tucked into the table or everyone is seated. When you decide to get up, and just leave your chair five feet away from the table, you fuck up the whole harmony of the establishment.

I'm sure you'd be the first to moan like a little bitch if you had to push chairs out of the way in order to get by, or if you tripped over a stray chair leg when carrying a bunch of stuff. So why the fuck do you make other people do it? Pushing your chair in shows that you're thinking ahead and about other people. Otherwise known as common decency – something you obviously lack.

I'll tell you another thing, if you came into my office for an interview, you could be the most charismatic person known to man. You might know everything there is to know about the role and the industry and you might be brilliant at your job. But if you do not push your chair in, upon getting up for that final handshake, it shows you have not learnt one of the earliest lessons you should have mastered as a child – leave shit the way you found it. So yeah, you've got fuck all chance of getting that job.

– [Pointless] Exercise –

If you still don't understand why you should push your chair in, you need to get your head checked. There's a good chance you're some kind of psychopath who needs careful monitoring to prevent your eventual, natural evolution into a serial killer. Okay, that may be an exaggeration. But, just be a decent person for once and push your chair in, will you? If on the other hand, you're the one having to deal with wankers who couldn't give a monkey's about their colleagues, get passive-aggressive. I don't normally condone passive aggression, but this is one instance where I actively encourage it. Push in their chairs really loudly just after they get up. Use those wooden floors and scrape to your heart's content. I want emails sent reminding the world and its mother of the need to be respectful. I want Post-Its on the chairs of the perpetrators. I want diagrams up on the company notice-board, explaining in excruciating, step-by-step detail, how to push your chair in. Show these people up for the inconsiderate prats they are. Idiot.

Know an idiot who needs to read this chapter?

- Scan the QR code
- Click the link
- Send it their way!

Adhering to reserved seating

Reserved seating sounds simple enough. We reserve a specific row and seat number, then all that's left for us to do is sit there! Unfortunately, you really do struggle with even the simplest of fucking notions, don't you?

Whether on an aeroplane, on a train, at the cinema, or any number of other places where reserved seating is used, you always somehow manage to not sit in your reserved seat. This has a domino effect, you stupid prick, and leaves the rest of us with the unenviable choice of either confronting you to ask you to move, or likewise choosing a seat not assigned to us, and risking the awkwardness and indignation of being asked to move ourselves.

For the average person, the shame of the latter is real. And even if the average person doesn't get caught in the wrong seat and asked to move, they will absolutely spend twenty anxious minutes, sitting on the edge of their unassigned seat, shitting themselves every time anyone comes anywhere remotely near them.

I need to keep reminding myself though, that you aren't the average person. You're an arsehole. You don't feel this shame. You don't give a shit that other people don't want the hassle and confrontation of asking you to move from your seat. You don't care that you are forcing good people to make a shit decision. In fact, you bank on the assumption that the average person won't have the balls to ask you to move.

And even if they do ask, you throw an exasperated look, as if we're in some alternate universe, where they're wrong for asking or going over the top. Or you pretend you've somehow magically, and extremely conveniently, lost your boarding pass/ticket stub. Or you get aggressive about the fact that anyone should dare ask you to fuck off from the seat for which they paid. Or you flatly say, "No". What the fuck do you mean, no?! You chose your seat. So fuck off and sit in it, you wanker!!

I don't really give a shit whether you like reserved seating or not. The fact is, you had to choose a seat ahead of time, and you still went anyway. Deal with it, preferably without taking the piss.

There are pros and cons to assigned seating, I don't dispute that. It does seem to cause more arguments than it resolves.

One of the problems is there is rarely anyone to enforce the seating plan. Why don't theatres have the same issue? Because they employ ushers who are shit-hot on the seating arrangements. Air stewards and cinema workers are nowhere near as stringent. It should not be left to the customer to enforce the rules or fetch a worker. Nevertheless, even a lack of ushers would not be an issue if you could just follow the fucking rules and stop constantly trying to take what isn't yours. Reserved seating would be a great system if twats like you could act slightly less twattish for the duration of the journey/film.

There are plenty of other reasons too, aside from common bloody decency, why you should adhere to reserved seating.

Imagine a young family of four, entering the cinema after reserving seats, so they can all be together, yet finding only single seats left all over the gaff. That is enough to piss anyone off. They're not just going to split up and sit elsewhere, they've got young kids for fuck's sake! Back in the day when reserved seating was far less common, they would have had no leg to stand on. They would have understood that they should have arrived earlier and may even have had to go home unless some kind souls decided to make room for them. Situations like this are exactly why reserved seating was adopted in the first place!

In many cases, people will have paid more, sometimes a lot more, for specific seats in certain areas that provide a better view or extra legroom. But you, you selfish prick, you just help yourself to these prime seats whether you paid for them or not. It's not "just a seat", as you are so fond of saying. There are not "plenty of others to choose from". The best seats get bought up for a reason. It's the buyer's prerogative whether they use them, not yours.

And what about those that are hard of hearing or have limited mobility? Reserved seating is an absolute godsend for them! They reserve some of the only seats that enable them to actually enjoy a film or travel safely. For you to ignore your reserved seat and potentially put your enjoyment above the actual *needs* of others...well, that just makes you a heartless bastard, doesn't it?

We know you've got your excuses for why you act as you do. Sometimes you highlight the fact that cinema screens and flights are rarely close to full. I take your point. But if this was truly the reason why you don't sit in your reserved seat, why can't you wait until you're sure no one else will turn up before picking and choosing? I'll tell you why, because you're trying your luck, trying to nab a better seat, and hoping no one says anything.

Other times, you will protest that you don't bother finding your own seat, in a cinema for example, because it's too dark to see the row and seat numbers. Well, how do you explain you doing the same fucking thing elsewhere on trains and aeroplanes, where light is bountiful? Oh, the numbers and letters were also too small? Put your fucking glasses on then, you lazy prat! Give up, mate. Stop attempting to portray your actions as anything other than pure selfishness.

At the end of the day, any excuse for ignoring reserved seating is utter bullshit. You're either trying to forcibly claim a better seat, wanting to sit with your family/friends, or you're just a stupid prick, unable to fathom the apparent rocket-science complexity that is your ticket. In any case, fuck off out my seat.

- [Pointless] Exercise -

The next time you go anywhere that employs reserved seating, look at your ticket. Do you see those numbers? Not the barcode, you mug! Yes, those ones. They tell you where you're supposed to sit. So find that seat and fucking sit there. And if you really want a specific seat, here's a crazy idea. Reserve it! I know, mind-blowing isn't it. Idiot.

Know an idiot who needs to read this chapter?

- Scan the QR code
- Click the link
- Send it their way!

Not using your vote

We all argue about politics at one point or another. And that's fine. Good even. Politics is about debate. Debate about our own life, about other people's lives, about society as a whole, about what we *should* be doing as a collective. This is why our vote is so important. Our vote is one of the most powerful ways for us to express our thoughts on a given matter. So it is incredibly frustrating when we ask the person we're debating with, who, or what they voted for in a recent ballot, and they say they just don't vote, because "there's no point". What the fuck are you on about?!

People died to get the vote. I don't care if you're fed up with hearing it. They died so they could have their voices heard. Working-class people struggled to get it, women struggled to get it. Those in power did not want anyone, other than like-minded money-grabbing wankers, to have their say.

Why didn't they want you to have a say? Because they were worried they wouldn't stay in charge if you did.

Knowing this, why do you still not fucking vote?!!

I get that you don't feel like any of the available parties and candidates really represent or fight for you. I get that in certain voting frameworks, such as 'first past the post', you feel that your voting power is severely diminished. And you're probably right on all counts. But, if everyone who felt this way decided not to vote, then the only people left voting would be those who are happy with the status quo. Which means things would only get worse for *you*! You can't just give up and not vote. What kind of exploited life will that leave you living? By not voting, you're basically saying, "Fuck it, have the power. Please, do continue to fuck me over".

Votes are the major barometer by which politicians measure whether what they're doing and proposing is met with positive or negative sentiment from the voting public. If you don't vote, they have nothing substantial telling them they're not doing the right thing! Yes, you can partake in protests. However, unfortunately, these actions have to be pretty bloody violent in order to have any chance of affecting politicians' lofty positions.

Think about it logically. What do politicians care about most? Power. What bestows this power upon them? No, not God, you muppet. Votes. If you don't vote, politicians will never take your opinions into consideration, because they don't *need* to. You've got to at least make them work for their power, surely?!

If you're still not convinced, thinking none of the parties mirrors your ideals, look at it another way. Voting for a party does not necessarily have to indicate your endorsement of that party. It can just be you are voting for that party because you think they are the least awful. Maybe they are the least likely to fuck up your life. Maybe they are the least likely to come up with economic policies that destroy other people's lives. Maybe they are the least likely to fuck up the environment. Whatever it is that they are least likely to fuck up, you've got to use your vote! Otherwise the most likely to fuck it up will probably be sworn in, and then we're all fucked. Don't get me wrong, the least likely to fuck it up will almost definitely still fuck it up. But at least they were originally less likely to…

- [Pointless] Exercise -

Wait for the next referendum or election. Get dressed. Walk to your polling station. Use the pencil provided and put a cross in a box. Simple. If after reading this, you still don't want to vote, stop debating politics with people. What's the point in others arguing with you about what is right, if you've already given up on doing the smallest thing you could in order to make it a reality? Idiot.

Know an idiot who needs to read this chapter?

- Scan the QR code
- Click the link
- Send it their way!

Voting Tory

Do you vote Conservative?

Are you also working-class - or some mug who thinks they're middle class, but has no other income other than their job?

If yes, THIS IS FOR YOU.

Do you genuinely believe it when the Conservatives say they're going to help you? Why? Because they're posh, so they must know what they're doing? If so, you're brain-washed. Or is it because you believe they care? If so, you're a thicko. No matter what policy they spout to portray their apparent willingness to help the working class, rest assured that it's absolute bullshit. They have proven time and time again that policies that would help you are double-edged or devised simply to get you to vote for them, you silly sausage.

Just use your common sense - assuming you have some. Why *would* a bunch of Tory millionaires help you out? They couldn't care less about the working class! Strike that, they care about the working class, but only in so much as they can use them. It suits them to keep you alive but struggling financially. They're never going to actually put policies in place that truly help you monetarily. If the working class suddenly had enough money, who else would work the shit jobs, for shit money, that so many industries are built upon so that millionaires can make yet more profit?

Tories don't understand you. They think you're a bunch of chavs who don't have any manners, and who don't know how to properly speak, read or write. They can never fully comprehend the life you lead and the daily struggles you go through because they've never experienced them. And they never will.

I know that you sometimes vote Tory because you think they are more convincing on a specific issue, like looking after the economy. Slap yourself in the face right now. Look, they may or may not be able to do things like reduce the never-ending deficit, make trade deals and lower interest rates. But these things mainly just bring in more money "for the country". Please tell me you are not stupid enough to believe you'll see any of it? Their economic actions, and the money they generate, only benefit people that are already financially stable - not you.

You might even vote Tory because of their "strength" and "leadership", openly expressing their lack of hesitation in pressing the red nuclear bomb button if needed. But c'mon. Seriously. Are you that much of a wanker that you believe this to be a good thing? Do you genuinely want someone in power who cares so little about human life, that they are actually happy to press that button? What does that say about you?

Other times, you vote Conservative because you believe you've moved up in the world. You now think you're middle class and so you want to ensure you hold onto more of your money, i.e. pay less tax. The one thing I would ask is, do you need your job? If you lost it, and couldn't get a new one for a couple of years, would you be in a bit of trouble? Then you're not middle class, you prat, you're working class. The clue is in the name. How have you not realised that the Tories want you to believe that you're middle class, so you'll start thinking you have something to lose, and therefore decide to vote for a party whose policies would benefit your own economic situation? Which funnily enough would keep them in power.

Furthermore, by voting Tory, you're also voting for a party that hates government intervention, and therefore a party that would love to dismantle any benefit systems that would support you if you ever found yourself out of work. Although, didn't we just establish that you would be in the shit if you lost your job? Voting Tory doesn't sound like such a good idea now, does it?

Please don't tell me about "all those benefit scroungers". They're a rarity, mate. Life is hard. If the opportunities aren't there, they're not there. It's not as easy as just saying the less well-off need to work harder. It's very convenient for you to say while *you're* doing ok, don't you think?

Give this a thought for one second. Even if you're rich. You're voting for a party that doesn't care about people less well-off. Just so that you can keep more of your money. Are you really, genuinely, that selfish? If you come to the conclusion that you are, good luck to you. But I think I speak for the majority when I say I really hope you end up falling on hard financial times, you prick. Might give you some fucking perspective.

- [Pointless] Exercise -

Ask yourself these questions. Do you need a job or your business for a living? Do you care about anyone other than yourself? Do you believe that you are not an arsehole? Do you need the NHS for healthcare? Answering yes to any of these questions means you are politically aligned with almost anyone other than the Conservatives. So, for the love of everything holy, please vote anything other than Tory. You'll have a much better chance of not fucking up your own life. Idiot.

Know an idiot who needs to read this chapter?

- Scan the QR code
- Click the link
- Send it their way!

Political correctness

Political correctness, what a topic eh? Very divisive. Some people incessantly promote it, others abhor it. And it's not difficult to see why.

Those who have been marginalised for any period of time as a result of their gender, sexuality, race, religion, or whatever it is, are very pleased with its adoption in society. Mainly because it has resulted in relatively widespread recognition that people from every sub-section of society should be respected and addressed, using neutral terms. Doesn't sound so bad, does it?

So why do so many people hate all this political correctness faff? It does seem weird, considering the bulk of them are definitely of the opinion that everyone should be respected. So why?

We need only be around overly politically correct people like you for a few days to understand the reasoning. I think the annoyance with political correctness can be summarised by simply saying that you are taking it too far.

I'm not talking about actions. Any action against someone, based on an aspect of their identity, is out of order. The vast majority of sane people would agree. I'm talking about words. What we are, and are not, allowed to say, according to political correctness. There are some words we obviously should not be using. But some are grey areas in my opinion, depending on the context. People being vilified for using the grey area words, without that context being taken into account, is plain wrong - yet it's happening far too often.

Let's look at some examples.

Imagine a boardroom with a bunch of blokes and one female on the board. She brings up an important and valid point. One of the male representatives starts off his response with, "What you've got to understand, love, is that…" Thoughts? It's quite clear that this is wrong. The word 'love' here could be construed as being used to highlight that this is a woman, to patronise her response and imply that what she is saying is wrong, simply *because* she is a woman. It doesn't matter whether what she said was wrong or not, none of that should be tied up in the fact that she is female. This may or may not have been the male board member's intention, but political correctness exists to ensure this kind of "mistake" can't happen.

On the flip side, imagine a supermarket. A woman is trying to reach something from the top shelf. A man notices her struggling and says, "Can I get that for ya, love?" Do you see the difference? If you're not a complete prat, of course you do. It's all around the context behind the use of the word 'love'. In this case, it is used to come across as non-threatening and offer genuine help.

The problem is, a PC muppet like you will have a go at the second man as well, just because he used the word 'love'. You will, because I've seen you do it. You are annoyed that he only used that word because she is a woman. Yes, 'love' *is* used because she is a woman. But the point I'm trying to make is this. So. Fucking. What. The bloke's intentions were good, he's being a nice person, offering his help to someone in need. He used the word 'love' because that's how he is used to addressing women and plenty of women do exactly the same thing. Yet, you're going to shoot him down for it. This is political over-correctness.

I heard a discussion on TV the other day about whether only LGBT actors should play LGBT characters. I get where they're coming from. In theory, only LGBT actors could possibly understand the history and subjugation associated with being LBGT. But again, this is going too far. By this logic, we could just as easily say only people who have killed other humans in the past should play the lead in a serial killer thriller – but that would be fucking mental.

In a similar vein, I understand why people do not feel comfortable being searched by security officers of a different sex, and why it has to be a member of the same gender. But what is the premise behind this? In essence, it's that the security officer might be getting some kind of sexual gratification from the search. But wouldn't that mean gay people should not be able to search other men? And lesbians should not be able to search women? And if we were to go down this route of being overly strict about the application of political over-correctness, we would need to declare our gender, sexuality and every part of our identity before every interaction with a human. Where does it end?

All I'm saying is you should be careful what you wish for. You think the world is crazy now, but it can get crazier, believe me.

Political over-correctness is even filtering down into day to day interactions that have got nothing to do with any social identity. For example, many of us use the word 'mate' to address every single person we meet. Some women get offended as it can seem more like a word reserved for men. Others get offended when we *only* use it for men. Women *and* men like you might also say to us, "I ain't your mate, mate". But what you don't realise is, I'm not saying I'm actually your mate, I've just bloody met you, you complete and utter dickhead. I use this term for everyone. Just sell me the fucking bottle of water and I'll leave the shop. Mate.

At the end of the day, political correctness is there to ensure that no pre-judgements are made or inferred, *where it matters*. That last bit is very important. In a given situation, if no judgments are being made or inferred, yet you are still contesting the meaning behind every single word people utter... that's where you need to calm down a bit. There's a difference between when words are meant in a sleazy

127 Reasons Why You Are An Idiot

or derogatory way, and when it's just a natural way people have been addressing others their whole lives.

I don't think it's necessarily the fault of political correctness. In general, it's a good thing, designed to make the world a fairer and less biased place. The problem is people like you, asking for political correctness to be applied way too literally. Your PC call outs are getting, frankly, fucking ridiculous. There is a middle ground that needs to be found.

You need to consider what happens if political correctness goes too far. If you keep shutting down people for discrepancies that aren't really discrepancies at all, like in the supermarket shelf-help example above, you will stop people from interacting or offering their help at all, for fear of being labelled as something horrible, like sexist. And what a shit world that would be.

You can already feel it right? That fear of saying the wrong thing. That fear of partaking in any quasi-serious discussions. That fear of addressing any issue you have, with anyone slightly different to you, lest you be labelled as having a problem with that social identity.

- [Pointless] Exercise -

Please stop taking things so seriously. Pick your battles. By all means, call out non-PC word usage where it matters, and where it is meant in a negative way. But stop having a go at blokes trying to help old ladies in the supermarket for fuck's sake. And to the wanky free speech protectors in society, please don't think I'm advocating for you to be able to say whatever the fuck you want, completely unchecked. Free speech is worth shit all if it's based on hatred, or negatively targeting specific social identities. Idiot.

Know an idiot who needs to read this chapter?

- Scan the QR code
- Click the link
- Send it their way!

Immigration

How many times have you moaned about the apparent plight of illegal immigration, saying something along the lines of, "They're taking our jobs!"

Well, it's not true. At least not in the way you think, you fucking muppet. What are the jobs that you think immigrants are coming over and stealing? Cleaning toilets? Shitty hand to mouth construction jobs? Picking strawberries? For an absolute pittance? These aren't jobs you would debase yourself to do anyway! At least, not for the money they're getting. The only other jobs for which immigrants are recruited are professional, skilled roles that aren't being filled by current citizens, and for which you almost definitely do not have the expertise to fill. So, what's the issue?

Have you ever stopped to think about how you first got the impression that immigrants were stealing all your jobs? Newspapers, social media, politicians, right?? Yeah, because these are great sources in which to place your trust... No ulterior motives to see here... When are you going to learn that you can't trust everything that you read or hear? Take this book for example. It's pure shit, one person's opinion, no substantiated evidence. Much like newspaper articles.

I know it's hard, but use your brain for a minute. Devil's advocate time. Why do you give any credence to the belief that immigrants are stealing your jobs? I imagine it's because you, or people you know, are struggling to get a job you want. And why are you struggling to get that job? Is it really because immigrants are stealing them? Or is it because there aren't enough of the jobs you want? Or is it because every job you want requires years of experience that you don't have? If this dire job situation truly did stem from something other than immigrants, like the economy or lack of entry-level opportunity, that problem would be your government's to tackle. I think we can all agree that politicians do not like to be blamed for things, and are more likely to try to deflect than actually find a solution. So wouldn't peddling an uncontrollable immigration problem, as the main perpetrator, be an easy fix? I'll remind you that the news, whether on TV, in newspapers or online, is hardly independent. They've all got their own agendas, as well as wealthy benefactors, including politicians and their mates, steering the overarching message of published content to their benefit.

Oh, by the way, we're not actually playing Devil's advocate. This is the truth, you numpty. I know it's upsetting to believe that your government would rather blame other people rather than try to actually solve the problem. But there we go, welcome to the real world.

Now, let's imagine that this immigration issue was a genuine problem. That we do, in fact, live in a world where immigrants are stealing your jobs. Would you really deny them those jobs?

Look at it from the immigrants' point of view. Maybe they *had* to come here to get decent wages and send money home so their families could survive – never mind the fact that these wages are considered by you to be too shit to warrant the labour. Or maybe they are refugees who came here fleeing war. Some of them had no money to travel here legally, so had to use rubber dinghies, the cargo space of criminal traffickers or something equally fucking dangerous to get here. What – did you think they simply hopped on a quick business class flight?

Would *you* get on a rubber dinghy to go and live in another country, with no work guaranteed, if your situation in your home country wasn't dire? No, of course you fucking wouldn't. People don't do desperate things like that if they're happy where they are.

It's pretty harsh, morally, to deny them work when they get here, don't you think? *You've* got the safety net of benefits if you can't find work. Many of these immigrants do not get anything like that back home. If, having considered the plight of immigrants, you would still shame them for trying for a better life, well, you need your soul checked, you evil prick. These are humans we're talking about. Just other people. Trying to look after themselves and their families. Let's hope you are never forced to leave your home eh? Arsehole.

- [Pointless] Exercise -

When you read the papers, try to actually think about what you are reading. Question it. Ask yourself who would benefit if this story was to be accepted as the truth. Don't take what is written as a given, because it's really not. Find an immigrant. Talk to them. Ask them about their life, what it was like back home, why they decided to come here. Give them a chance. Learn how to be more compassionate. Idiot.

Know an idiot who needs to read this chapter?

- Scan the QR code
- Click the link
- Send it their way!

Conspiracy theorists

Whenever you hear about anything new, why is your first thought always conspiracy? With every new vaccine, technological advancement, political policy, whatever it is, the only thing you seem to see is foul play. It must be fucking exhausting!

It's understandable to a certain extent. Governments and authority figures in general, have proven time and time again that they care more about their own power and wealth than the people they govern. Expense scandals, wars waged solely for oil or other material gains, economic collapses caused by banks and attacks on journalists, have hardly helped.

Then we also have recent technological advances that distort the truth even further. The rise of social media and fake news. The use of photoshop and deep fake videos to place people where they've never been, saying things they've never said. Technology using AI and undecipherable algorithms to make decisions on our behalf. All of this, and more, have muddied the waters of reality. How the fuck are we supposed to tell fact from fiction?

So it's really not surprising that the number of conspiracy theorists like you is growing. How can we trust anyone or anything when there are so many ways to pull the wool over peoples' eyes?

What's more, many conspiracy theories online are very convincing. A good proportion of them follow a logical train of thought, and come to a pretty reasonable conclusion, considering the information at hand.

So, I do have some sympathy for you as a conspiracy theorist. Obviously, I am discounting the absolute raving nutters who go on about having tea parties with aliens, the Earth being flat or hollow with civilisations living inside, Elvis and Michael Jackson being alive, Prince Charles being a vampire, a reptilian elite ruling us all and fake moon landings. Those lot are bonkers.

But for you, as someone who has no trust in your government, and thinks each new initiative has been brought about for nefarious purposes, it's a difficult world out there. I'm not going to tell you to just trust the authorities blindly. Healthy scepticism of people in power is a good thing, it keeps them honest. So how do you not drive yourself mad?

For me, you need to calm down first of all and not jump on the bandwagon. Look at each theory on its own merits and remember to always consider one fundamental thing. What governs our world at this moment in time? That's right, money. Money bestows power. Those in power understand this and will always seek more of it for that reason.

Armed with this knowledge, you can look at most things that are happening in the world and decide whether or not a conspiracy theory holds weight. Does the conspiracy you think they are covering up, generate more, or save them money? Most conspiracy theories can be dispelled pretty quickly through this logic.

If you've got a theory that passes this initial logic test, another good question to ask is, is it a conspiracy that would need to involve lots of people? Could it only be kept quiet if all of those people were also kept quiet? If so, you can also rest assured that it's probably not true.

If you ask yourselves these questions, yet still think a particular conspiracy theory holds up to scrutiny, it's then up to you to delve deeper into the facts, not just the one article you found on fucking Twitter. If you're that bothered, do the research. Don't just lazily assume things are true and share everything you see about it. Too many people like you share conspiracy theories and cause absolute tripe to go viral, without even asking themselves the simple logical questions above. You do it, almost always, without having done the due diligence to warrant you trying to convince others of the "truth".

All I'm trying to say is, there are enough problems and shady things being done in the world, without conspiracy theories, that hold no weight, diverting attention away from what matters, and from effectively holding those in power to account.

- [Pointless] Exercise -

If you're a crazy fucker who jumps on every single conspiracy theory going, no matter how mental, please take your alien landings bullshit and shove it up your arse. We've got no time for it - there are more important, real things happening in the world. Unless the aliens show up and start gunning people down with super lasers, I don't want to fucking hear it. The next time you read yet another article about yet another conspiracy theory, do us all a favour and ask at least the two big logical questions before believing it or sharing with others. Financial potential and how many people need to be in on the conspiracy are the key components. Help us all sort fact from fiction and try to regain some sense of faith in humanity. Idiot.

Know an idiot who needs to read this chapter?

- Scan the QR code
- Click the link
- Send it their way!

127 Reasons Why You Are An Idiot

Cancel culture

For anyone who has been living under a rock, cancel culture is all about shunning people and ostracising them from certain social, professional or other circles because of something they did. Examples of this ostracism might include actors being axed from TV shows or a musician's music being boycotted.

Cancel culture has always existed, it's not a modern phenomenon. But its success has never been so apparent before modern times, thanks to the internet and social media. It has never been so easy to amass popular sentiment behind a certain idea that someone should be punished. Before social media, you would have to call or email the complaints department of a TV network or a company, or even meet up to protest. It is much easier now for a keyboard warrior such as yourself to pressurise and call out people online, with the aim of creating a viral furore over a certain someone's actions.

Cancel culture is, therefore, a potent tool nowadays. And, in the words of Spiderman's Uncle Ben, with great power comes great responsibility. But as always, you refuse to take your responsibility seriously, jumping on bandwagons instead of calmly assessing and making a call.

Increasingly, cancel culture kicks into gear around things that people have said. But this is very dangerous territory. For one, punishing someone for their opinion is definitely moving into the realms of curtailment of free speech. For another, is what this person said really worth ruining the lives of them and their family? Some behaviours and opinions are clearly wrong, abhorrent and deserve to be punished. I have absolutely no issue with that at all, especially if the perpetrator is unapologetic; the problem with cancel culture is not that it exists. But, when calling for someone to be cancelled, you need to be absolutely certain it's warranted. And there is no doubt that cancel culture goes too far from time to time. Your calls for peoples' heads are sometimes unjustified and disproportionate, considering the circumstances and context.

Cancelling people for tweets they made and opinions they had years ago, is just bloody pointless. Everyone makes mistakes, for fuck's sake. We are all human beings and, as such, we fuck up from time to time. Sometimes mistakes need to be punished, other times there is an unwritten, yet logical, statute of limitations to which we should all be adhering. Can you honestly say you've never said anything controversial or told a dodgy joke when younger that if scrutinised in the public arena, could lead to you being vilified? If your answer is no, you're a fucking liar or a massive pussy who has never said anything out of turn.

Consider the difference between Katie Hopkins and Jared Bowen. Katie Hopkins, a media personality, called for a "final solution" to Islamic terrorism after the Manchester Arena bombing. She was vilified for these tweets *at the time*, and rightly fucking so. She is someone who actively spreads hate and absolutely deserves to be cancelled. Jared Bowen, on the other hand, is a professional footballer, who tweeted, "That one friend that thinks their black #N*****Please." While indefensible, mainly for the grammar, this tweet was made when he was fifteen. It was brought to public attention nine years after the fact, and only after he had established himself as a top footballer and was therefore in the public eye. It's no excuse for using the N-word, but it has to be considered that he does not actually mean to be offensive to black people in this tweet. If anything, he is being offensive to people of other races who appropriate black culture. It is also probably the case that, at fifteen, he just did not understand the history and connotations of the word, having grown up with black people all his life who use it among themselves. Does

127 Reasons Why You Are An Idiot

Jared deserve to be cancelled, just as much as Katie? I'll let you be the judge.

Similarly, compare these two situations and use that empty noggin of yours to work out who deserves to get "cancelled".

A black school security guard uses the N-word when telling a kid not to refer to him that way. Conversely, a white school security guard calls a black pupil the N-word simply because they were misbehaving.

I ask you, who deserves to get cancelled here? Logically, you should have no trouble working out that the white school security guard is the only one who is really in the wrong.

But what if I told you that the black school security guard, named Marlon Anderson, also got fired, despite having four kids to feed, simply because using the N-word is against school policy?

Do you see where your cancel culture is going fucking crazy? The school board was so shit scared of it and of being targeted themselves, that cooler heads did not prevail.

You don't seem willing to consider the circumstances or the prevailing mood at the time in which anything happened anymore. You don't seem ready to forgive anyone's innate fallibility as a human being. Your common sense just seems to have flown out of the window.

Cancel culture advocates like you are also making comedy very difficult. Comedy is often about coming close to crossing the line. But cancel culture is forcing that line to advance so close, that one wrong move equals the cancellation of a comedian's career. At best, it is becoming close to impossible to make risqué jokes anymore because there is no funny material available that doesn't potentially offend *someone*. In addition, I implore you to remember that in order for a comic to have been successful when making homophobic jokes twenty years ago, people had to have laughed. The prevailing mood at the time was that it was acceptable to make those jokes. Just because it is considered to be disgusting now, does not mean that we should punish the comedians who made those jokes, at a time when it was considered fair game. Unless of course, the comic continues to do so even nowadays, in which case do your thing cancel culture.

What about – prepare yourselves – paedophiles? It's weird that they find sexual gratification through children, right? However, can anyone really deny what gratifies someone else sexually? Obviously, this sexual gratification should *never* be acted upon, for a whole host of blatant fucking reasons. If it happened to my kids, I'd want to kill the perpetrator, no fucking doubt about it. However, there is something to be understood about the fact that someone "fancies" children – is it their fault that their brain is wired in this way? Maybe they need help to better abstain or deal with past traumas that influence their sexual desires? Remember, it wasn't so long ago that we largely shunned the LGBT community and enforced laws that discriminated against them, just because they had sexual desires that didn't fit in with society's consensus of what is normal.

You may well be going crazy right now at the insinuation that we give paedophiles the time of day, other than to lock them the fuck up. It's fair to say that the above paragraph is a minority opinion, don't you think? So can you imagine someone in the public eye putting it out in the wild, with cancel culture being as prevalent as it is? Displaying this kind of thinking to the masses, however logical, would probably result in the opinion-holder being deemed a paedophile themselves. Once that happens, they're finished. They will undoubtedly get cancelled. Game over. But should it be? After all, it's just an opinion.

I guess all I'm saying is, make sure you only use cancel culture to justifiably criticise and cancel people who actually deserve it. Or those who still hold the unacceptable views they held years ago. Or

127 Reasons Why You Are An Idiot

those who have actually done something wrong instead of having simply been put in a shitty position. You need to remember to consider the circumstances and allow common sense to fucking prevail, instead of using cancel culture to block free speech or logical minority opinions, just because they trigger you.

One last thing. High horse, cancel culture muppets like you tend to focus on one person at a time. You ruin one civilian life and then move on to the next victim, all the while thinking you're doing the world a service. But business goes on, as usual, you prat. Whether you get a TV presenter to retire or not, those in power *remain* in power, and all the major problems of the world *continue* to rage unabated. Wouldn't it be more useful to harness the power of cancel culture, the power to mobilise virtually and en masse, to actually do something that matters? Just a thought. Don't cancel me.

- [Pointless] Exercise -

Before you start thumping that keyboard, ready to jump on the bandwagon and get someone cancelled, think! Is whatever they've done or said, worth ruining their life? Did they mean it in the way it's being construed? Have you considered the context and circumstances? Is it an opinion that offends the majority, but nevertheless has a devil's advocate type merit? If you haven't considered any of these questions, what the fuck gives you the right to call for this person's head? Maybe we should get a private investigator to have a little dig into *your* past, you self-righteous wanker. I bet they'd find something that, by today's standards, would be cause enough for cancel culture to strike. Idiot.

Know an idiot who needs to read this chapter?

- Scan the QR code
- Click the link
- Send it their way!

Pandemics - COVID-19 special

Wearing masks

I think this generation of humanity is pretty well aware of deadly pandemics by now – thank you 2020s.

They're horrible, aren't they? They kill people. Lots of them. They cause lockdowns and economic recessions, which affect our mental health and create way too many job losses. Living through pandemics is not great.

However, luckily, we understand lots about how diseases work nowadays. There are things we can all do, collectively, to combat their spread. One of them is wearing masks. This allows us to limit the spread of disease-causing bacteria, especially to those who are more likely to die from it. Seems like a no-brainer right? A small, insignificant sacrifice by everyone to safeguard people with underlying health conditions.

But low and behold, despite it being a small, insignificant sacrifice, there are people like you who moan about needing to wear them. How much of a prick do you need to be?

Let's dive into that question, shall we? Why *do* pricks like you moan? It seems there are three reasons.

One, annoyance at your freedoms being restricted. Twats like you still seem to think you have a choice whether you wear the mask or not, even during the direst stretches of the pandemic, when it is explicitly made mandatory. I know this, one because I see you on TV talking shit on the daily and, two, because some mask-phobic arsehole in Asda argued this point with me, while simultaneously trying to lean over me, right next to my face, to reach the wine shelf. Let's get one thing straight: it's not your fucking choice; it's the fucking law because the disease is wreaking deathly fucking havoc. Wearing masks wouldn't be enforced if it wasn't.

And if you *really* want to go down this freedom rabbit hole, it's then also my choice to not get infected by your insensitive thick arse, pick you up and throw you to the other end of the aisle. Free country, mate, get over it.

I also happen to think you are actually well aware that you're *obliged* to wear a mask. Which is why you wear it around your neck, like a fucking pillock, just in case the police come calling. Why would you have it on you if you didn't think you were supposed to wear it?

But seriously, let's forget about the law for a minute. Imagine it wasn't law. Imagine you did have the freedom to choose. Why can't you decide to use that freedom to not be a dickhead? I'll tell you why. Because you don't have that in your makeup – you're a dickhead through and through. This is why, unfortunately, these things need to be enshrined in law. Wearing the mask isn't to save you, we all know you're not bothered about catching the disease in question, you never stop fucking going on about how super tough you think you are. Wearing a mask is to protect other people who *are* susceptible to it. They're worried, and rightly so, that they could die.

Two, it's too hot. Well, yes, your glasses might steam up. Yes, it can be uncomfortable. But so fucking what. There are doctors, nurses and a whole host of other people wearing full protective gear, much more than just a mask, for eight-plus hours at a time. To look after you, your families, your friends. It's not going to kill you to just wear your mask on the bus for a measly twenty minutes.

Three, you don't really believe that wearing masks will help slow down the spread of the disease. But it's not just politicians telling you this, it's medical experts, who dedicate their lives to helping people. What makes you think you have the right, or the brain capacity, to question them? You can't even work out how to stop your glasses steaming up from the bloody mask, you muppet.

Sounds to me that people like you, who refuse to wear masks, are just selfish wankers. Just my opinion.

– [Pointless] Exercise –

Stop being a bitch. Wear the bloody mask. I know it's hard when your whole life has been nothing but take, fucking take, but try thinking about what is best for other people for once, instead of just yourself. Idiot.

Know an idiot who needs to read this chapter?

- Scan the QR code
- Click the link
- Send it their way!

Vaccine fear

I get it, mate. Governments are seriously fucking untrustworthy. No arguments here. So, when they come out with a new, miracle vaccine that is supposedly going to get things back to normal, I get why you'd be sceptical.

But come oooooooon, fuuuucking hell. Don't be one of the muppets lapping up the bullshit, spouted on social media by people who know absolutely fuck all, telling you everything that is supposedly wrong with these vaccines. I've heard it all – from additives, crazy side effects and autism, to even microchips being inserted so the government can track you.

Side effects are of course possible. They're possible with *all* vaccines. I mean, fuck, vaccines typically involve you actually choosing to inject mild doses of the disease, into your body. If anything, I'm surprised these side effects aren't even more common than they are! At the end of the day, the incredibly slim chance of a side effect is surely better than getting the real thing. I'd remind you that this disease is killing people left, right and centre, and leaving plenty more debilitated for the unforeseeable future. Unless your argument is that the disease is a hoax created by the world's governments or some reptilian elite. In which case, you really can just go fuck yourself. Tell that to someone who's had a loved one die from it. They should not be held responsible for their actions.

Microchips... just no. No more discussion needed. It doesn't warrant further consideration. You fucking numpty.

Quick approval, however, *is* a little suspicious. It does make you wonder if enough rigorous testing has been done. This really is the only concern that has any legitimacy in my book. Maybe governments did rush the vaccine through to get their respective economies booming again? After all, a vaccine would enable all their worker bees to return to work and shoppers to go out and spend.

However, consider the logic here. Let me reiterate that governments *want* their worker bees to go back to work. They *want* shoppers to get out there and spend their dough. It's no good if workers all die out a week after returning to work and shoppers start dropping like flies in Primark when the vaccine fucks us all. The logic definitely dictates they'll make damn sure the vaccine is as safe as can be.

It's important to bear in mind that, while the approval process does seem quick compared to other vaccines and medical breakthroughs, rigorous testing *has* been done. In the midst of a pandemic, the *most* important thing is to find a way to combat the disease in question. So all the funding, manpower and support in the world gets thrown at it. It's all anyone is working on. Things that took a long time previously, when labs were working on any number of medical improvements, just don't take as long when everyone is focused on the same thing. There is normally a huge backlog of testing to be done, on a huge assortment of treatments, and it can take years to get around to them. There is nothing quite like a serious pandemic to ensure that a particular vaccine gets top priority status.

So, wind your fucking neck in, you government conspiracist. Instead of wanky social media influencers, try to listen to the advice of actual doctors and medical professionals. You know, those people who have taken the Hippocratic Oath and sworn to protect you all?

- [Pointless] Exercise -

Remember one simple thing. Despite any hypothetical, rare, almost-never-going-to-happen side effects, getting the vaccine will always be better than just letting the virus run riot. It becomes a real fucking no-brainer when you compare the death figures of the unvaccinated vs vaccinated. So stop using conspiracy theories as a cover for being scared of needles, you pussy. Get the fucking vaccine. Idiot.

Know an idiot who needs to read this chapter?

- Scan the QR code
- Click the link
- Send it their way!

Having a 'best friend'

I'm just going to come out and say it. Who the hell has a best friend past the age of twelve?! Weirdos like you apparently…

Whenever you refer to your 'best mate', I fully expect to see someone at about waist height, wearing dungarees, playing in the dirt with people their own age. So when the person, uttering something like, "The other day, me and my best friend were braiding each other's hair…", turns out to be you, a relatively clean, fully-formed adult with an unmistakably broken voice, it comes as a bit of a fucking shock.

You, and adults in general, shouldn't feel the need to rank your friendships. Why do you need to distinguish between a 'best' friend and your other, 'regular' friends? All of them are presumably friends for a reason - they all have their benefits, and you'll need the support of one more than the others at different points in your life. Some give great advice, some are always up for a night out, some are perfect for practising a weird role play you'll need to do at an interview. They're all as valuable as each other. Frankly, grading your relationships is fucking bizarre; certain dictators have, and continue to, grade people - something that never ends well…

Have you even spared a thought to what your seemingly, sub-par friends are going to think? Surely in their eyes, your snub only serves to diminish their loyalty to you. Don't get me wrong, I'm sure they're not crying too hard over it, as you're obviously a prat. But the next time you badly need one of your 'regular' friends, don't be surprised if they aren't available. Who could blame them?! You've let it be publicly known that they're dispensable.

If you *must* refer to anyone as a best friend, why can't you just have best *friends* - plural. The term 'best friend' should be a tier, not reserved for just one person. At the very least, spread that stupid, pointless, best friend love across multiple people. You don't have to, and shouldn't, limit yourself to one. What if that person disappears from your life for one reason or another? Shit happens I'm afraid, mate.

As cold-hearted as it is to say, you need to treat your best friends like your stock portfolio. You absolutely should diversify your holdings to protect yourself from any one bad investment. But holding too many positions makes it hard to keep track, and spreads you and your money too thin to make sizeable gains. For the thickos, the investments in this scenario are your friends. Got it? Good.

For another thing, this best friend bullshit is surely a smokescreen for debilitating codependency? Why do you need to label a particularly good friendship? Are you that desperate for feelings of safety, security and a sense of comfort? Grow the fuck up. As I say, this best friend rollox is what kids do. One, because they're constantly under the impression that they need a best friend, thanks to cartoons and their parents' insistence that they make one. Two, to cement an alliance that gets them through school and prevents them from ending up as lonely, easy pickings for bullies. And three, because they haven't yet developed the reinforcement and skills to be their own person and are still working out their place in the world.

You don't need your social life to mirror a pointless social construct, created by the media, to feel "normal". You're also not any less of a desirable person by not having someone you would call a best friend.

This best friend tripe brings up all sorts of connotations around jealousy. I'd lay money the green monster rears its ugly head every time you or your 'best friend' get pally with someone else, even if you might never admit it. The best friend label also puts unfair expectations on the other person. They will feel they have to be the one who shows up, every single time. After listening to all of your, probably plentiful, problems, they will feel the pressure to be the one to give solid advice that sticks, every time. They will feel they have to prioritise their friendship with you over others. They will feel bad turning you down for any activity you want to do, even if it doesn't interest them in the slightest. It's a lot to demand from just one person. Furthermore, it also means you are potentially neglecting other fantastic friendships by paying way too much attention to your romanticised BFF.

The term just doesn't work for the modern adult. People move away, they grow apart, they fall out, they develop completely different interests. If you still have a friend from childhood, great. But they're not the be-all and end-all, and they certainly don't have to be labelled your absolute 'best' friend based purely on longevity.

Most well-adjusted adults compartmentalise their friends; we've got school friends, work friends, gym friends, travel friends, abroad friends. Our mates are different depending on the setting, what we're doing and how we need to be challenged at any given time. No one friend can cover everything. Recognising this is being an adult. It's time you fucking acted like one when it comes to your platonic relationships.

- [Pointless] Exercise -

I get that some people find it harder to make friends. So it is feasible that you might have a 'best' friend by default, simply because you are each other's *only* friend. But I'm sorry to have to tell you that the title of 'best friend' is still fucking stupid, has no bearing in your case considering it was bestowed by default and is no excuse for not getting out there and making some more connections. In fact, the next time you feel the urge to utter the phrase 'best friend', go and watch some cartoons. It won't take too long to hear the first, "Aaaaahhh you're my best fwend". At which point you need to turn that shit off, before you fully regress to a child-like state, and slap yourself in the face as a reminder that using this phrase is equivalent to portraying yourself as an insecure kid, crying out to be liked. Idiot.

Know an idiot who needs to read this chapter?

- Scan the QR code
- Click the link
- Send it their way!

Making friends

Having friends is pretty bloody important, especially for our mental well-being.

With friends, we get to share stuff we might not always feel comfortable sharing with our own families. Work problems, romantic problems, in-jokes, dirty jokes, clothes, you name it. We can do stuff with friends that we otherwise might not have the courage to do on our own. Like going to a weird pottery class. Or making shitty Tik-Tok videos.

Anyway, having friends is the easy part. Finding and making friends is where it can get a little tricky. I'm not going to sit here in my hovel and say that it's easy. Because it isn't. Especially as we get older. I think it's pretty fair to say that, by the age of thirty, people are pretty much set in their various friend groups, with no real need for new friends. People have less time for socialising when working all the time, starting families and other adult shit.

When we were kids, it was simple. We would just walk up to another kid, ask if they want to be our friend, then throw mud at each other. Bang – friends for life.

So now that we're older, how *do* we make friends? The truth is, there isn't any one way. It's normally a case of trying to find people with shared interests and a similar sense of humour.

But, I can tell you one thing for certain. You will never find any friends sitting at home. You have to put yourself out there.

It drives me fucking mental when you say you don't have any friends – but don't do anything about it. How can you moan that you haven't got any friends, when all you do outside of work is sit there on your phone, scrolling endlessly and eating all day? What the hell do you expect?! Unfortunately, you muppet, new friends do not just appear out of thin air and ring your doorbell. You have no God-given right to make friends, you have to work at it.

Get up off the bloody couch, put your phone down, go outside, start a new hobby, join a sports club... just do something! In particular, try to do something you enjoy with other people – you're much more likely to find new friends this way, as the shared interest element is already pretty obvious. The bonus here is that the initial awkward conversation when talking to someone you don't know will be avoided because you're both already doing something you enjoy that you can talk about. I know it can feel weird, embarrassing even, that you're doing these activities for the express purpose of making new friends, but that's just something you're going to have to get over. There are a lot more people than you realise, feeling just as lonely as you.

If your excuse is that you can't think of anything you enjoy doing, well, your first task is to stop being a sad git. Secondly, I'm sorry, but you're just being lazy. Everyone enjoys doing *something*, it's just that you can't be bothered to even work out what that is. I absolutely empathise that you may be depressed and stuck in a rut, but you have to pull yourself out of it. At the very least, go to the pub, or somewhere you can talk to people in real life. You need to socialise if you are to have any chance of making a friend or two. It gets easier with time; talking to strangers is something you can practise and improve.

- [Pointless] Exercise -

Stop moaning about having no friends if you make next to no effort to make them. It's your fault. Stop feeling sorry for yourself. Actually leave the house. And talk to someone other than that girl on Babestation. Idiot.

Know an idiot who needs to read this chapter?

- Scan the QR code
- Click the link
- Send it their way!

Awful storytelling

We all love a good story. Listening to our friends' escapades, and reciprocating with tales of our own, are absolute staples of any good friendship. They allow us to live vicariously through our mates and share past experiences. They can be funny, sad, shocking; they can even be downright fucking bizarre, depending on the nuttiness of our friends.

And just as much as we all love a good story, we all love a good storyteller. Someone who adds in just the right amount of detail. Someone who knows their audience and what gets them going. Someone who brings their story to life and draws us in, so that we can imagine exactly what, and how, it went down. Someone who keeps us hooked right to the end. And most importantly, someone who knows which stories are worth telling.

A good group of storytelling mates makes reminiscing so much more fun. But a group full of such storytelling talent is not always feasible; storytelling is an art that not just any prat can master. Most friend groups have maybe one or two great bards. The bulk of a friend group is generally made up of average narrators; with the right story they can shine, but some of their tales fall on deaf ears or just don't have the desired impact. And then there is you – the awful storyteller of the group.

When you get going on a story, we all just *know* it's going to be utter shite. We are fully aware that the next five to ten minutes of our lives are going to be completely fucking wasted. Expectations are always low, yet you still somehow always disappoint.

You take fucking aaaaaaaaaages to tell the bloody thing!!

You'll include every, single, detail. You'll tell us that you need to set the scene and provide the context. Even if it adds fuck all and only serves to bore your listeners. Or you'll hop from story to story, going off on tangents that turn the original "story" into a monologue that bores the shit out of even the most stalwart of friends.

As an example, let's imagine you're talking about a time you got chased by a dog down a blocked alleyway – which objectively has the potential to make for quite an interesting story! But while we're all sat there, eagerly anticipating what happens next, you'll tell us all about the trainers you were wearing, where you bought them, that you got them sixty per cent off last spring, that that particular shop has now closed and you're gutted about it, what colour laces you had on and that it was a difficult decision that day between orange and purple, that you saw a few daffodils growing in the alleyway, that you stepped in six puddles and thought it was weird at the time as it hadn't rained for a couple of days. It's normally somewhere around the eighteenth pointless detail at which we, the audience, completely lose interest. Mainly because your story *never fucking ends*!!!

Although, it's not always the useless details that kill your story. Sometimes you take way longer than you should because of plain old, god-awful delivery. The incessant ermmmmmming that accompanies your storytelling is enough to drive anyone insane. "So, erm, I was, erm, walking down the, erm, street and, erm, I went back to, erm, my parents', erm, house and I realised, erm, this bit is funny, erm, I erm, forgot my, erm, keys!!"

What you haven't realised is that by the fourth erm, we're all wiped out. We may well be nodding our heads with fake amusement on our faces, but one thing's for sure. We. Are. No. Longer. Listening. Maybe you're nervous because you're speaking to the whole group – that would certainly explain your sudden inability to remember the names of the simplest objects on Earth. In any case, all I can say is shape the fuck up, you're just chatting with your mates!

Another of the more annoying traits of an awful storyteller like you is forgetting the story halfway through. You do this allllllllll the time. You'll tell us you've got a great one, you'll bring a stop to all conversation, you'll start off all excited, then you'll just forget what happened and tail off. I mean, what the fuck, mate. Get your story straight before you waste valuable social time!! In my humble opinion, forgetful storytelling, combined with any of the above traits that cause a story to go on and on and on and on and on and on and on, provides anyone forced to listen with a solid murder motive that, when explained to the judge, should get excused as self-defence.

But perhaps the most embarrassing trait is a complete failure on your part to even understand what constitutes a good story. You'll share every little thing that happened to you, whether it's worth sharing or not. Do you think it's bad having to read social media posts, where people talk about all the pointless shit in their day that happens to just about everyone? Well, listening to you is like that, but in real life. And it's a fucking nightmare.

Surely you understand that a story, not even an exceptionally good one, is one where something happens that does not normally occur on a regular basis?! Maybe you are simply playing a numbers game? You really can't tell a good story apart from the banalities of everyone's daily lives, so you just throw anecdote upon anecdote at your mates until you strike gold? Maybe you don't actually have any good stories, as nothing interesting ever happens in your life, but you just want to feel included in the storytelling? Look, if you need to embellish and add in a few extra elements to improve the story, please do so!! Anything to prevent us from having to listen to multiple recitals of that time you made toast for breakfast but forgot to buy butter!!!!

- [Pointless] Exercise -

Don't get annoyed if your mates end up ignoring your stories. Provided they're not wankers, if they stare blankly at you when you reach the climax or start up a separate conversation, treat it as an opportunity to learn. Don't take so fucking long to get through them, don't mention unnecessary bloody details, stop ermmmmming, and make sure your stories aren't shit before you tell them. Maybe tell your stories to a mirror before you release them to the wild. If you bore even yourself, then you probably need to practise some more or come to terms with the fact that a particular tale just isn't worth telling. But make sure you don't get caught talking to yourself in the mirror - that's an anecdote that truly will stand the test of time. Your friends *will* destroy you, as they should. Idiot.

Know an idiot who needs to read this chapter?

- Scan the QR code
- Click the link
- Send it their way!

Guaranteed mutual self-destruction

What is true friendship?

People will offer up plenty of different answers to this question. Being interested in the same things, for example. Or having a similar sense of humour.

Blah. Blah. Blah.

Yes, these are important elements to how people become friends in the first place, but they don't explain how the most durable friendships last so long. True friendships are based on guaranteed mutual self-destruction. Much like diplomacy between two countries is handled, when they both possess nuclear arsenals.

By guaranteed mutual self-destruction, I mean that the volume of dodgy anecdotes that we have about each other is enormous. And the sharing of those stories with outsiders would cause significant and irreparable damage. Put simply, true friends have dirt on each other.

Why is this true friendship? First of all, it shows that we have *that many* shared experiences together. But also, some of these shared experiences reflect pretty poorly on us - think drunken nights and stupid decisions. So we have no choice, other than to trust each other not to share these stories. This creates a very strong bond, as long as the stories remain untold.

Some clueless fucks like you don't seem to bloody get it though. You don't respect the principle of guaranteed mutual self-destruction. You bring up these radioactive tales willy-nilly just to get a laugh, even among new people. You don't understand that you're risking the friendship itself, plain and simple. You constantly risk a flare-up of tensions, between two warring friends, who wield powerful stories up to their eyeballs.

You shouldn't be sharing that shit with just *anyone*. These stories are for when we're sitting down together and reminiscing, not for outsiders. Who knows what someone we don't know is going to do with this new information. The sane among us would rather not fucking find out. At the end of the day, if you bring up *that* story about me, I will counter with *that* story about you. And then we're both fucked.

– [Pointless] Exercise –

Try implementing a rule between your friends for sharing stories when you're with outsiders. For example, in our friendship group, when one of our mates is about to bring up a tasty story in front of people that have no business hearing it, we quickly say, "Rule Number One", before they can get into their stride. When asked what this means by outsiders, we tell them it means, "Be Kind". But the true meaning is, "Don't You Fucking Dare". Failing that, you need to always think about the risk you're taking when bringing up a dodgy story about your friend. Consider all those mornings when you struggled to remember what happened the night before. Do you really believe your mate hasn't got something up their sleeve for a rainy day, maybe even photo evidence? Idiot.

Know an idiot who needs to read this chapter?

- Scan the QR code
- Click the link
- Send it their way!

Humblebragging

Humblebragging is basically saying something modest or self-deprecating and even complaining, to disguise what is actually a fat old brag. Ring any bells? A couple of examples for the thickos:

When people say the stock market is absolutely fucked at the moment and is down five per cent – they've lost sixteen grand as a result! Translation: five per cent of the money they had at their disposal to invest was sixteen grand, so they're doing pretty fucking well, thank you very much!

When people say they have had to spend a fortune, as all their clothes are hanging loose. Translation: they've lost a ton of weight and you should too, you fat bastard.

The problem with your humblebragging is *everyone* sees through it. Okay maybe not everyone, some people are fucking stupid. But most people see it for what it is – a blatant attempt by you to steer the conversation to yourself and the things you are most proud of.

But why do you feel the need to hide the brag? It would be better to just brazenly come out with it. At least then, you're not trying to conceal what you're proud of, behind a misty cloud of fake modesty. It's a simple case of sincerity vs. insincerity.

It's even worse for your mates. They have to watch you do it time and time again, especially when meeting new people. They wonder how you don't know that they know – because it's *that* obvious. They therefore assume that you must think they're fucking stupid. The fake, shy hair tuck and smile, the look down at the floor, the "I don't like to go on about it". Give us a break, mate!!!!!

The truth is, for the most part, you do know they know. But you just can't help yourself. It's quite sad actually. Humblebraggers like you would sooner lose the respect of your friends than pass up the opportunity to get the most prized aspects of yourselves out there to new people. There are only two reasons I can think of to explain why you feel the need to do this.

One is that you're just an attention-seeking motherfucker. You cannot *not* tell people how great you are and what you've accomplished. You want the whole fucking world and their mothers to think you're amazing. You've tried brazen bragging before, but people just told you to piss off because it was too much. So now you humblebrag, hoping against all hope that no one can tell, like the deluded muppet you are. But your friends see through it every time, without fail. You need to remember that what actually matters in genuine relationships is not based on the superficial: loyalty, kindness, respect.

The second reason is that you are too insecure about yourself and who you are. You are not convinced that your personality is enough. You worry that you need something, other than yourself, to be accepted when meeting new people. So you bring up the accomplishments you are most proud of, hidden in what at first glance are harmless statements, in the hope that they make people like you and excuse your perceived lack of personality. You use the humblebrag because you are nervous – you know bragging isn't the best thing in the world, but you feel you need to do *something* to get noticed.

– [Pointless] Exercise –

If you're an attention-seeking, motherfucker of a humblebragger, you need to try and hold that shit back. You are not getting away with it, your friends are fed up with it and people who hear it day in day out will start to pull you up on it. Instead of *pretending* you have some humility, how about just fucking having some? If you're one of the incredibly insecure people, who feels they need to remind everyone of what they've done or what they have, please remember that your personality and who you are is always more important than anything else. If you really believe you need to humblebrag for people to like you, and that your personality is just not enough, learn some bloody jokes. Idiot.

Know an idiot who needs to read this chapter?

- Scan the QR code
- Click the link
- Send it their way!

Baby talk

Having a baby is a momentous occasion in anyone's life. It should be celebrated, absolutely. No contesting that. But you really do not need to keep going on about it. We are all very much aware that you love your baby. You're *supposed* to love your baby! People have had babies in the past, people will have babies in the future. It's really nothing earth-shattering that you've had one too.

If you come and tell me that you've had a baby, I will be very, very happy for you. I will give you my heartfelt congratulations. But that does not mean that I want to hear about it 24/7.

For some reason, you want to tell us every single new thing that the kid has done, down to when it has eaten mushy vegetables for the first time. That's fantastic, but I don't really give a shit.

You take way too many photos on your phone and show them off all the fucking time, accompanied with a story behind each image. Yes, the photos are really cute, but you've just swiped through one hundred and thirty-eight of the fuckers, and I can't tell the bloody difference between any of them! It's enough to make anyone want to go back to a simpler time when two photos in a wallet or purse were all any parent had to show.

You think your baby's crazy building block skills are a sure sign that you've bred a future Nobel prize winner. On the contrary, mate, if your kid *wasn't* able to build that straight line, I'd be worried.

What you need to realise is that no one cares as much about your baby as you. Simply because it's yours, not theirs. It's nothing personal. It's just the way it is.

In addition, what makes you think that everyone wants to be around your baby when you do the rounds of your friends' places after the birth?

You start turning up to every function with the kid, without warning, and ask people to stop doing things that had never previously been a problem, and that you, in fact, did all the time! People drink and smoke at parties, that's never going to change. If you don't want your kid around that stuff, don't bring them! In what world do you think it's acceptable to ask your friends to change their behaviour, simply because you decided to get yourself or your partner knocked up!

For another thing, it's way too obvious that the main reason some of you bring your babies to your friends' houses, uninvited and without warning, is because you're looking for a little time off. You're hoping for a cheeky bit of free childcare from your mates, aren't you? The thing is, the child is your responsibility, no one else's. Your friends are at this party for fun, not for unpaid babysitting work, while you put your feet up and have a laugh.

Finally, not everyone is used to being around babies. Not everyone knows how to hold them, and more to the point, not everyone is comfortable holding someone else's baby. You shouldn't be putting that pressure on them. And if that person appears to be unfamiliar with the fucking rugby hold, you end up scolding them and taking the kid from their arms with a glare that says, "You're a terrible human being". Take your bloody kid elsewhere or keep them at home if you're going to tell people off! They didn't have a kid, *you* did!

- [Pointless] Exercise -

Stop asking your friends to change their behaviour at parties for your child. Either pay for childcare for the evening or stay the fuck home. While we're at it, if no one asks, yet you insist on bringing the topic of your baby up anyway, please keep it short and sweet. Thirty seconds maximum should suffice for telling your friends what your baby has been doing and no more than two new pictures at a time. Then move on to something more interesting. Idiot.

Know an idiot who needs to read this chapter?

- Scan the QR code
- Click the link
- Send it their way!

Always being late

Why are you always fucking late?! And I mean, *always* late. Apart from that one time you just about arrived on time, then had the absolute bloody cheek to point at your watch while shaking your head. Prick.

If we both set a time of 3:00 pm, we know for a fact that you're turning up no earlier than 3:30. In the A.M. Seriously though, it's out of order. You seem to love making us waste our time. Leaving us no choice but to loiter on the street, most likely sweating our arses off in a baking heatwave or getting drenched under a never-ending downpour. At which point we have to buy a coffee or a pint, that we never actually wanted, and sit there on our lonesome, bored out of our heads.

You *always* have an excuse as well. Yes, traffic can be a nightmare, but you'd have to be cursed for that many pile-ups to occur in your immediate vicinity, every time you leave the fucking house. No, you did not get held up by your neighbour for a chat – no one talks to their neighbours anymore, weirdo. No, you did not have yet another family emergency – how many family members have you got and why are they always ill? And no, you were not helping yet another old lady across the road – it doesn't take half an hour to cross the road, no matter how many canes are needed. Nobody's life is this dramatic mate, you are taking your friends for fools.

We love you, but let's face it, you don't really respect your friends' time. And the only reason you come up with excuses is that you know it's not on. Time is our most valuable resource, and you shit all over it on a daily basis, you tardy fuck. Don't tell me you just have a different relationship with time – you're not fucking Doctor Who. The truth is you just can't be bothered to make sure you are on time. You make it to work on time most days – enough not to get fired anyway. So you could absolutely be on time for us if you wanted to.

I do think that the rise of people like you being late all the time, could be something to do with being able to text your excuses. Nowadays, it's so easy to text someone, come up with a bullshit reason and say you're on your way when you're actually still in your dressing gown. It's much harder to lie to someone on the phone or face to face. Texting has taken away the shame of knowing you're leaving someone waiting. Nevertheless, it's still unacceptable.

There are people who advocate various tactics to manage the behaviour of frequent latecomers like you. Here are some of them:

- Starting without you – in other words, going ahead and ordering our food, getting the first round, whatever it is.
- Lying about the start time, so you end up unintentionally being on time.
- Specifying a minute rather than an hour – because, in your thicko latecomer brain, 6:00 pm means sixish. So we should tell you ten past six instead.
- Reiterating the importance of turning up on time to particularly meaningful events.
- Punishing you financially – telling you that, if you're late, you're buying the cinema tickets, the first five pints etc.

Now, these are all great ideas and, having tested them extensively on some of my more wanky mates, I can tell you that they do work from time to time.

But in all honesty, the onus should not be on *us* to manage and accommodate *you*. You should not need us to employ tactics, so you can keep to the timings of pre-agreed plans. You are a fucking adult – allegedly. You're not a fucking child whose behaviour needs to be scolded, moulded and rectified. You should not need to be told off. You should be able to recognise that you are being an arsehole and consequently modify your own behaviour.

- [Pointless] Exercise -

Get a fucking watch and use it. Stop making excuses. Know how long it takes you to walk to the bloody train station and start getting to your commitments on time. 6:00 pm does not mean 6-7ish. It means 6:00 pm. And if you are someone who is always waiting on tardy pricks, stop making excuses or using silly tactics to manage their schedule for them. They may well respect you as a person, but you need to realise the truth that they don't respect your time. They get to their job on time most days, don't they? Why can't they do the same for you? You need to let them know it's pissing you off. Explain how disrespectful it is. Sure, give them a couple of chances. But if they continue to take you for a fucking fool, it's time to shut them out and find new friends. Not nice to come to terms with, but it's better than standing on the street like a lemon, for an hour or two every other week. Idiot.

Know an idiot who needs to read this chapter?

- Scan the QR code
- Click the link
- Send it their way!

One-upmanship

Chatting with friends, telling stories and sharing successes, failures and heartaches are all some of the greatest joys of socialising. In fact, many people consider it as the only therapy they can actually afford.

However, the therapeutic benefits of sharing are somewhat disrupted when there is a one-upping prat like you listening in. You feel this innate need to try and beat our stories, whether happy or sad. Whatever we do, feel or achieve, you have always apparently done it better, felt it more or achieved bigger things.

When we tell our friends about something, you will decline to acknowledge any element of our story. You'll give us no praise, nor will you ask a single follow-up question. Instead, you use our story as a platform to bring up something similar that happened to you. Which completely undercuts us and makes us feel like pieces of shit who have nothing interesting to say. These are not the actions of a mate.

What I'm interested in is why you feel this need to one-up your friends?

Social awkwardness maybe? Perhaps you feel that you are, in actual fact, just trying to relate to other people and get in on the conversation by telling a relevant story? In some social situations, hearing a story that relates to something we've previously experienced, can be the equivalent of a social life raft.

But you don't need to use someone else's story to take over the room. Surely you can read the room, the awkward silence as you use someone else's story as a springboard for your own brag? Alas, it appears not, you seem to be the complete opposite of a social butterfly, more like a social slug with no ability to read social cues.

Most sane, socially adept people know that one-upping is *never* how you deal with any story that your mate has just told you. We all want, nay need, to be able to share and confide in our friends and feel like they have our back. If you truly are *that* socially awkward, you could have simply used the initial story to get involved by asking questions or making observations about it.

Sometimes, however, it is not even an issue of social awkwardness. I know plenty of one-uppers, maybe even including yourself, who are otherwise very accomplished in a social setting.

In this case, you are nothing other than a dickhead who just cannot *not* try to beat the story. You are *so* competitive that you can't even intelligently save your story for a more advantageous time to tell it. It's like you are in a perpetual state of social comparison, trying to ensure you "win" the game of life. Sadly, other people's success only serves to make you feel inadequate.

The thought of someone else succeeding and having the limelight just does not sit well with you. So, you simply do not let them have it – instead, you act out, like a child. You whip out your story to diminish the impact of that of the perceived limelight hogger. Sometimes your story will even be completely false, which is when things get really fucking sad. But regardless of whether your one-upping story is true or not, why can't you just be happy for, or commiserate with, your friends?

I can't see any reason for this competitiveness other than severely low self-esteem, though it may be hidden very well. But it's no excuse for shitting on other people's success and happiness. You should be able to keep your competitiveness in check – at least enough to acknowledge the story and pretend to be a good friend. You need to recognise that no one is telling their story to make you feel bad, you fucking twat. The vast, vast majority, are simply sharing a story. Not everyone thinks in a vindictive, vicious way like you.

– [Pointless] Exercise –

One-upmanship is much more acceptable if at first, you pretend to be interested and talk about the experience had by the original storyteller. Try to actually revel in their success. Failing that, ask at least one question about the other person's story for fuck's sake. After that, I have no issue with you eventually telling your story to add to the conversation, because it's not blatantly obvious that you're trying to belittle someone else's. For those who have to deal with one-uppers on a regular basis, the only thing you can do is go into the conversation expecting it. Start counting how many times they'll try to top your stories. Why not even get a sweepstake going? You'll still be pissed off, but pissed off with a little extra dosh is always better. Idiot.

Know an idiot who needs to read this chapter?

- Scan the QR code
- Click the link
- Send it their way!

Not introducing new people

Everyone loves meeting new people. At least, that's what every fucking boring person says in the hope that it makes them sound social and a little bit more interesting. Let's take it to be true, for argument's sake.

So in theory, when you bring someone new to the party, we're all eagerly anticipating meeting this new person.

Except it's nigh on impossible to meet them if you make no introductions. I mean, what the fuck are you doing, mate? You walk in with someone new in tow and just say nothing?!

You're leaving them to fend for themselves. There's no telling how shy that person is – your mates don't bloody know them! If they *are* relatively shy, they are just going to stand there awkwardly, until a good soul decides to say hello and save them. If they are more outgoing, they'll go round the room, embarrassingly trying to interrupt conversations between people they don't know from Adam. Either way, it's just not fair on them.

We all know what it's like in a group setting where everyone knows each other – an unknown quantity casts a shadow over the gathering. We're all in our cliquey comfort zone, and you're mad if you think we're going to allow some newbie, whose name we do not know, to take us out of it. For this reason, if there are no intros, the majority of people will not make that first approach.

Sometimes I get the impression that you think it's impressive just to have brought someone new to the party. Almost as if you think you're some kind of social butterfly, simply because you know one other person outside of your friend group. In your big head, you're so cool, you can just head into the party – you don't need to do any intros! Fucking mistake, you twat. You look like an absolute knobhead and you're potentially ruining the party.

Apparently, you never realised that when you can actually be arsed, and you have the decency to do introductions on arrival, everyone is more than happy and prepared to do the handshake with the obligatory, "Hey blah blah, so how do you know each other?" It's a nice, easy starter for everyone involved.

Unfortunately, you appear to possess similar manners to that of a fucking rabid dog, charging into the party without a care in the world for those you have forced to spend time together.

- [Pointless] Exercise -

You'd do well to remember that *no one* is too cool for social niceties. It's not even that fucking difficult, you ignorant arsehole. When you bring someone new to a party, who doesn't know anyone there, you quickly go round the room, pointing at people and introducing them, "Harry, Sally. Sally, Harry. Harry, John. John, Harry." And so on. Failing that, you don't have to do the whole room straight away, but at least bring the newbie with you as you work the room and introduce one person at a time. Idiot.

Know an idiot who needs to read this chapter?

- Scan the QR code
- Click the link
- Send it their way!

Phone fear

The original purpose of the telephone was to call people. To be able to hear each other's voices, communicate important details and get things sorted quickly, wherever we are. It must have been a revelation at the time and it was likely treated as such.

Back then, there were probably still people who were shit-scared of using the phone. But there is no doubt that with the advent of other forms of communication such as text, email and social media, more and more people now have minor panic attacks every time they need to call someone.

It's painful to watch when the fear impedes their whole life. Calling to book a table at a restaurant, or to ask if a shop is open until 10:00 pm, turns into a whole ordeal. They fall out with friends and family because they are so fearful of that menacing dialling tone that they end up never calling. God forbid they need to have an initial phone interview for a job… blood pressure through the fucking roof for nothing!!

I'm obviously not talking about those with true telephobia, who are equally afraid of answering the phone as they are of making calls and meeting people in general. This is linked to social anxiety and is a wider issue that needs work to overcome; that, I get.

I am, however, talking about muppets like you without social anxiety, who talk on the phone at work on the regular, and are fine chatting to your friends and family on the blower, but *only* if you are called first. If you have to actually make the call, well, for some bloody reason, that's a whole new ball game.

Let's take that first element, receiving calls at work. You have no problem with it! Someone calls you with an issue, you pick up, you either sort it out or tell them you can't and here's why. Simple. Yet when you need to call a company's customer service or call anyone for any semi-official reason, it's like you're being asked to arrange a ceasefire with some nutty warmonger!!

You get incredibly nervous. You rehearse how you imagine the call will go a thousand and one times before dialling. You make shitty excuses like, “No one makes calls nowadays” or, “What if they’re too busy to talk?”. But, people *do* still make calls. And if they’re too busy, well, they just won’t pick up, you prat. You would rather wait until the situation you need to resolve gets so dire, that you no longer have any other option. Sometimes you even get overly angry when asked to make a call and flat out refuse to do it.

One particular story comes to mind about someone I know, who bought an electric scooter and realised it didn’t work. But instead of calling and arranging a return, they just left it sitting in their house for four months, way past the thirty-day return window. They spent five hundred quid on the bloody thing!!! And no, they were by no means rich enough to let that kind of money pass them by. They just could not bring themselves to call up the retailer and organise a return. Five hundred pounds lost for the sake of one lousy, no-big-deal phone call.

All this hysteria… for what?

You’ve been the person on the other line for fuck’s sake, what are you so frightened about?! Even if you have never worked anywhere you need to answer phones, it’s still just another person on the line!! They’re not going to kill you, in fact, they can’t do *anything* to you, they can’t even *see* you!!

But look, I’m not a monster. I did help electric-scooter-person get their money back. I get your hesitancy to a certain extent. When talking to someone on the phone, there is no body language to work off, no social cues indicating how you should respond. I can understand being nervous about your voice, your accent, your ability to speak well. I see why you could be scared of looking stupid, worried about making a verbal mistake or stammering a little while having to think on the fly. And yes, it can absolutely feel like you're being judged, especially when speaking on the phone in front of other people, like at the office.

However, despite these valid concerns, they are not good enough reasons to explain why you are so petrified of answering the phone. No matter how bad your stammer or verbal slip up is, put it in context. The person on the other end of the line will hardly register it, they don't give that much of a shit about you. These people receive dozens of calls a day, if not more. Whatever happens on your call is a blip on their radar. Unless you really, truly fuck up. But even then, you will only ever be a funny anecdote for that person to tell at the pub. It's not the end of the world.

In my experience, whatever bullshit reason you give, the underlying explanation for the "terror" of making quasi-serious calls is fear of rejection. Too many people live and die by how people think of them. A negative response sends them over the edge.

You need to remember that no one *likes* rejection. It's how you define it, how you let it affect you, whether you take it as a slight upon your character, that determines if it stops you picking up the phone the next time. I'm here to tell you to get over it. Just get over it! You're not a fucking child. Rejection is a part of life and happens all the time, sometimes without you even knowing it. Being told no, when trying to open a savings account, or when returning that shirt that was delivered ripped, is not that big of a bloody deal, you numpty.

- [Pointless] Exercise -

To get over this fear of making calls, you need to do it over and over. Force yourself to make calls and you'll gradually realise that there is nothing to be afraid of. If you need to start off with the easier calls first, like ordering a pizza, do so. As you progress in call intensity, and you get rejected for the eighteenth time, you'll soon catch on that nothing earth-shattering ever happens as a result. Psychologists call this 'cognitive restructuring'. I prefer the words of a ruder Nike: "Just fucking do it". Remember all the benefits that you're missing out on by not making these phone calls. You'd get things sorted in real-time rather than fifteen emails back and forth, you'd maintain some much needed social contact in your life in a digital age, you'd be creating relationships with people that aren't based on words on a screen. You might even find you actually have a really pleasant conversation, while negotiating your new twenty-four-month phone contract, with Kevin from BT. Thanks Kevin. Idiot.

Know an idiot who needs to read this chapter?

- Scan the QR code
- Click the link
- Send it their way!

Telling it like it is…

There's always a twat like you in every friendship group who loves making sure the whole fucking world knows that you "tell it like it is", that you keep it real, that you always tell the truth to our faces.

You really give it the biggun', telling us exactly how you would have handled things in our place. "Yeah! Well, if I was there I'd have told them straight!" Shaaaaaaatup will you.

Using this phrase shows instantly that you just don't have a fucking clue. You either have no idea who you really are or no idea how to handle a delicate situation. There are so many instances in which "telling it like it is" is a god-awful thing to do. So many times when we don't know the full story or the perspective of everyone involved. Failing to recognise that, and harping on about your innate truthfulness, shows a complete lack of judgement.

Let me clarify.

Sometimes you say that you "tell it like it is" because you're actually a complete bottle job. You are trying to impress your mates by seeming more loud-mouthed than you actually are. When the circumstances finally call for you to be the strong teller of truth, there is never any doubt that you will avoid the potential confrontation that could arise, like the pussy you really are.

This is an embarrassing state of affairs, my friend. Not all of us are built for confrontation, there's no shame in that. But pretending to be tough, just to impress someone… maaaaate. Just be yourself, for fuck's sake.

Other times you overcompensate in your mission to constantly "tell it like it is". You are the kind of pillock who would reply to their boss after being asked how they are feeling today with, "Shit. I'm at work ain't I?". You would more than happily tell someone their fashion sense has died a violent death, while at a funeral. You would listen to a suicidal bloke on a rooftop, telling you all the things that he hates about his life, then agree, and tell him he might as well get on with it. On the way down, you'd shout down to the bloke and tell him to start fucking combing his hair in hell or he won't find a girlfriend down there either.

Obviously, these are exaggerated examples and are unlikely to happen. But the point still stands. You are unable to comprehend that there are times when it simply does not make sense to "tell it like it is". Honesty is not always the best policy. You have to judge each situation on its merits and work out what's needed. Is it an arm around the shoulders? Is it a comforting word or two? Is it a little white lie? Or does someone just need to hear the truth? There is no one size fits all approach to dealing with people. It's time that you realise it, you "tell it like it is" prick.

Most of the time though, you use the phrase simply as an excuse for being a gobby cunt. You genuinely believe you can insult anyone, in any way you like, as long as you justify it at the end with, "Sorry if you can't handle it, mate. I'm just telling it like it is". Bullshit, you absolute wanker. Half the time what you say is complete shite anyway, miles away from the truth.

Gobby cunts like you are also the most two-faced bastards on the planet. You think you always "tell it like it is" to people's faces, yeah? So tell me, why then are you constantly bitching away and slating people behind their backs?

- [Pointless] Exercise -

If you're someone who likes to talk tough, telling everyone you "tell it like it is", all the while hoping the moment never comes that you end up showing how much of a pussy you really are, just know that no one finds it impressive. Gullible muppets might not need proof that you're tough because, well, they're gullible muppets. But sensible, considerate people will know you're talking out of your arse. You're not built for confrontation - so what? You can get better at confrontation with practice, handling it calmly and with logic. You will never get better at it by pretending you're a massive prick. And for the times when you actually do find the courage to "tell it like it is", just so you can justify putting people down when you fancy a cheeky vent, I can't wait for the day you meet a gobbier cunt who "tells it like it is" much more aggressively than you. You are going to be shut down so hard. Everyone is going to realise what a nobody you are. You will lose friends and respect - things that you never truly had in the first place. And it will be sweeeeeet. Maybe it's time to start being nicer to people and to realise that, sometimes, just slating people because a thought popped into your head helps no one. Idiot.

Know an idiot who needs to read this chapter?

- Scan the QR code
- Click the link
- Send it their way!

Vaguebooking on social media

Never heard of it? It's a stupid name, which comes from connecting the words 'vague' and 'Facebook', and is the practice of making a post on social media that is intentionally vague and normally highly personal.

You've probably already worked out by now that this chapter is about muppets like you who post overly cryptic and/or emotional messages on social media, providing no details whatsoever.

So, why do you post intentionally vague messages? In most cases, it's because you are crying out for attention and sympathy. The lack of detail is generally designed to incite someone to respond and ask for more information. You are desperately begging for someone to care and ask what's wrong, for someone, *anyone* to be interested in what's happening in your life. Sometimes your wanky posts are vague because you want to refer to a specific someone or something without naming them/it.

Here are some example posts that I've seen from your accounts on way too many occasions:

- "Ahhh I'm so angry right now!"
- "Why does it always happen to me?!"
- "???"
- "How is this still a thing in the 21st century..."
- "People can be so cruel sometimes..."

When most people see posts like the above, they scroll right past with a scrunched nose and a quick, "Oh, fuck off will ya". But that somehow doesn't deter you.

Your posts absolutely reek of desperation. And most of the time, the "problems" being masked by your shitty, vague messages, aren't real problems at all. Yes, every now and then, there is a genuine cry for help behind them; you might be having a really bad time of it and just aren't quite sure how to express what you're going through. But on the whole, you are just feeling lonely at that particular moment in time and want someone to give you the time of day.

You have completely missed the point though, you sad vaguebooker. For one thing, when no one replies to your sorrowful, "please notice me", cry for attention, you're only going to feel worse. You might even end up having an unwanted conversation with that weird kid from primary school, who you last spoke to in real life fifteen years ago. Social media is just not the place to turn to when you're feeling down or lonely.

If you feel the need for a bit of attention, a bit of comfort, or just a bit of an arm around you, call up someone who actually cares – on the fucking telephone. If your friends and family are ignoring you, work out why that is. Moping about and posting absolute rubbish on social media, in full view of a bunch of people who mostly couldn't really give two shits about you, instead of actually doing something to fix your problem, is never going to help. In fact, it only serves to make you look like a child who hasn't learned the importance of proper communication.

Vaguebooking posts that call people out without naming them are just as fucking stupid. You're running the risk that people will simply guess what you're referring to. They might even assume you're talking about them. Though, even in this scenario, the most likely outcome is they will never give it a second thought.

If you really have to post about something in particular, at least stop being a pussy and name the problem. If it's a person, can't you just message them in private? We realise you are the kind of person who loves the drama of airing their dirty laundry in public – otherwise, you wouldn't be vaguebooking in the first place. But spare the rest of us the fucking antics will you – we don't care enough about your unspecified problem to have to keep reading your bollox. Unless it's particularly juicy gossip, in which case hand me the bloody popcorn – no salt, I'm not a fucking animal.

– [Pointless] Exercise –

The next time you're about to do a bit of casual, wanky vaguebooking, remember that it will not help you. No one cares about your fake problem, that you can't even be bothered to explain, and it will still exist when you've logged off. If you really have to post something, be explicit about your so-called problem. And if you're one of those people who reply to vaguebooking posts, please stop. You're just encouraging this pointless behaviour. It's a waste of your valuable finger-typing calories. If you're that worried, ask them directly off of social media. Idiot.

Know an idiot who needs to read this chapter?

- Scan the QR code
- Click the link
- Send it their way!

Taking the mick

Taking the mick, taking the piss, teasing, ribbing, banter, whatever you want to call it, is essentially the act of mocking someone. Admittedly, this sounds like something we should avoid doing. Surely there's no reason to mock someone, other than to be a prick and make them feel bad, right? Wrong. Well, normally.

Taking the mick is key to any solid friendship group. At the risk of sounding like a massive sap, it can be a wonderful way to bring people together, to make people feel comfortable and to show our affection for them. Insults become terms of endearment.

That's not to say it doesn't have its risks. It is absolutely an art form that must be honed. We need to understand when to take the mick, who it's fine to take the mick out of and what is acceptable mickey-taking material. This is where you go so wrong, you muppet.

You should never take the mick out of someone you have just met. It's just a complete no-no. Taking the mick should be reserved for people you know at least relatively well. By somewhat knowing who they are and what makes them tick, you've got a much better idea of what you could say in jest, that would not cross any lines. They are also much more likely to see the endearment behind your quips. When you take the mick out of someone you don't know, you run the risk of finding out, to your detriment, that this person is actually a nutty martial art specialist who fucks people up in cage fights on the regular, does not like to be ribbed and prefers breaking yours.

More than anything though, it shows a complete lack of respect to take the piss out of someone you encounter for the first time. You haven't earned the right to do it as you have no shared experiences to draw upon. You have no relationship to speak of. You can't possibly hold any affection for a person you have just met. Because you don't know them, there is absolutely fuck all for you to use as teasing material other than their appearance, accent or your first impression of them. Therefore, no matter what your intentions are when using this material, you're giving this person no option other than to assume that you're being a malicious twat and to interpret what you're saying as an act of aggression. A smack in your mouth would be more than justified.

Taking the mick is also generally only acceptable when the goal is to make everyone laugh, including the person you're taking the mick out of. If instead, you make everyone else laugh but cause the target to feel like shit, it's safe to say that you've royally fucked it. Unless you're a psychopathic prick, you're going to have that niggling feeling that you've been a bit out of order and burnt a bridge.

Taking the mick is about gentle ribbing. It's supposed to be light-hearted, nothing too serious. But what is considered light-hearted is admittedly very subjective. For every one person who takes a certain piss-take well, there will be another who is not best pleased about you bringing up a particular topic. I've seen ripped gym-goers take real offence to being called a "fat git" when ordering a burger, despite the joke being that they're not fat at all. It's all about perspective and history. There is a really fine line here and it's why knowing the person well is so important. How can you preempt that someone is going to take your joke like a champ and find it funny unless you know them? You can't, so don't risk it, you silly mug.

You also do not appear to understand when a joke has reached its expiration date. You'll happily tease someone with the same material every single fucking time you see each other. Most people take the mick out of someone about a specific thing a few times, and then move on once that person has proved themselves able to take that joke. But no, not you. You carry on and on and on. There's never any variation to your stale joke either, it's always the same recycled content.

First of all, come up with something else, mate. Be more creative. It was funny the first time, not the seventy-eighth. Secondly, ramming the same piss-take down someone's throat does not reflect well on you. It comes across like you're trying to turn this particular mickey-take into a complex for the other person. By incessantly bringing it up, it seems as if you are actually trying to get in their head. Maybe you're trying to make them crack and then bask in the false triumph of driving them nuts, about something that never actually truly bothered them in the first place. In any case, you're drifting away from light-hearted mickey-taking and into the realm of bullying.

Lastly, do not take the mick out of people if you can't take a joke yourself. Wankers like you can dish it out fine, but you lose your shit when you get a little ribbing back. No matter what the teasing is about, just the embarrassment of being the subject of a bit of banter in front of others brings out the worst in you. You'll get upset whenever anyone takes the piss out of you, yet ten minutes later you're back at the forefront of the joshing of another person, hoping everyone will overlook your prior tantrum. Being able to shake off a piss-take, or even partake in a little self-deprecation, is a non-negotiable prerequisite for the right to take the mick out of others. After all, why the fuck would you expect someone to take your banter in jest when your pussy response is to just throw your toys out of the pram?

- [Pointless] Exercise -

Stop taking the mick out of people you have just met. It may well be the reason why you think it's hard to make friends as an adult. It may also be the reason why all your current mates are fucking pricks, like you. We all look forward to the day you take the piss out of the wrong person and get destroyed, hopefully physically as well as psychologically. If you can't take a joke, but still want to partake in a bit of banter, get yourself a full-length mirror. Look at your reflection and take the piss out of everything you see. It might take you, in particular, a good while. But once you're done, you'll either be ready to dip your toes into the world of self-deprecation or you'll never leave the house ever again. Either way, win-win for humanity. Idiot.

Know an idiot who needs to read this chapter?

- Scan the QR code
- Click the link
- Send it their way!

In conversation

"Where did you last see it?"

Everyone has been in the position where they have lost something they need while in a rush to get out the door. Keys, wallet, purse, phone – whatever it is, after having looked for quite some time, in all the obvious places, we can get a little frustrated. Inevitably, we eventually ask for the help of those around us.

And it's at this point that a pillock like you pipes up with, "Where did you last see it?"...

My God – what a fucking stupid question.

Listen, mate. If I knew where I had last seen it, then it wouldn't be fucking lost would it, you utter twat. Why the fuck do you think I'm screaming at everyone around me, thinking I'm surrounded by nothing but a bunch of thieving bastards? Because it's not where I last saw it!!! I need you to help me find the thing, not stand around treating me like some prick with half a brain.

You might be shaking your head while reading this, thinking that sometimes the person who has lost something is in such a panic, that they haven't actually thought about where they've been or where they last saw it. And this is true for the numpties who don't realise their glasses are on their bloody head or who leave the fucking keys in the fridge when they make a sandwich.

But by the time most people are in a massive panic or have been looking for ages, there is little doubt that they have actually lost the item or it's been moved. They have already racked their brains for where they might have left it, checked there a hundred times and still not found it.

So if you believe that you're bringing some much needed calm and logic to the table with this question, think again. Consider your audience. Is the person who has lost something stupid enough to not ask themselves where they last saw the lost item? If not, just help look, and keep your thicko questions to yourself.

- [Pointless] Exercise -

Instead of wasting precious seconds asking, "Where did you last see it?", do us all a favour, get on your hands and knees and check under the fucking couch. Please. Idiot.

Know an idiot who needs to read this chapter?

- Scan the QR code
- Click the link
- Send it their way!

"Carrots help you see in the dark"

When you were young, what did your parents do to get you to eat food that is good for you, but that you didn't like? They said and did shit that made the food seem more fun, right? This in itself is not a massive problem. Your parents were just trying to look after you. The issue is you still believe what you were told while you were being coerced into eating your five a day and regurgitate these "facts" later on in life.

I'm sorry to break it to you, but your parents told you that carrots would help you see in the dark, simply because they hoped it would get you to eat your carrots. Not because they are special orange vegetables endowed with the superpower to magically help you see in the dark. I know, mind blown. While we're at it, peas on a spoon aren't actually little aeroplanes. Your parents made those propellor sounds with their mouths, you fucking prat.

Okaaaay, yes, carrots are a good source of vitamin A. If you truly struggle to see anything in low light, *anything* with vitamin A will help you. But if you have no vitamin A deficiency in the first place, you will not somehow acquire night-time infrared vision just from eating carrots, you muppet.

On the other hand, so many parents individually dreaming up the same notion that carrots help you see in the dark is a bit of a stretch. So, apart from the express purpose of force-feeding children, why else do you and so many other people say that carrots improve their night-time vision?

Turns out it's because the British Ministry of Defence wanted to hide their new radar technology from the Germans in WWII! It was getting a little suspicious how good they were at shooting down German planes at night, so they told the press they were feeding their pilots tons of carrots. So effective was this myth, the Germans started also feeding carrots to their pilots. The side effect was that thickos like you started believing this bollox and perpetuating the myth.

So, in short, stop believing all the bullshit from your childhood. Some of you will just not have it that your parents lied to you about anything. But you best believe that, when you have kids, you'll undoubtedly spout the same lies. Lying is a wonderful, underrated parenting tool. Get over it.

At the same time, parents should be wary about using this myth on kids who wear glasses. I certainly didn't appreciate being served this tripe, when I couldn't even see in the fucking daytime at just six years old! It's enough to give any glasses-wearing kid a serious carrot complex.

- [Pointless] Exercise -

Do an experiment. Judge your current level of nighttime vision. Then eat twenty carrots a day for two weeks. Then check it again. Did it improve? No – but your hands started turning orange? Idiot.

Know an idiot who needs to read this chapter?

- Scan the QR code
- Click the link
- Send it their way!

"Money doesn't buy you happiness"

I like the premise of this saying. But only when it is used for the right reasons. Unfortunately, too many dumbos like you take it too literally.

If you use this phrase simply because you're being a little bitch about the fact that you have no money, you're using it incorrectly. This phrase is not a comeback you employ to console yourself for the fact that you're broke, yet still unhappy. Trying to convince yourself that having more money wouldn't make any difference, just because you don't foresee a future in which you might be better off, is pointless.

Don't get me wrong, I completely agree that there is more to life than money. We don't *need* it to be happy. Happiness for most of us comes from surrounding ourselves with people we love and who love us, and also from feeling like we have a purpose. Of *course* this can be achieved without money. In fact, we *cannot* buy these things. This is the real meaning behind the phrase, "Money doesn't buy you happiness".

However, it must be remembered that it's a lot fucking *harder* to be happy without money. The truth is, sometimes we don't even see the happiness that we actually have in our lives, because of the monetary pressures of modern life. The pressure of trying to make ends meet and of trying to maintain a certain lifestyle. Unfortunately, we *do* need a certain amount of money to make life easier, and therefore make it easier to appreciate what we do have that makes us happy. But that does not mean we need to be rich and flush with cash.

Having a lot of money can also make happiness more difficult. In a world where everything is about money and making more of it, how do you continue feeling fulfilled? By making more? It doesn't make any difference at that point, because you already have enough. More money than necessary just buys you more stuff –

bigger houses, nicer cars, more holidays. These are nice-to-haves. But they won't make you happy. Another less obvious consequence of extra dosh is it becomes more difficult to know who around you truly cares about you. People, family, friends and strangers alike, will pretend to like you simply because you're loaded. That can make you feel on edge, suspicious, always looking over your shoulder.

At the end of the day, the phrase, "Money doesn't buy you happiness", is both true and false at the same time. The trick is to work hard enough, to have *enough* money. Just *enough*. You don't need more than that. Enough money will give you the time to enjoy the people in your life, yet stay fulfilled as far as possible.

– [Pointless] Exercise –

Work out how much money is enough for you. The amount that pays the bills, leaves you relatively comfortable and able to do things you enjoy and spend time with the people you love. Cut out the frills that make your life expensive, when it really doesn't need to be. You don't need the iPhone, you don't need the fancy car. Do the maths. It's not that hard. Idiot.

Know an idiot who needs to read this chapter?

- Scan the QR code
- Click the link
- Send it their way!

"God, you're blind!"

Why do people wear glasses? Why do they decide to put extra bits of ugly fucking glass and plastic over their eyes and head? It isn't for fun, I can tell you that.

Unless they're one of those weirdos who wears fake lenses for "fashion", it's because they can't fucking see properly without them.

So with your twenty-twenty vision, what the fuck do you expect to see when you ask to try on other peoples' glasses? I get that you're fascinated to see what the world looks like with them on. But surely you realise that you'll never see anything other than a blurry mess? Glasses are meant to *correct* poor vision. They distort what the eyes see by a prescribed amount. So it's a fair bloody bet that you will not be able to make out too much if you have clear vision.

I'm pretty sure you are well aware of this. So why bother asking to try on other people's glasses in the first place? And more importantly, why do you insist on pretending that the blurriness is such a shock?

"God, you're blind!" Every single time.

No fucking shit, Sherlock.

I get it, you're taking the piss. Trying to be clever. But people who wear glasses have heard this shit joke many times before – sometimes from the same person who forgot that they'd already tried them on. And it wasn't funny the first time, you thick prat. What you see through the glasses is always going to distort your vision and make the owners seem ridiculously blind, because that's what glasses do!! Fucking muppet.

- [Pointless] Exercise -

Instead of saying, "God, you're blind!", how about, "God, these glasses distort my vision the exact amount that they distort yours so you can see properly - amazing!" Otherwise, take your twenty-twenty vision, and shove it up your arse - you don't deserve it. Idiot.

Know an idiot who needs to read this chapter?

- Scan the QR code
- Click the link
- Send it their way!

Should of, would of, could of

If you have ever read anything, you will have seen contractions like 'would've', 'should've' and 'could've'. So you will be aware that these particular words include a 've' after the apostrophe.

What the fuck do you think the 've' stands for? What could it possibly represent?

The 've' is a replacement for the word 'have'. Should have. Would have. Could have.

Never 'of'. Never, ever, ever, has the 've' in these words ever been a replacement for 'of'. Why would it be – it's a fucking 've'. To quote Steve Carell in 'The Office', "Nooooo God. No God, please no, no. No. Noooooooooo".

I get it, you're thick. You're just about literate, so you write how you speak. I suppose that 'should've' does sound kind of like 'should *of*', 'would've' does sound kind of like 'would *of*', and 'could've' does sound kind of like could *of*'. But that's no excuse when there are reminders of how it should be written fucking everywhere! Newspapers, books, the internet, literally anywhere you bloody read anything. And don't justify these constant written mistakes by saying that you're not a reader. The truth is, understanding that 'would've' is actually 'would have', is something you *should've* learnt in Year 1.

It's obviously a bad habit that's set in. You can blame your parents for not being too hot on grammar or your teachers for being useless as much as you want. But I have no doubt that you've been told plenty of times by numerous people how to spell it correctly. How do you still get it wrong?!

Sometimes you'll even argue with people about it, saying they've got it wrong instead. Are you fucking mental? It seems you just don't listen, which was probably on all your report cards at school. Or you're just an ignorant twat. My guess? You're both.

– [Pointless] Exercise –

Stop fucking writing 'should of', 'would of' or 'could of'!! Get it in your thick head!! SHOULD HAVE. WOULD HAVE. COULD HAVE. Idiot.

Know an idiot who needs to read this chapter?

- Scan the QR code
- Click the link
- Send it their way!

"That's just the way it is"

The curious souls among us love to understand the 'why'. Why things are the way they are, why certain people take certain actions. 'Why?' is a very important question - it gets to the root of problems and enables us to come up with solutions.

So imagine our frustration, when you always answer this vital question with a shrug and a dismissive, "That's just the way it is".

What kind of an answer is that?! Surely you don't actually believe that there are no explanations for why something is like it is?

After all, *everything* happens for a reason. Nothing is ever just the way it is for nothing. It may not be written down or explained anywhere, but there's always a reason.

I'd half accept, "That's just the way it is", as an answer, if you were just not in the mood to explain it. For instance, if your kid had asked way too many questions about trains one day and you know you'll just get the same question tomorrow anyway. But most of the time, incurious wankers like you use this phrase for something much worse than fatigue.

Laziness. There's no getting around it, unfortunately. Unless you're spoon-fed the reason, you're the kind of person who would never work out on their own why something is the way it is. The very fact that you're using the phrase suggests that you have given the topic some prior thought, yet were unable or unwilling to delve deeper into potential explanations. This shows that you also obviously can't think outside the box. You'd rather just accept the negative things in the world as a part of life. You are a defeatist, willing to give up on finding answers if they're not immediately available.

You might even be a pessimist who does in fact understand the complexities and nuances of a situation, but who believes that nothing can be done to alter the status quo. However, using the phrase, "That's just the way it is", just because *you've* given up hope, is still pure laziness. What if the person you're replying to has the wherewithal to take up the baton and solve whatever problem is being discussed, yet you've just denied them the context that would enable them to do so?

What if throughout history, we *all* just shrugged our shoulders and said, "That's just the way it is"? We'd know next to nothing about the world we live in. Healthcare would be much shitter and more painful. The Nazis would have won WWII. The list goes on. One thing is certain – our lives would be much worse, were it not for curious people who asked themselves, "Why?", and then actually strove to find the answer.

This leads us to the worst thing about you using this phrase – the fact that it dims the curiosity in those around you. It's worth remembering that people are who they spend the most time with. Evidently, if people were to spend time with you, they'd turn into some bored fuck who knows nothing, blindly follows the status quo and simply accepts their lot in life. If someone has asked you, "Why", it's generally because they think you, in particular, might actually know the answer. You may even be a role model for them, whether you know it or not. Maybe you're a parent, a teacher or just a friend they look up to. In any case, providing the pointless non-answer, "That's just the way it is", is hardly inspiring…

In short, unless you're Bruce Hornsby belting out his absolute banger, stop fucking resorting to "That's just the way it is" answers. Have some balls and a bit of optimism if you know the answer, or admit to the gaps in your knowledge and actually work towards filling them in.

- [Pointless] Exercise -

Unless you're being asked why we exist or why living things die, I don't want to hear you saying, "That's just the way it is", ever again. Instead, how about, "I don't know, but let's find out together". Be curious, challenge yourself to actually think. Be a force for improvement, rather than an obstacle promoting laziness and ignorant acceptance. Idiot.

Know an idiot who needs to read this chapter?

- Scan the QR code
- Click the link
- Send it their way!

"New year, new me"

Every bloody year, the same shitty phrase rears its ugly head. For the whole lead up to New Year's Eve, there's no escaping the monotonous chorus of, "New year, new me". The media shoves all the best new year's resolutions down our throats. Advertisers peddle self-help notebooks that require us to visualise and manifest our goals by writing them down. Managers ask us to talk about our resolutions as a January meeting icebreaker. And for some fucking reason, you lap it up.

The conviction with which you use this annoying, self-obsessed, catchy phrase, every fucking year, makes it seem as though not having resolutions is tantamount to treason. You talk the talk about what incredible weight loss you're going to have. About starting that new business. About reading more books. About stopping drinking, smoking. I could name anything, you'd have a fucking resolution for it. But what actually happens with your "new year, new me" resolutions?

Unfortunately, very, very, very few people actually go ahead and walk the walk. You *definitely* don't.

You start off the new year with the best of intentions. And we're all oh so proud of you. Until you inevitably falter and drop off after week fucking one.

Sometimes you will make it to the end of January. Mildly less shameful.

You might even keep it up for three months. You tried I suppose – but you still fucked it didn't you? Better luck next year.

Very rarely will you still be going strong after three months, with your resolution now almost second nature. Congratulations. But please don't keep going on about it, trying to guilt-trip everyone you know into following suit.

Aside from having to watch stubborn conviction morphing into apathy, what pisses me off most about this phrase is the impression it gives – that important life changes need to wait until 1st January. Why? It's just another date on the calendar. It's not some magical day on which you suddenly develop some mental fortitude. If you want to make a change, just fucking do it!! You don't need to wait!! Do it on 21st November, 5th April, 28th February – I don't give a shit. If you think it's needed, which you obviously do, just do it.

You've probably gathered that I also can't stand the fact that this phrase pushes you to verbalise or publish your resolutions. Resolutions are all you talk about when the "new year, new me" bandwagon comes around. Social media is absolutely rife with it. But why do your resolutions even *need* to be broadcast?

I get that maybe you're trying to create a false sense of accountability; the thinking being that if other people know what you're trying to achieve, you'll feel the pressure to succeed. But most people don't give a shit about your resolutions. Your resolutions are for *you* to make a change that *you* know you need in *your* life. They are for *you* to take action on *yourself*. You're already guaranteed to fail if you believe you need other people to hold you accountable. Constantly talking about your resolutions does nothing except grate on everyone's nerves. No one is impressed by you simply talking about your potential transformation. Addicts say they're going to stop their addiction every other week. At least they don't bloody wait for the new year. All anyone is thinking when you lay out your new year's resolutions is, "Yeah, alright mate. I'll believe it when I see it. Let's see where you're at in a couple of weeks".

- [Pointless] Exercise -

You know that New year's resolution you keep harping on about, that you haven't done anything about yet? Yeah, that one. Shove it up your arse. Instead of boring our ears off about your "new year, new me" resolution bullshit, how about you just concentrate on actually following through? Idiot.

Know an idiot who needs to read this chapter?

- Scan the QR code
- Click the link
- Send it their way!

"One day, I'd love to…"

All of us have things we wish we could do or be. When we see people doing something which seems cool and appeals to us, it's natural to want to be able to do it too.

So what should we do in that situation? Well, we should start by learning how, practising, doing whatever we need to do to achieve it.

Lots of people do exactly that. They say they want to do something and they do it. Whether it's learning to play a musical instrument other than the triangle, learning another language, writing a book, or something else, people learn and do these things all the time.

However, there are far too many muppets like you who love verbalising your desire to be able to do something, without ever following through. Talking the talk, without walking the walk. You'll say you'd love to be able to play the didgeridoo or learn Russian. You'll exuberantly announce that you're going to finally do it. You'll proceed to make a shitty, half-assed attempt at researching what you need to do, maybe you'll even download Duolingo or actually buy the instrument. Then everything stops. You give up at the first bloody hurdle, which is actually doing the thing you want to do. The absolute worst is when you verbalise what it is you'd love to do, then sigh and say, "One day…", proceeding to do precisely fuck all about it.

Notice that I haven't mentioned unbelievably difficult things like being a rocket scientist or a Premier League footballer, things for which you need a massive brain or extraordinary talent. I'm talking about the things that anyone could actually do if they put their mind to it. Most of the time they simply require a bit of hard graft and dedication. Yet this is where you give up, unfortunately. You don't have that inner determination to push through and achieve something.

What I want to know is why. Because I am truly fed up with you uttering the phrase, "One day, I'd love to…", then not doing anything about it. Despite all your dreams, you're wasting your life and it's a really sad state of affairs. Especially as you get older, when you start coming out with all your regrets, saying you wish you had done this or that, all in the past tense. Watching you constantly come up with excuses and actively ignore your potential is awful.

I think there are a few different reasons why you do not follow through with actioning your aspirations.

Sometimes it's simply because you are a lazy bastard. No doubt about it. You want everything to come easy, without having to put in the effort. Maybe it is technology's fault, perpetuating and enabling your inner laziness. For example, people used to have to get up to change the channel on the TV, but now we just use remotes and sit there in our own filth. People are getting used to these comforts and unaccustomed to working hard at something. Nevertheless, technology's fault or not, it doesn't change the fact that you are a lazy fuck.

Sometimes you were just never really bothered in the first place. You didn't *really, really* want to do whatever it is – you just said that you'd love to be able to do it one day for the sake of it, almost as if you were trying to convince yourself that there is actually something you want to aspire to. In this case, why bother verbalising it? It's upsetting that you never try to achieve anything. In addition, if you keep telling yourself all the things you wish you could do, but you never do them, it's going to take its toll on you mentally, making you feel like a failure. So start verbalising your desire to do only the things that you are genuinely passionate about – then do them! Otherwise please refrain from talking about all your goals that are destined to become regrets… we're all fed up with hearing it.

Other times, you are just too tired. You need some downtime after working so hard. You've got kids. Everything is too expensive and you need the money more than you need to achieve your dreams. I completely get it. I am fully aware it would be easier to focus on your other aspirations if you had enough money to stop worrying about paying the bills. However, it's still no excuse. What's the alternative? I'll tell you – it's your life as is. Where you simply live to work and never do anything that could make you feel fulfilled.

Having said all this, I think the biggest reason is a crippling fear of failure. And it's understandable. It really is painful to fail at something, especially after dedicating yourself and so much time to it. It takes mental fortitude to shake off such a failure and move on to the next thing. But that does not mean you shouldn't at least try. So what if you fail? At least you tried. You can have no regrets. There are no what-ifs. You can never be accused of being lazy, non-committal and someone who only talks the talk.

- [Pointless] Exercise -

If you just have no idea how to go about getting started doing something you wish you could do, there's actually not much to it. You need to make a plan. You need to stick to it. And you need to actually start practising and doing whatever the bloody thing is. No one has ever magically woken up one day, suddenly able to do the thing they've always wanted to do. Remember that nothing worth doing ever comes easy or without effort. It's better than not trying, sitting on your arse with all your regrets and growing old ungracefully. Fear of failure is understandable, but not trying is inexcusable. There is also the possibility that you might actually succeed. Idiot.

Know an idiot who needs to read this chapter?

- Scan the QR code
- Click the link
- Send it their way!

Ignoring facts in arguments

A friend of mine loves the quote, "Never argue with a fool, onlookers may not be able to tell the difference." But sometimes we just can't help it! Fools like you are often so painfully bloody wrong that it's impossible to just let it go.

The problem with this is we'll never win the argument. We can't have a proper discussion with you, unfortunately, because you're not guided by the irrefutable logic that an argument, backed up by proper facts, is right. For some unknown reason, despite being presented with the evidence right in front of your nose, you will still say something along the lines of, "Yeah, well, that's just your opinion. Everyone has their opinion, I'm allowed to have mine!!"

No, you complete and utter prick. You are not allowed an opinion against an argument backed by facts. Facts are facts. They can't be argued. You can't argue against them. Because they are unarguable. Am I getting through to you yet? For fuck's sake.

However, I don't actually think you ignore facts in arguments simply because you are a total thicko. Well, not all the time at least. So the question remains, why do you continue to argue in the face of irreproachable truth?

One reason could be that you don't automatically put more stock in something just because it's written or proven by people with any official authority. You would trust an article you found on Facebook, written by some nobody, just as much as, if not more than, a paper written by a scientist in a medical journal with experiments galore. So when you get confronted by genuine evidence, you start thinking about all the conflicting "evidence" you've seen and read elsewhere. In short, the problem you have, with dismissing arguments backed by facts, could be rooted in your lower evidentiary standards.

Maybe you don't fully comprehend the amount of fake news content that is out there, written for nefarious purposes and to back up subjective opinion with false evidence. It's rife I'm afraid, mate. Fake news is news that is not based on real evidence – it's not just a term you can throw at anything that contradicts your point of view, no matter how much Donald fucking Trump claims otherwise. Facts are based on evidence provided by actual experts, and you have to make sure that your sources of information use them before you start spouting their conclusions. It is on you to do your due diligence if you're going to have proper discussions and dismiss other people's perspectives. You cannot keep using shitty opinion pieces, written by fellow idiots, as "facts" to back up your arguments.

On second thought, maybe the above gives you too much credit. In reality, I think, deep down, you do actually know when you are ignoring facts in arguments. But you just don't want to accept it because you can't stand the thought of being wrong. You are just too fucking inexplicably proud. Once you've been so stubborn in your convictions on a particular subject, you get so caught up in winning the argument, that your ego won't allow you to see the truth. You think that if you just keep going on and on spouting bullshit, and the other person just gives up arguing with you, that it counts as a win. But you haven't won, mate. It just makes you an impossible twat of a person.

– [Pointless] Exercise –

Start thinking of the words 'argument' and 'discussion' as the same thing. Neither *have* to be heated. The aim isn't to win. The aim is to get to the truth. You need to calm your tits and look at the evidence dispassionately, without emotion. Consider whether conclusions based on thousands of experiments constitute fact, at least more so than your shitty articles from Twitter. Have the humility to accept that you might be wrong. It doesn't mean you're less of a person - everyone is wrong sometimes. Idiot.

Know an idiot who needs to read this chapter?

- Scan the QR code
- Click the link
- Send it their way!

Veiled sentence starters

Look, I'm all for being honest - when it's the right time to do so. Finding the right time is difficult, especially when you know the recipient is not going to like what they hear. But if you are going to be brutally honest to someone, just fucking do it. You'll always get more respect for being open about it and owning what you are saying.

However, people like you don't have the balls for brutal honesty. You're a greedy fuck who wants the privilege of being able to say what you want to everyone, but in a falsely tactful way, to reduce the blowback on you seeming like a total dickhead. You appear to be so afraid of the reaction to what you're about to say that you therefore use, what I like to call, shitty, veiled sentence starters.

The kind of phrases I'm talking about include things like, "No offence, but…", "I'm not being big-headed, but…" or, "With all due respect…".

The problem with these veiled sentence starters is that they don't fucking work. You're the only one who actually thinks that they successfully dull the impact of what you are saying. When you use phrases like this, you might as well be holding a sign that says, "I'm going to insult you now, you wanker. And I expect you to take it well."

It really is mind-blowing that you could ever consider these sentence starters to be tactful when it is so fucking obvious that what is to follow will be hurtful. "No offence" is always inevitably followed by something offensive. "I'm not being big-headed" is always inevitably followed by something that shows you to be big-headed. "With all due respect" is always inevitably followed by something completely disrespectful. So what's the fucking point!! We all know what's coming, you insincere prick!!

This is precisely why I call these phrases, *veiled* sentence starters. They are employed, mainly by the pussies in society who claim that they "tell it like it is", to try, and ultimately fail, to pull the wool over everyone's eyes as to their true, obnoxious nature.

- [Pointless] Exercise -

The next time you want to call someone a cunt, in a non-friendly way, instead of saying, "No offence, but you're a cunt", just say, "You're a cunt". You need to recognise that, at the end of the day, you're still calling someone a cunt. By using veiled sentence starters, you are essentially trying to get away with tactfully being a dickhead to someone. If you're going to be a dickhead to someone's face, the least you can do is own your honesty. Idiot.

Know an idiot who needs to read this chapter?

- Scan the QR code
- Click the link
- Send it their way!

Overusing the word, 'like'

I don't, like, understand, like, why, like, you need to, like, use the word 'like', like, all the fucking time. It, like, makes you sound like a prat and it, like, drives me, like, fucking mental!

I mean, look at the state of what I've written there. Fuuuucking hell. But this is exactly what you sound like when you're speaking! I defy you to read what it sounds like to be you, overusing the word 'like' again and again, and still be content knowing that it's you, instead of some other random, uneducated, nervous muppet.

Speaking like this doesn't make you cool or easy-going. I mean, why would it?! Filling unnecessary gaps and pauses in your sentences, with a word that has no logical place, is just a waste of fucking time. It gives the impression that you have the vocabulary of a fish and that you're incredibly unsure of what you're saying. It also can come across as condescending, as if you're trying to slow down and chop up your speech to explain something as simply and stupidly as humanly possible.

I've been in job interviews, as the interviewer, and have had candidates speaking like this. For customer service roles no less. What makes you think you have any chance of getting hired when you sound as thick as shit? I can tell you for a fact, you've got no chance. I wouldn't hire anyone that speaks like this and I'm pretty sure that goes for most employers.

Now, I'm the biggest advocate around for young people, especially nowadays having been dealt a pretty shitty hand compared to previous generations. So it's with a heavy heart that I concede that this overuse of the word 'like', where it doesn't belong, does appear to be a recent phenomenon occurring predominantly among youngsters like you.

However, I'm not sure why that is. It's not as if you are simply less intelligent than older generations – in fact, I'd go so far as to say the opposite may be true. But the fact remains, that saying 'like' every other word, for no good reason, does not help your intellectual case.

I have but one potential explanation; that it's simply a new way of speaking. It's definitely very Americanised, and it comes from, as far as I can tell, watching reality TV and other shows, where the dumbest people in society are given a platform they really do not deserve. Too many young people watch this crap, and the way these numpties speak is slowly but surely being adopted as normal speech.

In any case, whatever the reason for the proliferation of overusing the word 'like', the point I'm trying to make is that it should not be happening. I don't care that you see people speaking like this all over Netflix. I don't care who your favourite celebrities are. Stop being a fucking sheep. Carry on like this and you are simultaneously running the risk of sounding condescending, never getting a job and portraying a distinct lack of confidence and vocabulary. That's a shit trade-off just so you can sound like some twat from '*Towie*'.

- [Pointless] Exercise -

If you suspect you may overuse the word 'like', open the camera app on your phone and set it to take a video. Take one video of you reading the first paragraph in this chapter. Then take another video, and read it again after removing all the instances of 'like' wherever they don't belong – if you don't know which 'likes' should be left out, go the fuck back to school. Then compare the two videos and tell me which one sounds more fucking stupid. Exactly. Keep the video with all the 'likes' as inspiration and re-watch it every time you feel like scratching the itch to use 'like' for no good reason. If for some reason, despite making the videos above, you still struggle to stop overusing the word 'like', you could take the more drastic step of teaching yourself like you'd teach a dog. Give your friends a bag of sweets and tell them to feed you one every time you manage a complete sentence without an unnecessary 'like'. You might get diabetes, but at least you'll get a job. Then you can buy a gym membership. Idiot.

Know an idiot who needs to read this chapter?

- Scan the QR code
- Click the link
- Send it their way!

“Oops, I’m so clumsy, hahaha!”

Everyone does mindless shit. Everyone has accidents. Everyone has, at one time or another, dropped a plate, knocked over a beer or done something equally stupid. It happens.

But what I *can’t* handle is you doing this stupid shit time and time and time again. And because you do these things all the fucking time and everyone knows it’s always you, you somehow get to laugh about it and excuse your uncoordinated actions with an, “Oops, I’m so clumsy!” As if that makes it all ok! For example, we have a running joke about a mate that spills at least one beer every time we go out. Without fail. Even when sober.

Well, I can’t abide by it anymore. Laughing and excusing your clumsiness, while you knock over my much-anticipated beans on toast and drench me in my own beer for the umpteenth time, will no longer cut it.

How about this. You just stop fucking being clumsy and making my life that bit more frustrating?

Don’t you dare bloody tell me you can’t help it. That is utter bullshit, you *can* help it. Unless you’ve got some kind of illness that affects your movement and/or awareness, clumsiness is not an excuse.

When you stub your toe on the wall or door, it’s not because you’re clumsy. It’s because you didn’t correctly judge the space needed to get past it.

When you trip over something on the floor, it’s not because you’re clumsy. It’s because you didn’t see the bloody thing!

When you put a cup or dinner plate on the edge of the table and it ends up falling off as soon as you remove your hand, it’s not because you’re clumsy. It’s because you couldn’t be bothered to ensure enough of the item was on the table to prevent the almighty force of gravity from taking over.

When you drop shit, it's not because you're clumsy. It's because you picked up said shit and somehow forgot how much finger strength you needed to pick it up in the first fucking place.

The above and thousands of other examples of "accidents", that "clumsy" people like you seem to have on a far too regular basis, are not accidents in the slightest. It's not clumsiness at play here - it's laziness and lack of awareness of your surroundings. Pure and simple.

It's time you started taking responsibility for your actions, you klutz. I don't want to hear you blaming these everyday accidents on your clumsiness ever again. I want you to actually use your brain, work out why you fucked up - again - then stop fucking up altogether.

Just a couple of seconds of reflection, after the next inevitable accident, should be enough for you to realise that you were simply being lazy or weren't adequately aware of what was around you. It's at this point you might hopefully also understand why I'm no longer laughing at your apparent inability to do the simplest of things.

- [Pointless] Exercise -

Stop saying, "Oops, I'm so clumsy", and laughing. It's not fucking funny. I want you to start saying sorry like you mean it. I want you to then tell me it won't happen again. Then I want you to fucking make sure it doesn't. Practice going about your life as though you're always behind the wheel. Concentrate. Be aware. Be consistent and deliberate with your actions. Constantly be on the lookout for potential hazards. And stop fucking dropping shit. Idiot.

Know an idiot who needs to read this chapter?

- Scan the QR code
- Click the link
- Send it their way!

Boring small talk

Small talk – an inevitable fixture at social settings, networking events and other functions, where those in attendance don't all know each other. Some people love it. Others really fucking hate it. I'm with the others, but only when it's extra boring and time feels like it's come to a bloody standstill.

At the end of the day, small talk is a necessary element of communication with strangers. Despite the fact that it involves the kind of questions that make us yawn, that bore us when they're asked and that we bore ourselves with when we ask them. It's the way humans interact to get comfortable with each other and to decide whether an ongoing friendship and deeper conversations are worth pursuing. It is essentially a vetting process, a social lubricant if you will – which makes it sound much more fun than it really is.

However, when small talk is done wrong, fuck me, that's time we're never getting back.

For one, you don't seem to understand that small talk is supposed to be a precursor to talking more in-depth. Obviously, we are all inevitably going to talk first about the weather, the traffic, what route we took, what we think of the food, how our families are doing, how work is going, what we're doing on the weekend. Blah blah, fucking blah. But the point is to then get to the good stuff afterwards! Yet you never do. You engage in the small talk and then simply descend into an awkward silence as you run out of small talk topics.

It's like, mate, where's the curiosity for your fellow human?! I gave you so many titbits you could have used to go off on an interesting tangent! Instead, you give me no follow up questions, no whys and multiple one-word answers, despite my open-ended questions. You sound like a fucking robot being put through a Turing test to convince the rest of us you're human.

If you don't want to be here and talk to people, in a social setting might I add, then go the fuck home. I get that it's a vetting process, a fact-finding mission in which you are simultaneously trying not to give too much away. But for fuck's sake, are you so shit scared of getting to know someone that you can't push yourself to move past the safety of small talk!?! It's not prying and you do have to give a little to get something back. It's *absolutely* normal to delve a little deeper after small talk has greased the wheels – that's the whole fucking point.

On the other hand, sometimes you seem to love small talk a little too much. You'll happily go on and on about yourself, what you've done recently, where you've been, what you like, hardly pausing for breath. You've got this huge fucking ego that causes you to assume that there is no one on God's green Earth who could possibly not be interested in you and what you have to say. In your self-obsessed eyes, small talk is your opportunity to shine; you feel under no obligation to take a break so that your conversation partner can contribute something to this conversation that isn't your shitty, rehearsed monologue.

An important part of successful and engaging small talk is working out what both parties like and are happy to discuss. This is why you should bring up topics and move on quickly if it falls on deaf ears or simply ask for the other person's interests. Most people will broach a topic, notice that the listener is not interested, then move on to something else or ask a question instead. Alas, not you. Incessantly talking solely about your favourite sport or your stock portfolio, purely because that's what you are interested in and feel comfortable talking about, doesn't fucking cut it if the other person couldn't give a flying shit.

You also seem to use small talk as a means to just fill the silence and make sure you don't look like that loner not talking to anyone. But if you're not actually bothered about talking to a particular person, then don't fucking bother! Talk with intention, actually try to get to know the person, not just for the fucking sake of it or because you're waiting for your friend to finish their own conversation.

Unfortunately, there isn't too much else to replace the standard topics of small talk – it's a necessary evil. And the questions we ask *are* useful, in so much as they elicit important initial details that allow us to get to know someone in a short space of time. But can't you at least try and do it in a more entertaining way! We're here, we're engaging in this fucking small talk, let's at least have some semblance of fun with it. Maybe a little humour, a smile, an indication that you can go a little off-piste, even some genuine interest on your face rather than this dead-pan seriousness that the socially illiterate muppet in you seems unable to shake. Come armed with a joke instead of incredibly wanky, "I've read a book on networking" questions about your biggest regret or current personal passion project. Please, prove to us you're not always genuinely this dull behind closed doors!

– [Pointless] Exercise –

When someone asks how you are, at a shit conference for example, instead of responding with the ultra-boring, unemotional, heard-it-a-million-times-before, "I'm doing well, thank you, how about you?", why not try a naughtier, "Bored out my bloody head mate, you?". Admittedly, this is going to go one of two ways. They're either going to be some frumpy, shit-conference-loving prick who thinks you're being out of order, or they're going to end up being your kind of person. In any case, at least it makes the small talk that follows more likely to be worth the bloody effort. And stop, for the love of God, opening up with, "So what do you do?". We get it, mate. All you do is work and your identity is fully wrapped up in your job. You're dying for the opportunity to tell anyone who will listen what you do for money because it's the only thing that you think makes you look good. Or you think it's a safe bet for a conversation starter as you probably both have jobs. But, please, try something different. Safe is also fucking boring. You're forcing us all to recite the same shit, which gets old very quickly. Idiot.

Know an idiot who needs to read this chapter?

- Scan the QR code
- Click the link
- Send it their way!

At the office

Company loyalty & living to work

We should of course feel some loyalty to our employers for hiring us and providing us with a living. But only to the extent that we do the work they hire us for to the best of our ability, within the timeframe stated by our employment contracts. We don't owe them anything other than that – something that some workers like you don't seem to fully understand.

If you got fired today, what would happen? Would your company crumble without you? Or would they just find someone else to do your job? I think you know the answer already. Get this in your head – *everyone* is replaceable. Whatever job you do. Get over it and ask yourself why you were ever dumb enough to care so much about a company that doesn't care about you. Because they really, truly bloody don't.

A company is not a person, it has no feelings. It is a machine whose sole purpose is creating profit. Companies will always demand more work from you in order to generate more money and will give the least amount possible in return for that labour to ensure it keeps more of the profit.

Have you ever stopped to think about where the profits of your hard work actually go? Have you ever wondered how much of that money goes to the people at the top rather than you, who generated that income? It's obscenely more than you think.

Nevertheless, yes, you should work hard. So that your company continues to earn money and so that you keep your job. But that's it! Working over your contracted hours, stressing about work projects outside of the office, all to get more money and a promotion... that shit is for mugs.

What do you think really happens after you work incredibly hard for your company, and you eventually get a bump in salary or that promotion? You'll be happier right? Wrong. You don't actually believe that more money buys you happiness, do you? That extra monthly income just means you can buy more. And, knowing you, you already spend most of your income on total rubbish anyway.

Please try to remember that you need work and money only so that you can survive and spend it on the things that you love, on the things that matter. No, not flashy cars, jewellery or fancy clothes, you prat. Family, experiences, moments. It doesn't cost as much as you think.

I know you've seen those wanky films where characters are on their deathbeds, complaining that they wish they'd spent more time with their families and less time at work. I know you then thought, "Oh, that's so true! I need to make sure I remember what's important!" But I am willing to bet my year's salary that you forget all of that when Monday morning comes around. You should be working to live, not the other way around.

I don't know the meaning of life - but I do know that you were not born to work harder than *you* need to, just so companies and shareholders can make more profit than *they* need.

- [Pointless] Exercise -

Think about how much money you made last week for your company. How much money came into your till? How much money did you make on that last deal? Work out how much of that actually sees the inside of your pocket. Then tell your boss that you want fifty per cent of the revenue you generate in the future. When they laugh and say no, at least you've got your excuse for why you tell them to piss off the next time they ask you to work late. You'll lose your job but at least you'll make your point. Idiot.

Know an idiot who needs to read this chapter?

- Scan the QR code
- Click the link
- Send it their way!

Delegating

Everyone gets stressed at work. Everyone thinks they need help with their growing to-do list. Most people just get on with it. They prioritise the urgent stuff and communicate what needs to get shifted to a later date.

But bastards like you plough through your workload in a completely different way. You get your colleagues to do *extra* work instead. You are what's known as a delegator; otherwise known as the wanker everyone else truly needs to watch out for in the workplace.

I'm not talking about the boss giving people extra work - they are supposed to delegate whether we like it or not. I'm talking about when you do things like call out your colleagues to help on projects that have nothing to do with them. In face to face meetings with top brass or via emails with the whole fucking world cc'd. With absolutely no regard for your colleagues' already bursting-at-the-seams workloads.

Now, in theory, it's up to us to communicate that we might struggle to get such and such done and won't be able to help at this time. Companies that take pride in their self-declared progressive nature even offer classes on the art of saying no - which is utter bull-shit by the way.

But, let's face it, the vast majority of companies reward those who appear to do work over and above their remit, and who shout from the fucking rafters about it. They are extremely unlikely to reward people who refuse extra work in front of the higher echelons. You know that we can't exactly say, "No, do your own fucking job, bitch". That won't go down well. We'll look like petty wankers refusing to be team players, while you look like a victim with too much work. Which makes it very difficult to turn this work down. And don't you fucking know it, you delegating arsehole.

The craftiest element of this delegation ploy is that, more often than not, what you delegate is your own fucking work. You present it as projects requiring cross-functional input, but they are really just part of your core responsibilities. You pass this work on to unwitting victims who end up doing your job for you.

A lot of the time, it's because you're just fucking useless at your job. If you don't delegate the work, it will never get done, because you can't actually do it. Basic shortcuts in Excel dumbfound you, so you pass the spreadsheets on to someone who isn't a technologically challenged muppet to ensure other teams aren't blocked for five weeks from doing their job.

One specific example of your sneaky delegation tactics is when you call meetings to brainstorm solutions to one of your many stumbling blocks. Some poor, eager sod will offer up an innovative way for you to solve your problem. You'll exclaim that it's an amazing idea. But instead of thanking them and closing the meeting to go ahead and resolve your issue yourself, you'll ask if they're happy to take responsibility for implementing it. The fucking cheek!! Your colleagues attended this meeting as a courtesy, in the spirit of collaboration, to give you ideas and help you intellectually. They're not there to do the thinking *and* the implementation for you. It's *your* fucking problem, *you* take responsibility, you lazy prick!!

But here's the worst bit. When it comes to presenting the results and findings from the innovative solution that someone else came up with and implemented, you are more than happy to jump in and say "*we* had an idea, *we* did this, *we* achieved that". You happily steal ideas and credit for work that you essentially had nothing to do with. It's sickening. And actually quite difficult to fight against, which is why you might get promoted left, right and centre. Then, in turn, you reward the same behaviour. And so this vicious cycle of delegation bullshit continues. Your managers probably think, "How do they get so much work done – impressive!" But you and I both know it's because you don't fucking do any of it.

– [Pointless] Exercise –

Go to the office. Do your own work, without palming it off on anyone else. Then fuck off home. Failing that, start treating your co-workers with a bit of bloody common decency. If your first approach was to ask for help nicely, most people would have no trouble finding time for you. But don't fucking call us out in meetings or cc the whole fucking company. Remember that revenge is a dish best served making you extremely fucking busy for the rest of your time at this company. Idiot.

Know an idiot who needs to read this chapter?

- Scan the QR code
- Click the link
- Send it their way!

Office temperature

Plenty of us have worked in an office where we feel the temperature is either too cold or too hot. Most of us are able to cope without too much fuss. If it's too hot for us, we'll take off our jumper or blazer or even bring in a fan to work the next day. If it's too cold, we'll put on an extra layer. Simple actions to take, right?

If the temperature is obviously too extreme either way, the normal, considerate people among us will address the whole office, asking if we could change the setting on the thermostat or switch the air conditioning on/off.

However, there is always a selfish prick like you who takes it upon themselves to change the temperature with no prior warning or consent. You'll get up from your desk, walk brazenly over to the thermostat and just turn the dial to whatever *you* want. You'll then return to your desk and sit back down, without a care in the world, as though it's the most normal thing to do. Five minutes later, the whole fucking building is complaining that it's way too cold or way too hot. All because you felt the need to change the temperature for *everyone* without a second thought.

More often than not, the temperature is fine. Maybe a little cold or hot either way, but nothing too extreme. And as mentioned already, there are plenty of other actions you could take to cater to your personal temperature preferences that do not affect everyone else. So the fact that your first move is to adjust the temperature for everyone, without asking whether enough people actually want it changed, shows just how much of an ego-centric dickhead you are.

Who the fuck do you think you are? Do you really believe that you are so integral to your workplace that the office temperature should be tailored solely to you? Because I guarantee you're not. Dickheads are rarely that important to the office; in fact, they're normally very fucking expendable.

Consider how spoiled you appear to the rest of us. This is basically what you're saying: "*I* want something, so *I'm* going to change everything for everyone just so *I* can have it. I'm not going to first seek a solution that will only affect me. I only care about my comfort, mine, mine, mine. Fuck everyone else". Still think you're not a dickhead, dickhead?

- [Pointless] Exercise -

The next time you're cold in the office, put on a fucking jumper. The next time you're hot, take off the jumper or buy a fucking fan. If you're a pussy and really can't handle the temperature, ask everyone if they mind the thermostat being adjusted. Chances are we'll be feeling it too and will thank you for bringing it up, but mostly for asking us first. Do not just get up and change the temperature setting on a whim. It's not all about you. Remember that unless the thermostat is broken, the temperature is basically always perfect for some, too hot for others and too cold for the rest. That's life. Idiot.

Know an idiot who needs to read this chapter?

- Scan the QR code
- Click the link
- Send it their way!

Emotional check-ins

As a manager, you really like to push the “this company cares about its employees” line, don’t you? You ask your employees how they’re feeling at every one on one meeting to “check-in” emotionally. You say you genuinely care and will help them if they’re struggling mentally. You make much ado about your willingness to make sure they’re happy at work and ask for honesty in these check-ins.

It all sounds great in principle. But it’s lip service in practice, isn’t it?

Companies are money-making machines at the end of the day. You, as a manager, are responsible for the success of your company. You are fooling no one by saying you care about anything other than the bottom line. You’re not truly bothered if your employees are feeling massively overstretched and burnt out, as long as revenue still looks good. Sure, you’d be worried if someone became too burnt out to work and needed time off. But only because that person could no longer contribute to the bottom line.

But more to the point in this chapter, do you think we’re all fucking stupid? You’re really trying to tell us that, if we said we were struggling at work, it wouldn’t bite us in the arse in the future? You’re really trying to tell us that we wouldn’t get passed up for promotion ahead of someone who appeared positive in every check-in? Rubbish, of course we would.

If someone was seriously struggling mentally, you and the company would absolutely think of that person as a problem, someone who needed to be gently pushed out before they became a liability and a blot on your happiness metrics. You don’t actually know what your next step would be in a situation where someone really needed help. It would probably be something unhelpful like providing some pamphlets on therapy, telling the person to take some unpaid time off, providing free access to some shitty wellbeing app, or installing some more fucking ping pong tables and beanbags. As much as I love table tennis and comfortable seating, they are no replacement for a reasonable work-life balance and good mental health at work.

Most employees understand this underlying truth, despite all the PR bullshit spouted by companies. This is why the answer that you normally receive when checking in with your employees is, "Yeah, not too bad". Some of the keenos will also include a few over-the-top phrases describing feeling energised and excited for the next project, some tripe like that. But very few people will give genuine answers.

And let's face it, if your employees were to really be honest about how they're feeling, answers would probably sound more like, "I'm feeling shit, I'm at work you numpty. If I didn't have to be here to pay my bills, you would never see me again."

Ridiculously, I actually think you fully understand that your company's policy of checking in on emotional welfare is a load of bollox. You ask how your employees are because you *have* to. You know you're not going to get the truth. And you are more than happy with that because it means no further action is needed on your part to help struggling employees. You can safely tick the checkbox and say that your employees are happy at work as a direct result of your "wellbeing program".

What an awful state of affairs though! Everyone tip-toeing around each other, not being completely honest and pretending they're happy to be there. There's not much more that can be done, however. Work isn't really the place to discuss emotional problems or our mental states, despite spending eight hours plus a day at the office. And I don't really think it's incumbent upon you to look after your employees' mental health. HR departments very rarely comprise any mental health professionals. And a business is a business, meant to make money. Employees are only there as cogs in the wheel of that process and get paid a tiny fraction of the profits in exchange for their labour. As horrible as it is to say, mental health has got nothing to do with it really.

So if you're not going to have a proper wellbeing program in place and a concrete plan for what to do if someone is in trouble mentally, why even bother asking how your employees are? You ask for honesty, but don't actually want it. Those who are genuinely struggling will feel worse every time you ask how they are because they know they need to hold back their true feelings for fear of losing out at work or even getting pushed out. Genuinely honest answers would showcase the honest yet unfashionable truth that few people are actually happy at work, which would sow doubt about the whole system of work and capitalism at large. God forbid, eh?

- [Pointless] Exercise -

If you're an employee and are curious to see what would happen if you were to be honest in your next check-in, just go ahead. Tell your manager all about how you hate being at work, that you'd rather be doing something you enjoy or care about, but you can't because you need to pay the bills and it's affecting your mental health. See what happens. Equally, managers, if you genuinely care about your employees' happiness, why not try some anonymous polls that include some proper questions? Instead of asking how we are feeling at work, ask if we would rather be at work or elsewhere. Cut the crap, lift the veil and get to the truth. But you wouldn't dare do that, would you? You're scared of what you'd hear, or rather you already know and don't want the incontrovertible proof weighing on your conscience. Idiot.

Know an idiot who needs to read this chapter?

- Scan the QR code
- Click the link
- Send it their way!

Heavy walking

No one is *so* important at work that they need to announce their arrival at the office with a mini-earthquake. But that doesn't stop you and your fucking footsteps from creating one. Normally we only hear people before we can see them because they're loud, gobby bastards – but with you, it's your heavy walking.

How are we supposed to drown out your bullshit at work when your heavy walking tremors keep making our headphones fall off? And how are we supposed to tolerate listening to your bullshit in meetings if you keep making our morning coffees spill over?

Exaggeration aside, I struggle to understand why wankers like you need to walk so loudly in the office. Your heavy footsteps are overkill! Okay, it's not earthquake-level, but the floor definitely shakes enough to induce heightened anxiety when you walk around.

I do wonder if you are just a genetic freak with heavier feet, ankles and legs. If that were truly the case, I would apologise for calling you a freak. But it's not the case, is it? I've seen much bigger, thick-set, seven-foot blokes walking around at the same pace as your midget arse, yet making nowhere near the levels of excessive noise that you do every time your feet hit the ground.

I've heard plenty of excuses for this loud walking, mainly to do with physiology. For example, some will advocate that you lean forward too much, so you are constantly braking so as not to fall over. Or that you drive your legs downward instead of forward, wasting energy bouncing up and down. Or that you slap the floor, rather than drawing your foot backwards as you land.

However, I call bullshit to every single one of these excuses. These are basically saying that you don't know how to walk. And while that may be true, it's not that hard to remedy your technique so you don't make as much noise. I've also seen you walking at a perfectly reasonable decibel level outside of the office.

So the question remains, why do you insist on walking so loudly in the workplace?

I think it absolutely has to do with you having a bloated sense of self-importance and a craving for attention. You want people to notice you and that you are there, in the office. You want people to know you've arrived. What you don't realise is that no one cares, knobhead.

In a similar vein, you might be trying to assert your authority. After all, heavy office walkers do tend to hail from higher up the food chain that is the corporate hierarchy. In your mind, heavy walking makes you seem bigger and more powerful, as if the alpha is in the house. But that doesn't necessarily translate to power. Yes, it raises anxiety - but that's the inevitable result of all loud noises. Unfortunately, the heavy walking just makes you seem like a loud bully that needs squashing.

The final element is you trying to appear busier than you really are. Loud walking often comes from walking fast. So your hope is that, by dashing in and out of the office with loud, heavy steps, people start thinking that you're super busy and you've got important stuff to do and calls to take. All I can say is that I hope, for your sake, that your colleagues never work out what you actually do when you heavy-walk out of the office: sit on the shitter and scroll through Instagram for an hour. Actually, I do hope you get found out, maybe then you'll stop with the fucking stomping like a spoilt child.

- [Pointless] Exercise -

If you think heavy walking enhances your prowess and fear factor within the company, why don't you ask your colleagues? I know for a fact, if they're being honest, their responses will be along the lines of, "No, I whip my head round to see who it is, I see it's you, then I just think, what a twat". It might be time to start wearing some fucking slippers at work or at least some padded soles on the outside of your shoes. Idiot.

Know an idiot who needs to read this chapter?

- Scan the QR code
- Click the link
- Send it their way!

Passive aggression

Everyone has encountered at least one passive-aggressive arsehole at work. By which I mean someone being confrontational, but indirectly, and therefore never actually dealing with the reasons why they are angry. I could go into a whole psychological rant about general passive aggression, but I'm going to restrict this chapter to one of the more common and fucking annoying outlets: email. Or Slack, for the super chic, wanky, modern workers. For the thickos who don't know what passive aggression is, let's talk about what it can look like.

Firstly, you've got your passive-aggressive email sign-offs, which are particularly effective in an email chain where you start with genuine, polite sign-offs and gradually get shorter and less courteous.

For example, first email = "Best Regards". Follow up email = "Kind Regards". Second, follow up email = "Regards". Third, follow up email = "Many Thanks". Fourth follow up email, when you want to smash the fucking person's head in = "Thanks". For added dickheadishness, you sign off with your first name initial rather than wasting all that time writing the whole thing.

Note: Some people prefer to go the other way here and get longer and more courteous. It's a judgement call, both work wonders. I just prefer going shorter so the other person knows I haven't got the fucking time of day for them. God forbid they think they've got in your head.

Secondly, you've got your general phrases that show off your best and most petty, passive-aggressive flair.

Examples with translations:

- "Correct me if I'm wrong" = "I'm not wrong, fuuuuuuuck you"
- "Let me clarify" or "To put it simply" = "Are you fucking stupid, mate?"

- "Just to reiterate", "As discussed" or "Per our last conversation" = "When I write something, you're supposed to read it, you lazy fucking twat"
- "Thanks in advance" = "Just fucking do it, you prick"

Thirdly, grammar is king. What you put after words is what really matters. Just think about the difference between, "Great!" and "Great." The exclamation mark says all is well, no problem. The full-stop variation is pretty much an expression of pure and utter hatred.

Now, there are many other levels of passive aggression, such as cc'ing the big boss and their mother, but I'm sure you now get the gist you silly fuck.

There are but two types of people in the world of email and Slack. Wankers like you who employ passive aggression almost as their default tone. Then the rest of us use it only when it's called for. If you think you've never been passive-aggressive, you're either a fucking liar, drastically self-unaware or you somehow still don't know what it is.

As a prick whose default setting is passive aggression, you will tell us that it's just the way people talk on these platforms. Well, that's just not true. If everyone did their fucking job without moaning, if no one was asked to do more than their pay dictates and if no one tried to palm work off on others, then there would never be any need for passive-aggressive behaviour. Unfortunately, we all know that this is nothing other than an unattainable utopia.

The default passive aggressors are generally prats like you who feel overly stressed whenever they're asked to do something, even if it directly relates to the job they are being paid to do. The problem is you know you can't simply reply to the request by blatantly asking the requestor to fuck off, otherwise you'd lose your job. So you vent your frustration and tell them to fuck off in a "professional" way: by being passive-aggressive.

Yes, sometimes you're genuinely asked to do too much and work has been unfairly palmed off on you. But on the whole, you're just being a lazy twat. There might even be stuff going on in your personal life that exacerbates your passive-aggressive tendencies. But I don't really give a shit, you shouldn't let it influence your interactions at work.

In any case, as a result of your passive aggression, nothing gets done. From experience, there is no point in persisting with a fully professional, nicey-nicey approach; this just makes you think you've got away with not doing any work. This is precisely where you force the rest of us to resort to passive aggression. Because, what gets default passive-aggressive pricks like you to sit up and take notice? That's right, reciprocal passive aggression.

- [Pointless] Exercise -

Don't get me wrong, the temptation to employ passive aggression as your default is monumental. Having a go at someone, knowing there'll be no repercussions because you haven't been blatantly out of order? One of the most satisfying fucking things in the world. Nevertheless, the next time you're about to be passive-aggressive, consider first why you're doing it. Is it because you're a lazy bastard who doesn't want to do the job? Are you just being a stubborn prick for the sake of it? If so, why don't you just fuck off and get a different job, as you're obviously not enjoying this one. If you've got a genuine complaint, stop hiding behind passive aggression as a way to vent your frustration. You're creating a shitty work environment and forcing sane people to also resort to passive-aggressive behaviour. Don't be a pussy, speak your mind. If you've got a valid point, it'll be heard. Idiot.

Know an idiot who needs to read this chapter?

- Scan the QR code
- Click the link
- Send it their way!

Waste of time meetings

Bloody meetings eh…

Sometimes they can be useful as a tool for discussing finer details and brainstorming. But in general, what a colossal waste of fucking time. Yet you still love to call them! And you make damn sure you find other ways to make them even more excruciatingly pointless.

One problem is the sheer pointlessness of the majority of meetings.

On the one hand, sometimes there is no reason for you to have arranged them in the first fucking place! It's truly bewildering how many times we have all turned up to a conference room, just for you to start talking for an hour, without communicating any clear aim for the meeting, then we all leave none the wiser and having achieved sweet fuck all.

On the other hand, sometimes you arrange meetings that are simply not needed! Too often, we'll discuss a particular point on Slack or email, then you'll suggest having a meeting to "discuss further", or "consolidate our thinking". No, mate. We've already discussed this at length, the consolidated thinking is all there in black and white on your fucking screen. If you actually read the shit everyone sends you, you'd know there is no need for a bloody meeting.

Another grievance arises after actually having had a rare, productive meeting. We find that we're a little excited about our job for once. Clear outcomes were communicated and everyone knows what their next steps are – we're all finally going to get something meaningful done!!

So we sit down to get on with our next steps, but then realise we need one of the other meeting participants to send over a crucial document or bit of info first. Needless to say, we made it abundantly clear in the meeting that we need it to complete our part of the project. But, being the obedient worker ants that we are, we understand that people are busy and the company's "culture" encourages us to "assume the best" of our peers. So we decide not to follow up just yet, assuming you've added it to your to-do list and you'll get round to it.

Three hours, two days, a week goes by – nothing. So we decide we've had enough and we send you a quick message to follow up. Your response, almost without fail, is, "Oh yeahhhhh, thanks for reminding me, completely forgot about that, will send it now". Then we get it in our inbox twenty seconds later. We're left thinking that if it was *that* fucking easy, why didn't you just send it straight after the fucking meeting?! And why did we have to remind you, you procrastinating twat?!!

The final atrocity regarding meetings is the way people like you conduct yourselves. In a meeting of five people, there is always at least one of you wankers who just cannot help talking over everyone else. You love the sound of your own voice and have no interest in hearing from the other participants. Your only aim in meetings is to talk and make your ideas heard, regardless of whether they're any fucking good.

In too many companies, it appears that whoever shouts the loudest wins. It's much worse when top brass is involved, which leads me to think it could be a career-driven person problem. I remember one meeting in particular. It comprised the CEO, VP of Europe, VP of North America, Europe Regional Director, Europe Marketing Director and a lowly, old Associate me. Fuck knows why I was in this meeting, but I was present all the same. I then proceeded to spend one of the most pointless, shitty hours of my life listening to these "experienced leaders" just shouting at and interrupting each other. Not one person managed to speak quickly enough to get their whole point across before being cut off.

You don't realise that this is fucking hell on earth to us normal, considerate folks. Observing you in meetings is like watching a really overgrown, fat bully child trying to run a company. It becomes very clear that one of the important elements of how knob-heads like you climb a corporate ladder is just by being the fucking loudest. But that's by the by, the pointlessness of meetings is the point of this chapter. And the way you act in these meetings makes it impossible to get a clear, democratic consensus on any decision. Which in turn renders your meetings, as always, a complete waste of fucking time.

- [Pointless] Exercise -

Take your meetings, shove them up your arse, then let's convert the time saved into a three-day working week. Idiot.

Know an idiot who needs to read this chapter?

- Scan the QR code
- Click the link
- Send it their way!

Torrid training

Let's face it, starting a new job is a bloody nightmare. New twats for colleagues, new names to try and fail to remember, new inefficient systems and new, but equally shoddy equipment.

But getting to grips with a new role is made even harder when new starters have got arseholes like you training them.

You make it abundantly clear that you don't actually *want* to be training them. You consider it a complete waste of your time. To you, they are an inconvenience on which you'd rather not have to expend energy.

So inevitably, because you don't want to train them in the first place, you do a really shit job of it. You talk through brand new processes in seconds, expecting new starters to instantly pick them up. You leave no time to take notes, nor do you provide any pre-prepared instructions. You refuse to help them step-by-step to ensure they've got the hang of things. Essentially, you waste their precious probationary time and leave them none the fucking wiser.

If they dare protest that they don't yet fully understand something and want to go over it again, you get annoyed and feel that they are questioning your professionalism. On a good day, you'll retort with some variation of, "It'll make more sense when you play around with it yourself, it just takes practice." In other words, you're telling them to fuck off and learn it in their own time. On a bad day, you will just say that they obviously aren't cut out for the job.

What you fail to grasp, or conveniently forget, is that you were also once in the same position, you thick, self-absorbed muppet. You are not some genius who didn't need any training or time to adjust to a new role. Maybe you got a trainer who wasn't a complete prick and who gave you the time of day. Or maybe you were indeed trained in the same shit way as you train others. But one would think you would have the wherewithal to break the cycle and improve the way the training is done, to make sure no one else has to endure the same stressful experience.

The other bugbear is with the quality of the actual content of some of the work training you force down people's throats. Some of the worst culprits include online safety, data privacy and safeguarding.

Don't get me wrong, training people in these aspects of work life is obviously very important. The problem is that you, as the manager or head of the company, don't seem to think so. You provide pointless video courses that teach people fuck all about anything, narrated by the most boring, monotonous person on earth. Elsewhere, the whole office is subjected to half a day of role-playing, where everyone takes the piss out of the designated "safeguarding officer" and it's all just a big fucking joke. And while, once again, no one learns anything, everyone's work pile has doubled in the meantime and we all have to stay late to get it done.

If you're going to do this training simply to tick a box, just fucking forget it. If you want it done properly and taken seriously, invest in the training. Get a proper, engaging instructor in and get rid of the bloody videos and role play.

- [Pointless] Exercise -

Stop being a fucking twat in your responsibility to train new starters. Try to remember how hard it was to get comfortable using new tools and systems when you started. Alternatively, just use some common sense and realise that the people you are training have joined the company for a reason. The quicker they get up to speed, the quicker they can take away some of your workload. Idiot.

Know an idiot who needs to read this chapter?

- Scan the QR code
- Click the link
- Send it their way!

Office loudmouths

Look, only weirdos like complete silence when there are other people in the room. Why? Because it's unnerving.

So a little office chatter and general background noise is a good thing in a workplace. Only gravediggers want to work at a graveyard.

But, there is a fine line between a healthy amount of noise and pissing people off while causing them to lose their concentration.

And you just do not seem to fucking comprehend the delicate noise balance at play.

One minute, everyone is happily working away at their desks, maybe a couple of colleagues having a quiet natter in the corner. Then you, Billy Big Bollocks, decide you need to shout a question at a colleague on the other side of the office, "JOHN, HAVE YOU GOT THOSE NUMBERS FOR ME YET?".

Shut. The. Fuck. Up. Dickhead. This sounds, very fucking loudly, like a question for John, and John only. And it being a question for John, inherently means it is *not* something the rest of us need to hear about. Nevertheless, you've now forced us to listen to John's reply and the subsequent shouting match over numbers that mean nothing to us. In the meantime, we can't get anything else done because you're both so fucking loud.

Has it never occurred to you that John might not want to shout his answer back to you in front of everyone? Now everyone's up in John's business thinking, "Fucking hell John, get the numbers and shut 'em up will ya!"

It begs the question, why the fuck do we bother signing up for other communication channels such as Slack, if you aren't going to use them for the simplest of questions, you loudmouth prick? If your question does happen to be time-sensitive, which it never truly is, get off your arse and go speak to whoever you need to in a quiet manner. No raised voices are needed.

Another incredibly frustrating element of you being too loud at work is when you take calls and video meetings in communal office space. When I say communal office space, I mean where the desks are; where the majority of people sit, heads down, actually doing the work that keeps the company afloat.

Do you really not understand that this is not the place to take your calls and meetings?! You're making it nigh on impossible to fucking concentrate while forcing us to eavesdrop on the most boring conversations known to humankind!

It's a bit more understandable if you get an impromptu call, but surely you could still just take it outside? In fact, most half considerate people do just that!

But the video meetings, fucking hell. There is no excuse, you lazy prat. You almost certainly knew the meeting was coming and you knew what time it would start. You had ample time to book a meeting room or find another space. Yet you still decide to take it where everyone has to listen in!

Your loudness at work really shines a light on your bloated sense of self-importance. You think the world revolves around you; the rest of us are just there, unimportant. You like to take the calls and video meetings in front of us because you think it shows us just how impressively in-demand and busy you are. You consider being blocked out for the day as a badge of honour. You like to bark your questions to people across the room because it's a power move. It's a, "You come to me, I don't come to you" mentality. You want to show that you need the info *so quickly*, that getting up to walk over to the person you need it from, or simply using Slack, just doesn't cut it. You truly believe you are *that* busy and *that* important, and being loud is your chosen method of showcasing it.

The problem with this is, most sane people do not think you are important or busy just because you have a lot of meetings and talk loudly in front of everyone, all the fucking time. You forget that we all have meetings too – we know how completely pointless most of them are. So, instead of something to be lauded, these should-be-private meetings actually portray just how much of a loud, time-wasting wanker you really are.

- [Pointless] Exercise -

I'd tell you to just fucking be quiet, but somehow that just never works. You'll be apologetic, but you'll carry on right where you left off. Being noisy is ingrained in your way of working; it's an impulse you have. You are just that self-absorbed. So, my recommendation here is for those who have to deal with you. Ensure you have headphones on. When they shout a question at you from across the room, ignore them. Do not give them the satisfaction. Force them to get up and come over to you or use an alternative communication channel such as Slack. These people are like children, they need to be trained day after day to behave appropriately. If someone next to you nudges you to respond, act surprised, take off your headphones and look at the shouting prat dead in the eye, put your index finger to your mouth in a shushing action and beckon them over with a wave of your hand, then put your headphones back on and return to your computer. Has never failed me yet. Idiot.

Know an idiot who needs to read this chapter?

- Scan the QR code
- Click the link
- Send it their way!

Taking it offline

Wanky business-speak and corporate jargon are inevitable when working in an office. Most of it is bloody pointless and used to falsely imply that the speaker knows what they're talking about. But it's normally relatively harmless. However, the phrase, "Let's take it offline", is one I am extremely fucking fed up with hearing you utter.

First of all, taking something "offline" logically requires someone to have been, and then stop being, online. In other words, deciding to talk about a topic face-to-face in real life instead of on a video call with others. But what if you're already offline, in a meeting room, facing your colleagues? How do you get more offline than that? You're mad if you think I'm having an extra off-the-grid meeting in the fucking jungle – the pay raise would have to be astronomical.

Also, I don't know if you've noticed, but a lot of people now work exclusively online and remotely. *Especially* in industries and companies with copious, pretentious, corporate prats where you're more likely to hear the phrase, "Let's take it offline". How do you take it offline when you only work remotely? Apparently, the answer is, you keep it online and have yet another video meeting… online…

You might say this is a stupid argument. That this phrase has nothing to do with being on the internet or talking in person. That it simply indicates the intention to discuss a particular topic at another time. Maybe you're right, but I would still argue that you sound like a complete muppet. In any case, the semantic problems with "taking it offline" do not end with whether or not we are online.

When you say, "Let's take this offline", what do you really mean? What are you really trying to say? The phrase has so many potential meanings, that your true reason for using it can be easily misunderstood. It also very much depends on the person who used it and how much of an arsehole they have decided to be on any given day. Context, as always, is key.

Let's dive into some of these possible reasons.

Frequently, you use it as a way to simply avoid further discussion. The reasons why you might want to are endless. Maybe you want to put a stop to an uncomfortable situation. Maybe you want to save the blushes of someone asking a painfully stupid question that has nothing to do with anything. Maybe you think it's none of their fucking business. Maybe you want to move on when it becomes too painfully obvious that you are in the wrong. Maybe you want to make sure that you don't crash and burn while trying to explain yourself in front of people who actually know what they're talking about. Maybe you are just reasserting your control over a meeting that has veered in a direction you had not intended.

However, one thing is for sure. Whatever the reason for you wanting to "take it offline", there is rarely any doubt that the topic is actually being shut down for good. You are hiding behind business-speak to avoid accepting any accountability for the topic.

In your mind, this phrase has the added benefit of giving whoever raised the topic the illusion that they have been heard. In reality, you just want them to shut the fuck up, move on and forget they ever brought it up. Although what I would say is shame on those who don't realise this from the outset. They are the kind of numpties who believe company values are anything other than lip-service and PR bollocks.

Sometimes you use, "Let's take it offline", to professionally disguise your blatant anger at the gall someone must have had to make a given point. What you are really trying to communicate is, "Who the hell do you think you are, asking that question?! I don't want to berate you in front of everyone else. So, instead of telling you to piss off, I'm respectfully saying we'll take this offline. But I have fuck all intention of doing so." Again, it's an issue of accountability and on us to read between the lines.

What you don't seem to realise though, is that the majority of your colleagues aren't thickos. They *can* read between the lines. They are all very aware that you're doing your utmost *not* to discuss a particular topic when you use the phrase, "Let's take it offline". Every time you employ this tactic, you're imparting an air of secrecy around the topic in question and your role in it. You're kicking a can down the road that you're much better off just dealing with in the meeting.

Once in a blue moon, you'll use the phrase appropriately. For instance, when there are more pressing items on the agenda and you're running out of time, when the team is going off on tangents, when topics are not relevant to everyone in attendance or when they require non-attendees to weigh in. And as much as yet another meeting makes most of us want to throw up on our keyboards, it is always good to see you taking a topic offline and actually chasing it up.

The sad truth is that examples of you properly taking matters offline are few and far between. Unfortunately, 'let's take it offline' are four of the most simultaneously hollow, charged and pointless words you utter in the office, and you utter them way too often.

- [Pointless] Exercise -

Instead of saying, "Let's take it offline", why can't you just be specific about your issue with the subject at hand. If you want to schedule another meeting so all the Karens can join, say that, and then schedule the bloody thing. If it's confidential and none of the attendees' business, say that. If it was a stupid fucking question, say that. If the meeting is going off-topic and there isn't much time left, say that. If you're just not in the mood to discuss it and want the protagonist to kindly fuck off, say that.

It's also worth remembering that the phrase, "let's take it offline" is inherently a little threatening. At the end of the day, you are putting a full stop to a conversation and forbidding further discussion at this time. This could be interpreted as a direct challenge to your colleagues/employees, daring them to continue pursuing their line of questioning. Why don't you just go the whole hog and say, "Let's take this outside", instead? Let's go primal, forgo the veil of professionalism and sort things out the old-fashioned way. Idiot.

Know an idiot who needs to read this chapter?

- Scan the QR code
- Click the link
- Send it their way!

Being born well-off

When spending any substantial time with people like you who have always just *had* money, thanks to your family, it becomes horrifically clear that you genuinely believe you are better than people without it.

Now, those of us with any sense know that you are wrong – fucking stupidly so. But why do *you* believe this?

The quick answer is that you have been brought up by equally wanky parents. You were raised under the assumption that wearing nicer clothes, having a posh accent and having more money, automatically means you are a better breed of person.

Logically, this is absolute bullshit. Why would these things make you a better, kinder, more tolerant person? In my experience, they tend to make you more of an arsehole.

We should bear in mind though that it's not completely your fault. From day one, you've probably only ever mixed with other well-off people. Your family, or friends from your paid-for school. Your belief in your "kind" being superior has been reinforced by everyone you've ever known.

You don't understand the real world. You've never spent time with "normal people". You don't and can't comprehend problems or struggles that are the direct result of a lack of money, because you have never experienced them. It is much more convenient to assume that poorer peoples' problems are their own fault, an issue borne from a lack of financial know-how, budgeting or brainpower. You therefore never make the intellectual leap that the only difference between you and these people is the amount of money into which you were born.

However, this lack of real-world experience does not excuse you. If you did indeed hail from such an apparently amazing, intelligent breed of humanity, surely you would have the wherewithal to see beyond your own experiences and appreciate how difficult things are for people without money? Surely you would be able to realise that you yourself have always had money, a better education and that you were simply *lucky* to have been born into it. Because that is the truth. You have nicer clothes and that posh accent because you are lucky, not because you're better.

I get that it's painful to acknowledge that luck is the only reason you are in such an advantageous position. Because what are you supposed to do with that knowledge? Unless you're willing to make peace with the guilt and responsibility of such privilege, it's much easier to accept what you're constantly told by your peers – that you're just superior to the average person. It's fucking wrong though.

Another thing that fucks me off is you believe that you "pulled yourself up by your bootstraps". In other words, you think that *you* are the reason for your good financial situation. Ok, yes, you may have made a lot of money in your own right. Yes, you may have invested wisely and made your money work for you. But what you don't understand is that none of this would have been possible without money in the first fucking place. For the most part, people make a lot of money because they were given money to start a venture, they were given money to get the education/connections/accent that allowed them to get a job unavailable to those without them, or they had the backing to go and spend time in a field where it takes some time and luck to succeed - acting being an example. And the most obvious one, you cannot invest any money if you don't have any!!!

So, true story - I was having a conversation with a well-off friend, upon whom I tried to impress the difficulties poorer people have. I explained how having money from birth means you get a good education. How your accent and school connections then open up job opportunities that are unavailable to the vast majority. How having money from birth means you can invest some and make your money make more money. How you can only afford to do unpaid internships and follow your dreams into more creative fields if you have the safety net of a family with money to support you. Yet he maintained that there is no excuse - he thinks the rest of us should still be able to invest and save some money to start building a better future. Intrigued by this perspective, I asked him what he thought my family earned. He said he reckoned fifty thousand pounds per year!!!

Let's unpack that… So firstly, a fifty thousand pound annual salary, to him, meant poor. That's how out of touch he was with the reality of our situations. Secondly, he also assumed that we squander *that* kind of money. That's how financially inept he thought we all are.

I told him that my parents raised four kids on fifteen thousand pounds per year, in London, between the 1990s and the 2010s Not fucking *fifty*! He was absolutely shocked - he couldn't believe it. In fact, he *didn't* believe it at first! I told him to build a budget there and then at the pub, on a fifteen thousand pound salary, that catered for four kids, mortgage payments and everything else. Needless to say, he could not make ends meet. Not even close. He finally came to the realisation that most people without money are actually incredibly good at managing budgets, simply because they *have* to be to survive! Here was a well-needed reality check that I think you and all well-off people could do with.

In the end, it's pretty fucking simple – you are nothing special. Plenty of poorer people would thrive if they had the same opportunities! It's truly mind-blowing how thick and unaware so many well-off people like you really are.

– [Pointless] Exercise –

Really think about how you earned any money you have – if indeed you earned it at all. Consider any help/support you were given in order to do so. I guarantee you will have had some – you've just never had the inclination to realise it. Don't automatically revert to the fall-back position that you did it all yourself. And to the rest of us, think about the fact that we are trusting well-off people, like my friend above, to lead companies, set budgets and even run countries! If that doesn't send chills down your spine, you're just as thick as the well-off people who think they are God's gift to humanity. Idiot.

Know an idiot who needs to read this chapter?

- Scan the QR code
- Click the link
- Send it their way!

Settling your debts

You know exactly who you are. You're the one who issues IOUs to their mates like they're giving away fucking Tic Tacs. The one who always apparently forgets their wallet or purse. The one who somehow always leaves their card at home. The one who says they'll pay for everyone's drinks on the next night out, then conveniently gets too pissed to remember after round two. The one who never pays people back.

Of course, sometimes there are legitimate reasons for having to borrow cash and settle a debt in the first place. Maybe you're short near the end of the month. Maybe you actually did forget your wallet or card. Although I can't understand, for the life of me, why you would take your card out of your wallet and then not put it back.

Most people are really embarrassed when something like this happens and they pay the money back as soon as they can. But not you.

You take aaaaaages to settle your debt. There's always an excuse and a delay. You know you owe money, you just don't feel the need to pay it back as soon as you can. You don't give a shit how much of a struggle it was for your mate to be able to give you this money in the first place.

You will wait until you yourself are on good financial footing again before settling your debts. But that's not how this paying people back malarkey is supposed to work. As soon as you have the money, you should be paying it back. As soon as you get paid, you should be paying it back. If it's a larger amount, you pay it back in fucking instalments and keep your mate informed. If we really have to wait for you to be on good financial footing, we might *never* see the money you owe us!

You use the same old diversion tactics bullshit every time, always in the following order. You insist you don't owe anything in the first place, hoping we'll let you off the hook. Then you lie about money we owe you from some other time, fifteen years ago, that no one remembers. Then you say, "Ah come on mate, it was only a fiver!" Fuck you arsehole, those fivers add up. And this is all in an attempt to try and convince yourself repeatedly that it's not a lot of money, so you feel no guilt. One day, it won't be a night of beer you're looking for help with. You're going to need real money, and fuck you if you think we'll be footing your bill.

In addition, you constantly need reminding that there is even a debt to settle. Six paydays will go by and you'll say nothing. Whether we need that money paid back ASAP or not, you'll say nothing. We'll call you to ask for it, all the while feeling shitty for asking because money is a touchy subject. And then you'll tell us that you "forgot". *You fucking forgot!?* That's your excuse while I've been sitting here, unable to go out or pay the fucking rent! Wanker.

Listen, you devious twat. You are not supposed to be reminded. You shouldn't have to be asked to pay up. You should be telling me when you're going to pay me back and then do it. If you have a legitimate reason why you can't, you tell me what it is and you tell me when you can. You do NOT wait to be asked, hoping to get away with it. You do not "forget". You pay the money back, simple. I understand no one likes parting with their hard-earned cash, but the reason why you even have a debt to settle is that your mate parted with theirs to help you out. So stop being a tight prick – settle your fucking debts.

- [Pointless] Exercise -

The next time you ask for help paying for something and are expected to repay the money, try putting a reminder on your calendar. Most people don't need to, because they feel bad asking in the first place, so the unsettled debt doesn't leave their minds until they've paid up. But you don't seem to give a shit. So set up that reminder and stop fucking about. Idiot.

Know an idiot who needs to read this chapter?

- Scan the QR code
- Click the link
- Send it their way!

Splitting the bill

Why are you so fucking stingy when it comes to paying the bill? Like, seriously. It's pathetic how awkward you're willing to make a situation, just to save a few pennies.

I just can't stand it. You'll go out for a meal with friends. Everyone will have burgers and a beverage, so the bill is pretty much going to be the same for everyone. Nevertheless, without fail, when the waiter comes round with that little bloody plate, you'll want to check it and make sure you pay the exact, correct amount that you owe, down to the last pissing penny!

Put your calculator away, you tight prat. No one, other than stingy fuckers like you, gives a fuck if they pay thirty pence more. We just want to pay the bill and get out of the restaurant. Why do we need to do this, "Who had the chicken burger and G&T", bull-shit?

LET'S JUST SPLIT THE MOTHERFUCKING BILL EQUALLY!!! It doesn't matter! If you haven't got a lot of money, I understand you counting the pennies - shit can be tight. But then I also question why the fuck you are going to restaurants in the first place. If you can't really afford it, don't go.

The vast majority of people do not like wasting time poring over a receipt to work out exactly what they owe. It puts a real dampener on the evening. We're happy to pay a tiny bit more if necessary, we're all mates here for fuck's sake. It'll even itself out at the next meal or the pub. And don't humiliate yourself by citing something like that '*Friends*' episode, where someone only orders a side salad and then is asked to split with those who ordered a lot more. That's completely different and it rarely happens like that.

Some technology companies are even creating apps to solve this splitting the bill "problem". This appar-ent epidemic of friend groups feeling hard done by.

This super complicated task of working out who had what and how much they owe.

Get the fuck over it. Splitting the bill isn't the problem and nor is the arithmetic – well, it shouldn't be, you thicko. Stingy bastards like you are the issue. The notion that we need technology and apps for social situations like this is embarrassing.

- [Pointless] Exercise -

The next time you go for a meal, try suggesting that you all split the bill equally. Feel the relief wash over everyone at the table. Throw your card on the little bill plate without delay and calm your shit. And to those who are fed up with bill-splitters, try having a rule in your friend group that if anyone suggests splitting the bill to the penny, they have to pay the whole bloody thing. Hopefully, that'll show the stingy fucks. Idiot.

Know an idiot who needs to read this chapter?

- Scan the QR code
- Click the link
- Send it their way!

Money bragging

Look, money is important. I'm not going to deny that. But, only in so much that we need it to survive, to buy food, to pay bills and to have a roof over our heads. But twats like you pay much more homage to your dough than you should.

And you go on about it all the fucking time. You'll never miss a chance to mention your bloated salary. Or in a misguided, shoddy attempt to be more discreet about your earnings, you'll mention all the things you have bought recently while attaching the monetary amount. The monetary amount is imperative, otherwise, how would we know that we could never afford it and that you can? Prick.

The problem with all this, my well-off wanky friend, is that what you're trying to do is painfully transparent. You're doing your utmost to impress others, you want them to idolise what you have, you may even be trying to make them jealous. For you, money is the unit by which you measure success in life.

You're overly competitive about dosh and you think everyone else is too. You've been fully indoctrinated by capitalism and bought into the belief that money, nice houses and cars are proof that you've done it right, that you've made it.

But grounded people, rich or poor alike, won't give a shit how much money you make or have. They'll be pleased for you, but they won't think you're a better person as a result. Most won't understand why you feel the need to shove it down their throats, because they know that money is not the be-all and end-all of life. The rest will just feel sorry for you.

"Why would they feel sorry for me?" I hear you ask. Well, it's quite simple really. Either you're so thick, immature and inexperienced that you haven't grasped the notion that money isn't everything. Or you're peacocking through money as a cover-up for some element of insecurity. Maybe you don't truly believe you deserve what you earn, maybe you inherited it. It could even be nothing to do with money. Maybe work is all you have, maybe you've got a small penis, who knows.

Whatever it is, sort it out, for fuck's sake. Because this money chat is getting fucking boring. You make a lot of money, you have a nice car, you have a nice house. We get it. So bloody what. You're still a wanker. You still have to live with your insecurities. And guess what, you're still going to die one day, just like the rest of us.

What you're failing to realise is that most people measure their lives through another unit, happiness. It might sound corny – in fact, I'm sure you're thinking that that's exactly what someone with no money would say. But it's not, I'm afraid. Go talk to good people who have been wealthy for a long time. They'll tell you sure, money enhances their experience of life and allows them to do, and buy, more shit. But they can still get bored and they can still get lonely. When it comes down to it, the fact that there are people you love and who love you, how much time you get to spend with them and how you will be remembered, is all that really matters.

– [Pointless] Exercise –

Talk to me about what you've done, not what you've bought. If you really need to keep on about how much money you have, show me how you're using it to benefit people other than yourself, in ways that people without money can't. Because you're boring the shit out of me, mate – read the fucking room. Work on your insecurities. Ask yourself why you're bragging about your money. Why can't you just be pleased that you're doing well for yourself? Why do you need to broadcast it? I think you are more aware than you realise that, if you were truly happy with your life, you would not hint at your bank balance so often. Idiot.

Know an idiot who needs to read this chapter?

- Scan the QR code
- Click the link
- Send it their way!

Tailgating

Why - the fuck - do you feel this need to drive so close behind other cars? What do you think you're going to achieve through tailgating? We're not dogs - you don't need to lick our arseholes to get to know us. We're not your boss either, you bloody brown-noser. So why do you insist on getting so up close and personal?

Maybe you're so thick, you don't actually know what the speed limit is? Maybe you believe you're a poor man's Lewis Hamilton? Maybe you have a small dick and feel like you have no option other than to be a prick to get through life? Maybe you just genuinely like licking arseholes? Or maybe, aww diddums, did you have a bad day?

No, it's obvious why you tailgate. You're an impatient fucking wanker. You want the car in front to go faster, just so you can go faster - despite the fact they are normally driving at the speed limit. You're dying to overtake but you just don't have the space. So you find solace in putting pressure on the car in front.

What you don't seem to get, you absolute knobhead, is how fucking dangerous driving up peoples' arseholes really is. However tempting my arse is, you don't have super-human reactions, knobheads rarely do. There is no doubt that, if I suddenly had to brake really hard, you'd have no option other than to go through the back of my car or veer off the road. Either way, someone is going to get seriously hurt, or worse.

How would you feel if you were to kill someone, simply because you were impatient? You would have to live with that, you twat. You may even go to prison. Additionally, if you go into the back of my car, *your* insurance will be paying, not mine. That's a lot of risk, mate, all for the sake of impatience.

To the good drivers out there, I hope you might consider adopting my preferred response to an arsehole driver/licker. Never, ever, under any circumstances, bow down to the pressure and reward arsehole drivers by driving faster. Instead, DRIVE SLOWER! When they come up behind you, automatically slow down at least fifteen miles per hour. For added emphasis, give the prick behind a nice little fright, with a quick slam on the brakes, before continuing on your way. Look back in the mirror straight into the eyes of the petrified wanker behind. Enjoy the view and don't forget to smile.

- [Pointless] Exercise -

The next time you find yourself wanting to drive up someone's arsehole, remember that this absolutely infers some desperate need on your part to lick arseholes. If that doesn't phase you, because you genuinely do like licking arseholes, remember instead that driving bumper-to-bumper, at anything above fifteen miles per hour, makes you a wanker who hasn't considered the fact that you could kill someone. If the potential to suffer from perpetrator trauma doesn't phase you, then you're a fucking psychopath. Idiot.

Know an idiot who needs to read this chapter?

- Scan the QR code
- Click the link
- Send it their way!

Road rage over learners

How does someone end up being able to legally drive on the road? They have to learn, right? Everyone who has ever been given a driving licence has had to have driving lessons.

It's very easy to forget after you've been driving for a few years, but I'd bet good money that you also made some God-awful mistakes when you were learning. Everyone does. That's how you learn. You were a fresh-faced prat of a driver at one point too, holding up drivers and stalling like a motherfucker at red lights on a hill.

Yet, that doesn't stop you from swearing and getting frustrated when you get stuck behind a learner. I know it can be annoying - the learners appear to be going too slow and you've got places to be. But so fucking what? I know you'd rather they weren't on the road, but how else are they going to learn?

You'll even automatically give them a few honks on the horn. I mean, how much of an arsehole can you be? Fuckwits like you will say that the learners have got to learn. But learn what? What does bibbing learners teach them, when they haven't done anything wrong? That you should bib other drivers for no fucking reason? That impatience is a virtue? Fucking prick.

Another automatic reaction you have to getting stuck behind learners is overtaking them straight away - even when they are driving at the speed limit. What the fuck does *that* teach them? That they should fucking speed, otherwise they'll be overtaken?! They're learners, they might even be on their driving test for Christ's sake! They simply aren't allowed to go any faster. And for that matter, nor are you, you speeding wanker.

We all have a responsibility, as legal drivers, to exemplify good driving. That is how we ensure learners become good legal drivers and that the roads are a safe place to drive in the future. Treating learners with disdain is not going to help with that, you prat.

- [Pointless] Exercise -

The next time you get stuck behind a learner, don't overtake them or honk your horn for no fucking reason. Give them the time to learn by taking a deep breath, staying calm and letting them do their thing. Idiot.

Know an idiot who needs to read this chapter?

- Scan the QR code
- Click the link
- Send it their way!

Zebra crossings

The official rule: when a pedestrian *moves onto* a zebra crossing, drivers must stop and let them cross to the other side. But fuck the rules. Do you really expect an old granny to just step brazenly into the road? Even though drivers ignore rules and speed limits, all the fucking time? No chance. I think we all know the unwritten element of the zebra crossing rule – that drivers should stop when someone is blatantly *waiting* to cross. After all, if a driver hits someone on a zebra crossing, they're going to be legally destroyed whether the pedestrian was already on the road or not.

With this in mind, I have two really big fucking bugbears about zebra crossings.

The first is to do with pedestrians. I don't know about you, but when I was a kid crossing the road, even at a zebra crossing, my parents told me to raise my hand to the driver in appreciation. The driver has done a nice thing by letting you cross the road. It only cost them a few seconds, but still, they stopped, for you.

You, as a pedestrian and the person who has received that goodwill, should therefore say thank you. These are pretty standard fucking manners. So why, why, why, do you think you're such a Billy Big Bollocks that you don't need to raise your hand? Is it that your hand is just unnaturally heavy? Do you feel embarrassed being nice? Or have you just been raised as a complete arsehole? I realise that saying thank you to a driver who is *supposed* to stop is not strictly necessary – but manners never are!

You have no idea how this simple action can affect a nice driver's state of mind for the rest of the day. To be clear, not saying thank you can easily piss well-meaning drivers off for the rest of the day. Those drivers might then decide not to stop for other people. They might inadvertently be a wanker to everyone they meet that day. In short, not getting recognition for a kind act from the beneficiary, just leaves a really shitty taste in the mouth.

The second issue is with drivers. Stopping and letting people cross the road at zebra crossings *is the fucking law*. Yet it would appear that you are one of the dickheads who are somehow unaware of this rule. Don't give me the legal bullshit that you only stop if the pedestrian is already on the crossing - it's pretty fucking obvious when people want to cross. So why don't you stop? Is it because you're a petty prick who didn't receive proper thanks from those for whom you previously stopped? Is it because you expected to see an actual zebra? Or is it because you're in a rush?

No one is too busy to stop at a zebra crossing or drive safely for that matter. Instead of thinking selfishly about the few seconds you'll lose by stopping, think how you'd feel if drivers didn't stop for you, your mum, your nan, or any other loved one who might struggle with crossing the road.

I've seen it happen! Wanker drivers like you roaring past while elderly people try to use a zebra crossing, leaving them frightened and unsure of themselves. It's disgraceful. And what's worse is when you do actually stop, but you do everything you can to intimidate the pedestrian to get a move on. Revving your car and inching forward slowly while pedestrians cross. Dickhead.

Why can't you just do your bit to make the world go round a little more smoothly? Stop being a wanker on the road, whether you're playing the role of pedestrian or driver, and take responsibility for your actions. When a driver lets you cross the road, say thanks and raise your hand. When you come to a zebra crossing and someone is waiting to cross, slow the fuck down and wave them across. Simple.

– [Pointless] Exercise –

The next time you arrive at a zebra crossing and someone is waiting to cross, slow down on your approach, wave them across and wait patiently. It'll feel good to not be a prick for a few seconds, trust me. However, if you don't get a thank you, feel free to run the fucker over. Idiot.

Know an idiot who needs to read this chapter?

- Scan the QR code
- Click the link
- Send it their way!

Crossing the road

Driving a car in the city is bloody stressful. Road rage is rife with busy commuters cutting each other up to try and get to work on time, there's traffic in every bloody direction, potholes galore, cyclists and scooters swarming all around you, every other road is one-way, never-ending construction and road repair prompting diversions every half a mile, cars parked on both sides making many roads far too narrow… I could go on. Needless to say, therefore, drivers do not need pedestrians creating additional, unnecessary hazards by crossing the road as if cars were actually slow-moving, fluffy fucking pillows.

Yet that is exactly what you do. Without a care in the world, and seemingly no regard for your own and others' safety, you walk into the road whether the green man is lit or not. Listen, I am by no means a jaywalking nut or health and safety advocate; I think people should be allowed to judge for themselves whether they can cross a road without traffic light permission. However, if you're going to do it, you've got to at least check both fucking directions for on-coming cars beforehand. But most of the time you *don't* look, do you? You don't even throw a cheeky glance over your shoulder when you're halfway across, and an approaching car has had to screech on the brakes in order to let you carry on living.

The truth of the matter, that you seem unable to fathom, is that if you cross the road and force an oncoming car to slow down, you've messed up. You only made it across unscathed because a kind soul *slowed* down instead of *mowing* you down. Obviously, you either haven't adequately checked for cars or haven't judged the time needed to cross properly.

I don't care whether or not you've got the right of way as a pedestrian. This is your life! You should be preserving it, not throwing caution to the wind based on right of way rules that are hazy at best. Where the fuck is your personal responsibility?! You absolutely have a duty of care to yourself and drivers to realise that they might not see you in time, considering all the other hazards they have to contend with, or might be going too fast to brake in time when you cross at the last fucking moment. If you don't fulfil that duty of care, your life is fucked, maybe finished. And a forgotten factor here is that the driver's life is also fucked. Yes, they might get hurt. But if they survive the crash, they're also going to have to live with your death/injuries on their conscience for the rest of their life. Honestly, I wouldn't blame them for reversing and running over you again, for being such a selfish, ignorant, unaware arsehole.

Your lack of responsibility as a pedestrian is dangerous enough in the daytime when there's sunlight and shit. But at night, poor visibility gets added to the long list of things drivers have to deal with and makes every hazard that bit more hazardous. What makes you so sure that drivers are going to see you when the sun goes down? They've got enough problems making out the bloody road signs and markings. At least cars have big, beaming headlights announcing their impending arrival to help you work out whether you should be crossing or not. What do drivers get? You, crossing the road like a wanker, without checking both directions or judging the required time, most likely while wearing dark clothes with a fucking hood on.

Special mention now for when you cross the road without due care at a junction. Yes, in theory, you have the right of way at junctions if you're already on the road. Yes, drivers will check if someone is crossing before they turn a corner. But if you decide to cross at the precise moment that a car turns the corner, you make it very fucking difficult for the driver to react quickly enough. Ignoring right of way for a second, is it too much to ask that you just check to make sure it is safe to cross first? How about you use your brain for once and decide to cross a little further down the road, away from the junction, to give drivers enough reaction time? Or better still, if you are *that* shit at judging the traffic or just can't be bothered, wait for the fucking traffic lights, you muppet.

Finally, we come to the occasions on which you just follow other people into the road without doing your own checks, like sheep following their compatriots and the shepherd. Has it never occurred to you that it's ok for sheep to be sheep, as shepherds have fewer cars to deal with, being in the fucking countryside? It's also a fair bet that shepherds actually care about their flock. The person you just followed into the road does not give two shits about you, mate. They've checked the road and judged the time needed to cross for *themselves*, not for *you*. Just because they've decided to cross the road, does not mean you will also make it across in time, however closely you follow behind. Someone else crossing the road also doesn't inherently mean the green man must be on. You should always check first, you fucking plonker.

- [Pointless] Exercise -

Read the Highway Code and get familiar with the rules of the road for pedestrians and drivers alike. Then take your copy and throw it in the fucking bin. Use your bloody common sense instead - I'm assuming it's somewhere in that thick skull of yours. Forget the right of way for pedestrians bullshit. Only cross the road after checking left and right, giving yourself ample time to make it, or waiting for the green man. While we're at it, start helping drivers out by making it obvious, with your body language, that you intend to cross. Stand at the edge of the kerb and make a show of looking down the road in both directions. You could even make a cheeky bit of eye contact with the oncoming driver. It doesn't need to be fucking romantic, it just needs to get their attention. Idiot.

Know an idiot who needs to read this chapter?

- Scan the QR code
- Click the link
- Send it their way!

Cyclists on roads

Almost daily, I get sent a new video of a cyclist having a big old row with a driver. It's never absolutely clear who was in the wrong, as that bit never seems to make it to the final cut, but the argument is always hilarious. Normally between two pussies threatening to fight, but never quite having the bottle to get out of their car or off their bike. One thing is clear – there are two sides to the eternal debate regarding cyclists on roads.

On the one hand, I can understand why a driver might hate you as a cyclist. You do seem to frequently take the piss. It's like you think that, as you are not in a powered vehicle, especially not with those scrawny legs, you do not need to abide by the laws of the road. THIS IS NOT TRUE.

For the lack of attention that you pay to them, traffic lights might as well simply be the world's shittest light show. On too many occasions, I've seen you drive straight through them at various crossroads and junctions, and nearly cause crashes in the process. I've even seen you mount the pavement at traffic lights, just to avoid waiting for one fucking minute.

As I'm sure you are aware, traffic lights are a traffic management signalling tool that tells road users when to go or stop. And what are you, as a cyclist? That's right, you are a fucking road user. As you are on the road. And as such, you are subject to the rules of the road.

Your seeming inability to understand this leaves the rest of us wondering whether your helmet is somehow preventing the neurones in your brain from firing properly. Even more so when you neglect to use hand signals, ignore the indicators of turning vehicles, forget to wear bright or reflective clothing or use bike lights, and drive in the middle of the fucking road instead of next to the kerb, sometimes even when there are designated cycle lanes!!

On the other hand, it's worth remembering that this hatred between drivers and cyclists isn't all down to cyclists. When you're behind the wheel, you assume that all cyclists are dickheads who flout the rules, just because they ride a bike. Which is also not true.

I've seen cyclist-phobic drivers like you drive way too bloody close to cyclists when overtaking, bib them like crazy when they're doing nothing wrong and conveniently forget to indicate or check your mirrors when turning, even before crossing over a cycle lane. Let's face it, when you moan about cyclists, it's normally because you are actually just an impatient bastard with a little dick, who hates being stuck behind something moving slower.

At the end of the day, reckless cyclists like you need to start abiding by the rules. But when you take the car instead, calm your tits and recognise that it's not every cyclist's fault by association.

- [Pointless] Exercise -

Here's a thought - if you stop doing whatever the fuck you want on the road when on your bike, maybe drivers will also stop being wankers! If you don't know the laws of the road, piss off to a river path or I'll drive over your bike myself. Equally, when you're behind the wheel, remember what it's like being a cyclist. Nearly dying each time you saddle up, despite following the laws of the road, is no fun. Start looking at things from both perspectives. Idiot.

Know an idiot who needs to read this chapter?

- Scan the QR code
- Click the link
- Send it their way!

Electric scooters

Do you know what, I get it. These electric scooters, or e-scooters, are brilliant. It's amazing that we can now stand and zip along at the push of a button, on something that we previously had to use our own legs to get moving. Technology is advancing. Wonderful. I can think of more important things for tech geeks to spend their time on, but, whatever. Electric scooters are fun.

However, as with anything new, people inevitably ruin it by being prats.

The first problem/cringe-moment is most definitely with adults like you who try that bit too hard to hold on to their youth. You latch on to every new fad, desperate to stay relevant, but ultimately and inevitably failing.

You would love to use scooters to get to work if it was in any way practical. But, even in full mid-life crisis mode, you would never use a normal scooter to get to work considering how much you've let yourself go.

I can just imagine your delight when you found out about the e-scooter and the lack of physical effort needed. "Yes, Donald/Barbara/Ned/Patricia/Harold/Edna/any other old person's name!!! We can pretend to be young again! The youngsters at work are going to think we're well sick!!"

I'm sorry Arnie, it's not going to happen. An E-scooter is still a scooter, meant for kids. Move on.

The second issue with e-scooters is you go waaaaay too fast around other people and use them on the road.

You are a fucking nightmare on these things. You seem to have no regard for anyone's safety. Actually, there's no "seem" about it, you obviously couldn't give a flying shit. The way you ride around on e-scooters in populated areas is an absolute disgrace. Everyone else has to have eyes in the backs of their heads to survive your reckless whizzing about. You make everyone else feel nervous, even when they're walking on the fucking pavement. Weaving in and out while people are out for a nice walk in the park, turning at the last possible second and avoiding knocking them over by mere fucking millimetres… there's just no need.

These things are illegal on pavements for the time being – not that that stops you. But incredibly, they *are* legal on the roads. Some of them even without a driving licence. Which is lucky because, from the way you ride them, we could be forgiven for thinking you have never even had a fucking driving lesson. I have yet to see a wanker like you on an e-scooter fail to break the laws of the road at least once.

Unfortunately, dickheads and e-scooters look like they are here to stay. Which leaves us looking for the silver linings in life. One such silver lining came one boring, grey day in Burgess Park, South London. Two young prats were going way too fast in the park, weaving in and out of people as usual. They turned their heads to laugh at each other and very nearly smashed into an elderly couple who were hand in hand, just out for a stroll. One of the riders had to jerk the handlebars to avoid the couple. He fell off, skidded to a stop and the back tyre blew out. It was a wonderful sight. He had to sheepishly walk away, wheeling the scooter with him while his mate rode slowly alongside him. The icing on the cake was everyone in the vicinity cheering at him when the tyre blew out. "Whhhhhhheeeeeeeeeeeeeyyyyyyyyyyyyy!!!!!". Slightly restored my faith in humanity.

– [Pointless] Exercise –

Before you buy that e-scooter, as someone over twenty-eight years old, I want you to remember one thing. The kids at work don't and won't ever think you're cool, hip or trendy. So why don't you go ahead and drag that scooter out of your shopping basket. You're a fucking adult, al-

127 Reasons Why You Are An Idiot

legedly. And if you're that wanker who loves riding along like an imbecile on the pavement and in public places, I'd buy some shoulder pads. People aren't going to accept you driving like that for much longer – "accidental" shoulder barges are coming your way. Idiot.

Know an idiot who needs to read this chapter?

- Scan the QR code
- Click the link
- Send it their way!

Walking on busy streets

Most people will have heard of Oxford Street. For those living under a rock, it's one of the most well-known shopping streets in London. It's also one of the busiest, in an already incredibly busy city. And I fucking hate it.

Now, it isn't just because it's a busy street that I hate it. It's because of the way people act. It is seemingly full of more wankers per capita than most streets.

However, it probably isn't the case that there just happens to be more wankers visiting Oxford Street – although people that care about designer clothes are invariably much more likely to be wankers than not. Rather, it is the fact that busy streets highlight just how many knobheads don't know how to walk down one properly. Anyone who has lived in London, or any big city, for a good while, will know exactly what I mean.

First of all, no one owns the fucking pavement. So why do you act like it? If you're walking in a group, why do you insist on taking up all the space? I know you want to talk to your friends in a horizontal line and that this is precious social time. Nevertheless, on a busy street, it is your responsibility as a group to get out of the fucking way. If you want to chat, go sit down in a park in a bloody circle. People have shit to do. You should not be walking arm in arm down Oxford Street and making others veer into the fucking road to get around you. All I'm saying is, don't be surprised when someone decides to smash straight through your group to get to the other side.

Remember though that this is one of the *only* occasions on which it's acceptable to collide with people on a busy street. Yet you seem to think you have some inherent right to barge into everyone, whether the victims are in a large group or not. You knock

127 Reasons Why You Are An Idiot

into anyone who dares come anywhere close to crossing your direct route through the crowds. Who the fuck do you think you are? You aren't the lord of the fucking street! Your anger at people crossing your path isn't justified in the slightest. Busy streets just aren't that simple. Veering off your route and making tiny little adjustments constantly are unfortunate inevitabilities, if you want to maintain your speed. I'd be careful if I were you with all the barging. One day, you're inevitably going to come up against a like-minded, six foot five guy having a bad day, who's going to send you spinning into the fucking road. And we'll all be there to laugh in your face, make no mistake.

On the subject of making tiny little adjustments to keep speed, navigating on busy streets is much like driving on busy roads but without rules. You should be thinking ahead and continuously evaluating potential hazards. Just because you are using your own legs rather than an engine, and unlikely to run anyone over, doesn't mean you can be completely fucking oblivious to your surroundings and those around you.

It's comparable to getting in the right lane at a large roundabout or pulling out on an A-road at the opportune time so as not to make the oncoming car slow down. If you see fewer people on the opposite side of the pavement, move your arse over there. Use your body language to make it clear what direction you're going in next. Check behind you and your blind spots before moving to the side or ducking into a shop. And do not, for the love of fuck, just stop abruptly. Would you just stop for no reason on a motorway? No. So don't fucking do it on Oxford Street.

I am genuinely considering creating a course that teaches considerate walking on busy streets. Or better still, I would happily condone a government-mandated walking licence that qualifies people to walk in busy areas. I've heard of shopping malls, in certain countries, where people have to walk in straight lines designated by arrows on the floor. Sounds like a utopia to me. If an authoritarian state is what it takes to get noobs like you to walk courteously, then please, take my freedoms, O Mighty Leader, take them all…

– [Pointless] Exercise –

If, having read this, you think I'm talking shit, please fuck off to the countryside. Otherwise, the next time you walk on a busy street, please think as if you were behind the wheel. Would you do what you are about to do if driving a car? Would you not look where you are going and plough right into the person carrying that fresh coffee? Most people walk much slower than seventy miles per hour, so you should have more than enough time to make sensible fucking decisions. Idiot.

Know an idiot who needs to read this chapter?

- Scan the QR code
- Click the link
- Send it their way!

Using umbrellas

If I had a pound for every time a fucking brolly wally like you nearly poked my bloody eye out, because you didn't seem to understand how to use one of the simplest instruments known to man, I'd be a fucking zillionaire.

Look, I haven't got too much of an issue with umbrellas. If you want to use one, go ahead. Walking to your destination and arriving like Noah forgot to build his ark is no picnic. But do us all a fucking favour, don't use the thing like a knobhead.

For one, why do you insist on taking out your umbrella in the slightest of drizzles? You. Don't. Need. It. You certainly don't need those fuck-off golf umbrellas you swear by, that are big enough to accommodate golfer, caddy and clubs all at once. Most of the time, when it's "raining", the volume of water that is actually falling on top of your precious hairdo hardly warrants the word. Are you really that fucking petrified of a little bit of water? Plants love that shit - why can't you?

On a separate note, when you're walking down a busy street, it'd be bloody lovely if you could remember that there are other people around you, for fuck's sake. If you're a midget, i.e. anyone under six feet, and you're coming up on someone relatively tall, that piece of shit in your hand is probably more or less at their head and eye height. If you don't tilt or lift it out the way and they don't see it coming, it's no exaggeration to say that it could take their eye out. An umbrella is not a bloody weapon! It's a device for keeping you dry, not blinding other people!

Here, you might protest that I just asked you to remember that there are other people around you. You might say that other people should do the same and see the umbrella coming. No, mate. You're the prick who has made the decision to bring a lethal shield onto the streets. Tilt it out of the motherfucking way!

It's also time that you refreshed your understanding of gravity. Let me simplify for the thickos. When rain falls onto your umbrella, where the fuck do you think it goes? It falls off onto the floor, yes? Which is fine when you're walking. But when you're standing still, in a queue outside or at a busy bus station, your umbrella water will drip in the same place the whole time you're waiting. So if you're standing right next to someone, it's probably constantly dripping on them, you silly fucker! I had this happen to me once. Went to put on my hood later and felt like I was diving into the world's tiniest fucking swimming pool. Not best pleased. So, once again, be aware of who is around you when using umbrellas.

Some other quick-fire umbrella issues to address:

- Do not text and wield an umbrella. In my opinion, it's just as bad as using your phone while driving. It should be made illegal and, if I catch you doing it, your phone will be snatched away and dropped in a puddle.

- If using an umbrella, take a wide line around street corners. If I get a face full of parasol one more fucking time, just because you're an inconsiderate, thick twat…

- When you're on public transport, put your wet umbrella by your feet, not on the seat next to you. Someone has to sit there at some point, you self-absorbed dickhead. Your minimally dirty umbrella does not trump someone else looking like they pissed out of their arse when they arrive at work…

I sincerely hope you get the point…

- [Pointless] Exercise -

If it isn't torrential outside, stop being a pussy and brave the weather, or accept just how much of a pussy you are and call a taxi. If you absolutely have to use an umbrella, remember that holding one does not automatically mean you should be afforded the equivalent of the width of your umbrella in space on the street. Unless you are actually that big, in which case you need a gym more than you need a fucking parasol. You don't suddenly own the street just because you have a bit of fabric on a pole above your head. If you need to tilt or lift the umbrella to avoid poking someone's eye out, and you end up getting a little wet for a millisecond, so be it. Trust me, it's a small price to pay for the peace of mind that comes with not being a complete arsehole. Idiot.

Know an idiot who needs to read this chapter?

- Scan the QR code
- Click the link
- Send it their way!

Public transport etiquette

When regularly taking public transport to get around in big cities, we become acutely aware of a distinct set of unwritten rules that everyone follows. However, there are still too many local wankers and tourists like you who have somehow yet to catch on. So, here's a reminder:

- Don't fucking talk to me.
- Don't make fucking eye contact, for Christ's sake – you're making it awkward for the both of us.
- Create space for people, you knobhead. When standing, put your fucking backpack on the floor between your fucking legs. Similarly, don't you fucking dare put your bag on a seat next to you. It will be launched off at the next stop.
- Wear deodorant if standing and holding rails above shoulder height – I've seen too many small people faint from overexposure to foul body odour when breathing into your fat armpit during rush hour.
- Getting the escalators underground? Stand on the right and walk up or down on the left – how fucking difficult is it? Similarly, when walking down the tunnels between changes, walk on the fucking left. Simple.
- See someone who's pregnant, elderly, disabled? Get the fuck up and offer your seat. Don't avert your selfish eyes and hope someone else makes the offer, you lazy, selfish prick.
- Let people get off the train before you try to get on. They have right of way, and you should fucking know it.
- If you're by the door when people are trying to get off, disembark before them and stand to the

side. Don't let them struggle and push past, just because you're a dickhead who's terrified of losing their spot.

- Have your ticket/payment card ready at the barriers will ya, bloody hell. Let's keep this fucking rat race moving.
- When it is extremely busy, don't force yourself on if there is no obvious space. This is the city, there'll be another bus, tube in a minute, you muppet. If I'm the one you're pushing into as you force your way on, rest assured, you won't be getting on.

These rules are all about creating space and making life easier. This is what we do as city dwellers to make public transport that little bit less unbearable. We try our best to be helpful and civilised. Public transport is shit and cramped enough as it is without you being an inconsiderate arsehole, especially during rush hour.

So learn the fucking rules and abide by them. Otherwise, you will incur the wrath of your fellow commuters - mainly tuts following you wherever you go, with the odd nutter smashing you up.

- [Pointless] Exercise -

Next time you take public transport, remember that you are a nobody. You do not deserve any more space than the next person. And nor does your fucking bag. Idiot.

Know an idiot who needs to read this chapter?

- Scan the QR code
- Click the link
- Send it their way!

Being first off the plane

Why, in the name of fuck, do stressy bastards like you feel the need to start rushing about on aeroplanes, as *soon* as they stop, to try and be first off?

The plane has just come to a halt. The seatbelt sign hasn't even turned off yet. Nevertheless, without fail, there you are, already standing up, taking your bags out of the luggage compartment overhead, jostling for position with those on the other side of the aisle, who are doing the same fucking thing. Even worse is when you stand up in the window seats, pressuring the poor folks in the aisle seats to hurry up and join the melee.

Firstly, surely you realise that no one actually enjoys being stuck in a stationary vehicle. Everyone would love to be first off the plane, or at least get off as quickly as possible. Everyone wants to start their holiday, get their business trip moving or get the hell home. But not everyone rushes about, acting like a selfish wanker who has an inherent right to be first off.

Secondly, you've been on planes multiple times, mate. How have you not realised by now that it's a pointless fucking exercise to try and be first off?!

How long do you generally need to wait to disembark from a plane, even after it has come to a complete stop? I'd say a good fifteen minutes – sometimes longer, rarely shorter. I know it, you know it, we all know it. Planes are not fucking trains, buses or trams. The doors never simply open as soon as the bloody thing reaches its destination. For all your rushing and impatient jostling, you're never getting off before the doors are manually opened.

How much quicker are you truly able to get off a plane, by being among the first to stand up and retrieve your luggage from the compartments above? You can maybe push forward towards the exit and gain two or three rows before there are too many people in the way. But really, how many extra seconds are you going to gain by being let off slightly earlier? The vast majority of people end up getting off precisely zero seconds earlier than if they had just sat down and waited. Everyone tends to get off the plane more or less row by row anyway, whether you decide to sit calmly in your seat or stand with luggage in hand, sporting a stressed, sweaty face.

"Hold up, Yann?! Are you telling me, I've been standing up for fifteen minutes on stationary planes, holding my bags, for no reason what so fucking ever?! That I pissed off all those nice, calm people in the aisle seats for nothing?!"

Yes, that's right, thicko. The mind boggles that you have not put two and two together from all those times you've previously been on a plane.

My hope is that one day, everyone is going to just think logically and the world, including air travel, will run like clockwork. We'll all sit down and wait patiently on the plane for fifteen minutes, then, when the plane doors are opened, we'll calmly take our stuff down, row by row, and disembark relatively stress-free. Unfortunately, such a utopia is probably impossible - you are way too stupid.

It's interesting to consider what twats like you believe you might gain by trying to be first off the plane.

Maybe you want to be the first to get your luggage from the conveyor belt in the airport. But, as we've already established you don't get off the plane any quicker.

Perhaps you just really need a shit and the plane toilets don't tickle your fancy. But that can't be it either. Whether it's a domestic one hour flight or a seventeen hour trip to the other side of the world, there always seems to be a similar proportion of pricks like you who try to get off the plane first.

There can't be that many people with dodgy stomachs and bloated bladders who urgently need the crapper after just sixty minutes.

No, it would appear that you are just a stressed-out muppet, who finds the stress in everything and wants to make sure everyone in your vicinity is aware of just how stressed out you are. You are the kind of knobhead who turns everything you do into a big hullabaloo, simply because you don't want to be doing it. You are the kind of pillock who cannot relax long enough to distinguish between logic and the stupidity of doing something pointless.

"But, Yann! There can't be that many stressed people on every single plane, can there?!"

Well, my friend, there's one thing you've forgotten. Too many people like you are sheep. You are followers, without the resolve to judge situations for yourselves. So instead you copy those who seem to be taking action because you just assume that's what you're supposed to do.

- [Pointless] Exercise -

The next time your plane lands and comes to a stop, instead of standing up early and holding your bags for nothing, try just sitting down and waiting for your row's turn to get off. Anything else is fucking pointless and stresses out everyone around you for no reason. You've got no right to get off earlier than anyone else anyway, you selfish prick. Idiot.

Know an idiot who needs to read this chapter?

- Scan the QR code
- Click the link
- Send it their way!

Reclining plane seats

Anyone who has ever been on a plane knows just how awfully uncomfortable the seats can be. We're talking about the budget airlines - that economy class life. Any rich fucks reading this who fly business class won't have the foggiest what I'm talking about. By the way, what's the price of a pint of milk nowadays? No, not in Waitrose, you pillock!

Back to plane seats. They're really shit. Minimal padding, too short for tall people to rest their heads - unless they enjoy staring upside down at the freaked-out family in the row behind, tray tables that hate anyone with half a beer belly, seat widths that are adequate only for size zero anorexics and, worst of all, a distinct lack of legroom for anyone other than midgets. We're not in fucking Tudor times anymore, there are plenty of people over six feet who should be catered for!

So, knowing how terrible it is to spend anything more than twenty minutes strapped into these shit awful plane seats, I have two questions.

Question one is for the reclining-lover: What the fuck makes you think it is acceptable to recline your plane seat when there is someone behind you that will be affected?

Before you go off on one, you self-absorbed prat, I'm not arguing your right to recline. There *is* a recline button at the end of the day, it does unfortunately exist. What I am arguing though is the extent to which you are a fucking arsehole. Are you a fucking arsehole in every facet of your life and in every human encounter? Or are you just a complete fucking arsehole on planes and then you go back to being a standard arsehole as soon as the landing gear touches solid ground? My gut tells me you're an arsehole all the time, as that is the only plausible explanation for why you could think it is acceptable to recline your seat onto someone's lap. Just because something is possible, doesn't mean it's ok to do it. The button is there, doesn't mean you should press it.

I understand that you want to recline your seat to make the journey a bit more bearable. But do you not think the person behind you wants to do the same? Of course they fucking do. But *they* don't want to make the person behind them uncomfortable, *just* to cater for themselves. You, on the other hand, obviously couldn't give a flying shit – pun intended bitch.

It's worth remembering that we're all in this tin can in the sky together. Each one of us is having to deal with the lack of comfort, some more than others. Can't we all just get through it in similar discontent, instead of wanky fucks like you deciding it's worth making someone else's journey a complete misery just to make their own slightly better? At the end of the day, the real enemies are the vampiric clusterfucks that are capitalism and the aviation industry, working to try and determine that fine line between customer discomfort and maximum profit.

Question two is for the airline chief: Why on God's green earth do you even bother providing seats that have the ability to recline? It seems to be the most pointless engineering addition I've ever fucking seen. We know you haven't provided the ability to recline out of the goodness of your hearts for fuck's sake. We know you couldn't give a shit about our comfort, or you would have stripped out all the tiny seats a long time ago and installed replacements that conform to at least some basic human rights. So it's like you've said to each other, "If we're going to make the seats this shit, we've got to give the people something. I know! A recline button! That causes arguments on a flight-ly basis and provides little to no comfort anyway! Hehehe…"

There is no doubt that you care about nothing other than more bums on seats, more tickets sold and more profit. It's common knowledge that you have actively conspired to reduce seat space on planes to maximise the number of flyers you can pack into each plane. This process has even got a fucking name, densification. So why don't you just go the whole fucking hog and at least remove or jam the reclining function on your seats? Don't give obnoxious reclining wankers the option! You'd save yourself a lot of ball ache from complaints and your staff would be much happier not having to deal with these twats and the stupid bloody arguments they cause.

- [Pointless] Exercise -

If you really want to recline your seat, but you know it would affect the person behind, then just don't do it. Forget this 'ask first' bullshit. It's very simple - don't recline your fucking seat, or do anything for that matter, if it would cause discomfort to another person just to alleviate yours. Your comfort is in no way more important than anyone else's. If you desire a lifestyle that allows you to recline your seat, then piss off, earn some more money and then piss off once more to first class. If you do end up trying your luck and reclining your seat anyway, don't you dare fucking moan when the person behind asks you to put it back up. Get your fucking seat off the poor person's knees behind you and take your medicine, you cheeky prick. You took a chance, it backfired, fucking move on. And argue back at your own risk, mate - even on a plane with limited people, there is a good chance one of the other flyers is a nutter. Personally, I hope the nutter is the one behind you, has dodgy knees and ultimately knocks your cocky head off. Idiot.

Know an idiot who needs to read this chapter?

- Scan the QR code
- Click the link
- Send it their way!

Bad losers

Whatever the game being played, there will always be a knobhead of a bad loser like you to ruin it.

You just cannot accept losing! When you play Monopoly, you would rather flip the board into the air and scatter the pieces, than pay to get out of prison again. You would sooner walk straight off the pitch after conceding a last-minute goal than shake hands with the winning team's players. You can't help but turn every fun game with friends into a competition, that becomes so important in your own mind, that it's no longer fun.

And it's never your own fault that you lose, is it? It's never that the other player or team is just better on the day. It's never that it's just a game where luck plays a major part and sometimes you win, sometimes you bloody lose! There is somehow always apparently some form of cheating going on or a problem with the ref being bent, blind, or both.

You need to get the fuck over it, you childish muppet. Losing is a part of life. We have all lost more times than we care to admit. At the same time, most people come to the sobering realisation early on, that we often learn more when we lose. We learn about our limitations and our character. We learn what we could or should have done to win, and we try harder next time. It's pretty difficult to take advantage of the benefits of losing if you're always too fucking fixated on the simple fact that you lost.

If you never take responsibility for your improvement and continue to blame your losses on something other than yourself, then guess what – you will continue to lose. And I will be there to laugh my arse off every time.

When it comes to playing sports seriously or for a living, you'll argue that it's actually good to be a bad loser. You'll tell us that all top athletes are terrible losers, which is why they succeed in the end. But I don't subscribe to this bullshit. There is a difference between a bad loser and someone that hates losing.

I agree it can be useful to hate losing to make it as a top athlete in your sport. That's where the motivation to become one of the best comes from. You hate losing, so you work like a Trojan to make sure it doesn't happen that often. However, hating losing doesn't mean you have to be a bad loser. You don't have to put your disdain for losing on full display to those who won. By all means, when in private, kick everything in sight, scream the house down. But when the game ends, you shake hands and say, "Well played". Show a bit of sportsmanship, you spoilt wanker.

– [Pointless] Exercise –

The next time you're playing a game with friends, try to remember that it's just that. A fucking game. Enjoy the act of playing. If you lose, you lose. Move on. Idiot.

Know an idiot who needs to read this chapter?

- Scan the QR code
- Click the link
- Send it their way!

Gamesmanship

“Some people will do anything to win. Including being a right twat.” This is my not-so-official dictionary definition for gamesmanship.

The real definition is: “The art of winning games by using various ploys and tactics to gain a psychological advantage”.

So still basically being a massive twat. My definition is better.

Anyway, gamesmanship between mates, during a friendly game, is all well and good. Standing in the way of the shot when someone’s on the black ball. A few quiet words in the ear of your opponent, letting them know they always bottle it in the end. Even making a mate think twice with an “accidental” cough and smile when they are about to land a devastating checkmate or call an all-in bluff.

These things are just plain funny. When we tell our mate they’re going to bottle it, and they do, they will never live it down. As I say, funny.

What’s not funny is employing gamesmanship when playing a sport professionally or during a serious game, such as for money. The integral element of a good, serious game is the respect opponents have for each other. The hope is that the respect remains at the end, with both sides having given their all within the rules of the game.

We want to see talent winning games. We want to see good managerial tactics and hard graft winning games. We don’t want to see gamesmanship winning games, i.e. professional fouls, berating the officials, time-wasting and generally being an arsehole. Gamesmanship is not an “art”, as the official definition reads. It is being a prick who is afraid they can not win on merit alone.

Wanky gamesmanship advocates like you will call it fair game. That you *should* do anything to win. That winning is all that matters. That fans just want to see their team or favourite sports person win.

That may be true for the idiot hardcore fans who live and die by their team. But it's not the case for the majority of fans who love the game itself, not just their team. Fans want entertainment – that's why there are fans, dummy. Entertainment in sport, in most peoples' eyes, is the sport being played to a high level. Entertainment is not rolling around on the floor, screaming like a pussy and feigning injury, trying to get people sent off. Entertainment is not constantly going mad at the referee after every decision, trying to bully decisions your way. Entertainment is not checking your football boots for mud or that your socks are pulled up to your throat, all in the name of time-wasting.

Take José Mourinho for example. For those who are not familiar, he is a football manager who is well-known for getting his teams to do the horrible things well. He actively encourages diving to get free-kicks and penalties, fouling people on the halfway line to stop counter-attacks, taking the ball to the corner flag to waste time, among other dirty tactics. In the midst of all this gamesmanship, his teams play boring football, defending with too many players, simply hoping to get a chance to score rather than crafting one. The truth is, no one enjoys watching his teams play. It is simply shit to watch. Games built up to be blockbuster entertainment pieces between two top teams are reduced to snoozefests the likes of which could easily turn people off the sport entirely.

Another problem is the ethics of winning through gamesmanship. It feels empty. No one likes people who win like this. You might think it doesn't matter as long as you win. But you will regret it. You're teaching kids and other thicko adults that it's fine to act like a twat, as long as you win. There is undoubtedly a role model element to sport, in terms of the spirit in which a game should be played, that professionals need to take more seriously.

What gamesmanship dickheads like you do not realise is that, if everyone used these shit tactics, no one would ever watch the sport again. You're just lucky there are ethical people willing to play properly, fairly and in an entertaining enough fashion, to keep whatever sport it is alive.

And professional sport aside, if you do think it's fair to stand in the way of my shot on the black during a pool game for money, rest assured I will not pay you a fucking penny.

- [Pointless] Exercise -

Just before you do that dickhead thing you think might help you win a serious game, ask yourself if it would be frowned upon. Not by you or your arsehole mates. But by nice, rule-abiding people. Would it be within someone's rights to say that it was out of order, even if you went on to win? If so, don't fucking do it. Failing that, try playing for fun beforehand. Get all the arsehole out of your system. Wind up your opponent to your heart's content. Then settle down and play the serious game without being an arsehole. The hope is that you will have had so much arsehole inside you, that you will be too tired to be an arsehole during the serious game, after letting so much out when practising. Idiot.

Know an idiot who needs to read this chapter?

- Scan the QR code
- Click the link
- Send it their way!

Passionate football fans

Quick disclaimer: I love football. It's my favourite sport. I grew up playing and watching it. And I get how someone can be so passionate about the beautiful game. But bloody hell, when you morph into a red-faced wanker of an adult who screams, shouts and swears from the terraces – that's enough to turn anyone off…

Why do you scream and boo the players on the pitch when they make a mistake? Why do you treat other humans like complete shit, just because they're on the opposing team? In essence, the question is, why do you care that bit too much?

I understand it to a certain extent. You want your local team to win. You've supported them all your life. It's a matter of pride in your local community and you want the players to represent you with pride too.

However, nowadays, this local way of thinking doesn't make any sense. Think about it. Why would you expect the players on your team to take pride in representing your community? I could appreciate this thought process thirty or forty years ago. But the majority of players now hail from all over the country, sometimes even from abroad. They have little to no connection to your local community. In fact, it's pretty rare to have a player, born and bred locally, playing regularly in the first team. This is even more apparent in the big money leagues, such as the Premier League in the UK.

So when you scream at these footballers to have some pride and play harder – why would they? They are there because they are good at football and because they are getting paid. Not because they care that much about your team or the local area. You need to get over it.

It makes more sense to have pride when watching international football when your national team is playing. Only then can you be assured that the bulk of your team actually loosely represents you. But not club football. Getting incredibly upset when your club doesn't win is a mug's game.

I sometimes think that you don't even like the actual game of football. You don't seem to care whether your team plays well or that they play enjoyable football, just that they win. It's almost as though football is your religion, your escape from normal life. It might even be that you want them to succeed because the club is imperative to the local economy. I get it.

But whatever the reason for your misplaced pride, don't you think it's all a little sad? You rely on other people, who get paid crazy money and who don't really give two shits about you or your community, to win a game so that you can feel happy. Isn't it time you took back a bit of control over your life and your day to day emotions, you muppet? Maybe choose something other than a game to affect your mood?

- [Pointless] Exercise -

Attend your team's next game. When one of the players inevitably makes a mistake, and you start screaming and going red in the face, hold up a mirror to yourself. Yes, that's genuinely what you look like to other people. And yes, you look like a fucking twat with no life. Calm your tits and remember the advice you would give to a kid who loses a game and starts throwing a tantrum: IT DOESN'T REALLY MATTER. BECAUSE IT'S A FUCKING GAME. Idiot.

Know an idiot who needs to read this chapter?

- Scan the QR code
- Click the link
- Send it their way!

Everyone's a football pundit

People who love football, also love to talk about football. All the tactics, upcoming fixtures, who's going to win the league, a bit of ribbing here and there to a rival supporter. In fact, the first question out of their mouths when they meet someone new is normally some variation of, "So, who do you support?" And I love the sport myself, so I've got no problem with people talking about it frequently. I do, however, have a problem with people like you who talk absolute shit in the process.

You'll shout at the TV screen and tell everyone within earshot that so and so is a useless prick who can't control the ball to save their life. However, put you on a pitch and ask you to do ten keepie uppies, it's like watching a fucking goat trying to do them. Not the "Greatest Of All Time" kind of GOAT. Like, an actual pregnant goat that's forgotten it has eyes and the power to control its own feet.

What makes you think you are qualified to pass judgement on a football match when you are so diabolically embarrassing when you play? How do you even know if a player meant to do a particular bit of skill? How could you understand that they should have passed to a different player? You don't even seem to understand that a football is a fucking sphere, judging by the way you kick it!

Nevertheless, you still genuinely expect other people to listen to your opinions on football… Surely you've worked out by now that, even if you do manage to say something that makes sense, no one can be bothered to listen. At the end of the day, a broken clock is also right at least twice a day. When you run your mouth, all we can see is your awful penalty miss at the work five-a-side. You were like a poor man's Peter Kay in a budget John Smith's advert, for fuck's sake.

If football is going to be a big part of your life and you're going to want to talk about it – all the fucking time – maybe you should have to pass a test. Similar to how coaches have to show they have decent enough technique and can actually play the game before they pass their coaching badges, so should people like you who want to give their footballing opinions.

By the way, I don't truly believe you should have to take a football test, you mug. I just can't take any more of you insisting that not all professional footballers can do kick-ups.

– [Pointless] Exercise –

Find a mate. Give them a football. Ask them to throw the ball to you. If you can't softly trap it back into their hands a hundred times out of a hundred, either keep practising until you can or piss off and stop talking to me about your Fantasy Football team. Idiot.

Know an idiot who needs to read this chapter?

- Scan the QR code
- Click the link
- Send it their way!

Splashing in the pool

Doesn't it just drive you crazy when you go for a nice, calm swim in the slow lane, then someone accidentally splashes you? Who do they think they are, right?

Well no, mate. You're in a bloody swimming pool, you moany fuck. What do you expect? Getting wet is a guarantee. Get. Over. It.

Listen, I used to be a lifeguard. I've heard all your complaints before. I understand that you just want to complete your daily exercise without being bothered. Even though your "exercise" involves imitating a drunk frog, performing the slowest version of breaststroke the world has ever seen. I am also fully aware that you swim with your head above the water for the express purpose of not getting your hair wet.

The problem is, I just don't give a shit. Going to a swimming pool, where there is loads of *water*, then complaining about getting a part of your body wet, is fucking ridiculous. It's the equivalent of putting your arm in the mouth of a gigantic, wild alligator and moaning that you got a scratch. I can't help but look at you as a complete fuckwit.

What do you want the lifeguard to do about it? Do you really expect them to go over to the kids and ask them to stop splashing and having fun? All because some grouchy bastard is in a mood?

You have to remember that these are kids. They are never going to simply move delicately through a swimming pool. They will splash. And so they bloody should. They are not doing anything wrong and they have just as much right to be there as you. I guarantee you if you can remember back a few hundred years, that you also splashed as a kid.

I know sometimes your whining is directed more towards the faster swimmers, splashing while they do lengths in the fast lane next to you. Well, I have news for you. It is nigh on *impossible* not to splash when swimming fast. Have you ever watched the Olympics? They splash. A lot. I know the fast lane in the local community pool is a far cry from the Olympics, but at least they're trying. Unlike you, you slow twat.

If you don't like the splashing, take your shit technique and piss off home.

- [Pointless] Exercise -

Buy some goggles and a swim cap. Put your head under the water. Swim properly. And try to remember that your local swimming pool, indeed the world, does not revolve around you. It's not there just for you and your enjoyment, you entitled wanker. Idiot.

Know an idiot who needs to read this chapter?

- Scan the QR code
- Click the link
- Send it their way!

Sweating at the gym

You dirty bastard. You dirty, sweaty bastard.

You'll sweat your fat arse all over the treadmill. You'll finish your run, panting like a rabid dog. Then you'll simply hop off, leaving your sweat all over the buttons and handles, pooling on the treadmill belt.

After that, you'll waddle over to the drinking fountain. You'll lean over the basin to get your fill, all the while allowing your sweat to drip all over the tap.

Then you'll wobble over to the weights section. You'll pick up a shitload of free weights and perspire all over them. You'll make the obligatory grunting noises, then let the weights crash down, sending sweat droplets flying across the room.

Then you'll toddle over and choose a mat from the rack. You'll sit your damp arse down and do a couple of stretches. You'll lay down on your even damper back and do a few crunches. Then you'll get up and walk out of the gym, without picking up or cleaning the mat, leaving behind a foul, stinking imprint of yourself for others to enjoy.

Do you not realise, you sweaty fuck, that people need to use the equipment after you? Do you feel no shame that those waiting patiently for you to finish, know full well that the sweaty perspiration they now have to deal with came from you?

I've got nothing against sweaty people – I'm a sweaty person myself. Frankly, in my book, if you haven't been sweating, you haven't worked out hard enough. And I'm also no clean freak or germaphobe. But for fuck's sake, there's nothing worse than touching equipment covered in white, dried sweat rings and fresh, salty water. Especially knowing that it comes directly from the pores of an overheating wanker like you.

- [Pointless] Exercise -

Bring a hand towel with you or locate the paper towels that gyms provide. Then wipe down the equipment you use. Just be a tiny bit considerate of other people. Just a little bit. It doesn't take much. Idiot.

Know an idiot who needs to read this chapter?

- Scan the QR code
- Click the link
- Send it their way!

Bar & pub etiquette

Buying rounds

At the end of the day, when all's said and drunk, we are all one of two kinds of people. Those of us who buy our rounds without fail and then people like you, who shirk the responsibility.

For those of us who buy our rounds without fail, it's simple. We've been brought up correctly, so we're well aware of this integral element of drinking. We keep track of the rounds and, when it's our turn, we also keep track of the drinks. When the majority of the group are nearing the last quarter of their drink, we say the magic words: "My round, same again?".

But pricks like you, who shirk their round responsibilities, portray some or all of the following characteristics.

You genuinely believe you buy your rounds properly. And, admittedly, you do buy your round *sometimes*. But more often than not, you go missing when it's your turn. You don't keep track of the rounds, so you don't even know how many you're missing. People with this characteristic tend to be financially better off. It's as though you don't keep track because it doesn't really bother you whether you buy the round or not, simply because you could afford *all* the rounds if need be.

It's a fucking nightmare though because it leaves the rest of us having to recall all your recent missed rounds and feeling like whiny wankers. But it *is* a big deal because we can't afford to keep buying your rounds, you dickhead! Especially not when you *can* afford it!

Another characteristic is *always* challenging whether it's your round. Every single fucking time. Every cycle, you need to be prompted with a "Mate, it's your round". You'll exclaim, "Oh is it?! I thought it was blah blah's round?". Then it needs to be explained to you, for the sixth time that night, that blah blah has already got their round, etc fucking etc… It's tiresome for the whole group, particularly when we all know that you're just feigning surprise. You know full well it's your round, you knobhead. You just question it because you're upset to be parting with money. But no one gives a shit I'm afraid – we've all bought our rounds, so just shut the fuck up and go get us some drinks. You are the kind of person who would never, ever buy the first round upon entering a pub. Carry on like this, mate, you won't be invited anymore, trust us.

The worst characteristic presents itself when you do know it's your round and you're happy to pay for it. However, your way of buying the round is to wait for someone to get up for the loo, then ask them to head to the bar to get the drinks on your behalf. It's fine though because you hand over your bank card to pay… NOOO! It's not fucking fine. Part of the respect element of getting a round is physically going to the bar, waiting in line, and then carrying the drinks over for your mates. You have *not* fulfilled your round if all you do is provide your card. I don't care if you can't be bothered. I don't care if you hate standing in line. Do you think any of us actually enjoy that part? Of course not, but you don't see any of us trying to shirk it.

You're the wanker who thinks they're better than their drinking partners, maybe someone a little posher, probably born with a shitty silver spoon up their arse. You think that bit too highly of yourself and so consider yourself to be above waiting for other people. Or maybe you simply feel like you're having too good of a time to leave the table right now. In any case, it's worth remembering that your drinking buddies are your mates, not your fucking lapdogs.

Whatever characteristics make up your evasion of rounds, one thing is for sure. It constantly puts a downer on the night and, as far as I'm concerned, it shows a complete lack of respect for your mates and the art of drinking itself.

- [Pointless] Exercise -

Next time you go to the pub with your mates, keep track of the rounds. When it's your turn again and most people are nearing the end of their drinks, get up, go to the bar and buy fresh ones. It really is that fucking simple. If someone has to tell you it's your round, remind yourself that you can be a bit of a shirker. Don't start bloody moaning about it or saying it's someone else's round. Give a quick, "Sorry lads", and shift your arse over to the bar sharpish. Idiot.

Know an idiot who needs to read this chapter?

- Scan the QR code
- Click the link
- Send it their way!

Round stinginess

Some people think that the height of stinginess at bars and pubs is when someone simply does not buy their rounds. And don't get me wrong, not buying your rounds does indeed make for a disgraceful human. However, buying your rounds but being stingy in the process trumps not buying them in the first place. It's the slyness of it that irks; when you appear generous but are the complete fucking opposite.

Here are some examples.

You'll buy a round, but you'll miss one person's drink "by mistake". Or you'll assume that one person was lagging too far behind so wouldn't need a new fresh pint. To the naked eye, it would appear to be an accident or even you just being considerate. But when this starts happening way too often, and the missing drinks are never actually bought, the underlying stinginess soon becomes apparent.

You'll buy a round and come back with half-pints. You apparently thought we were moving on to the next establishment soon. You took a judgement call that we would be happy with half pints so we could leave on time. We'll say you were wrong and you'll apologise. But you won't buy the missing halves. Because in your eyes, you've already bought your round.

It's your round and you've asked what everyone is having. And it just so happens it's that time of the night when we might feel like switching it up. This is a frequent occurrence, perfectly normal and acceptable. Maybe it's too many bubbles from the beer, the sheer volume of liquid or just for the sake of something different. We might ask for a glass of wine, a vodka lemonade, a whisky coke, or something else. You'll nod your head as you note the requests, you'll go to the bar and return with a tray. On this tray are the regular beers for the hardcore stomachs. But next to them are tiny glasses of wine and mixed drinks that, when tasted, are so diluted, you could be forgiven for thinking the bartender had mistaken water for vodka. It turns out you asked for *small* wines and *single* shots in the mixed drinks. You'll say you thought people switching things up meant your mates wanted to slow down a bit. What a thoughtfully stingy wanker.

Last example. You're a little peckish. You'll buy a packet of crisps or nuts with your round. You'll return to the table with the tray and the nibbles. You'll lay the tray down and take your seat. You'll open the nibbles and eat some. Then you'll eat some more. And you won't put the packet down until all the nibbles are gone. You'll fail to pick up on, or choose to ignore, the expectant sideways glances. Nothing is ever said. But we're all a little disappointed that the packet was never opened up on the table or at least offered to the rest of the group. Just would've been nice, you know? "Never mind, they must've been really hungry", is the unspoken, yet suspicious group consensus.

In my humble opinion, stingy bastards like you are the worst kind of stingy. You know how important it is to everyone that you get your round, so you oblige. But your rounds are an absolute joke. You just can't help trying to save a couple of quid here and there. Nevertheless, you get away with it, because you did buy the rounds at the end of the day.

You would never be so generous that you open up your crisps and nuts to the table or buy more than one pack. God forbid you don't eat your fill or pay anything above what is strictly and socially necessary to save face.

Well, fuck you. No longer will your sly, stingy, shit rounds be accepted. You have been called out, we know what game you're playing. You are a stingy fuck, simply masquerading as a cultural stalwart round-buyer, and it ends here.

- [Pointless] Exercise -

Stop thinking you're getting away with your shady stinginess. You're not. It's just that no one can be bothered to speak up about something so fucking petty when you haven't overtly done anything wrong. But just know that *everyone* notices and you *are* getting a reputation. Buy your rounds properly and share your nuts or don't bother coming. And if you are still somehow, unfathomably confused about the switch-up, listen here. When someone asks for wine, you get them a *large* wine. If someone asks for a whisky coke, you respond to the bartender's inevitable, "Single or double mate", with, "Double please". Every time, unless otherwise specified. Idiot.

Know an idiot who needs to read this chapter?

- Scan the QR code
- Click the link
- Send it their way!

Non-patrons using pub toilets

Picture the scene. You're dying for a piss or you have a full-scale emergency shit show on your hands. You look around. No public toilets. "What a fucking surprise", you think, exasperated. You see a pub. What's your next move?

Well, I can tell you what it shouldn't be. Walking into that pub, pretending to look around for a few seconds for some non-existent friends, maybe taking a quick peek at the taps behind the bar to intimate you *might* buy a drink, then relieving yourself in their toilet and walking straight back out again.

I don't care how desperate you are, you do not walk into a pub and use their facilities with no intention of purchasing a drink. It might sound counter-intuitive, to get a drink when you need a piss. But I don't give a shit.

I realise that in a lot of places, especially when it's busy, if there are no bouncers or if you don't have to walk past the bar to get to the toilets, you could easily get away with using their facilities for free without anyone noticing. But that's just the point isn't it - you're "getting away with it". And you know it. You also therefore inherently know you shouldn't do it!

There should be no need for any 'toilets for paying customers only' signs. Pub staff should not have to stop people like you from using the toilet - their job is tough enough. What I'm suggesting is that you should be decent enough to buy a drink, or at the very least purchase a packet of crisps or pop a pound in a charity box, without being told to do so!

At the end of the day, it's a public *house,* not a public *toilet*.

The lack of the latter is the responsibility of the arseholes of local government. It should not be incumbent upon pubs, and businesses like restaurants and cafés for that matter, to pick up the slack for the failures of our civil servants.

The former is completely misunderstood by too many thickos like you. Pubs are not a public convenience, like libraries or parks. In direct contradiction to the name, they are actually private buildings, open only *by invitation* to the public. This is why you can be asked to leave with no reason provided, and also why it is not illegal to refuse entry in the first place.

Make no mistake, despite it being a "public" house, a pub is still a business owned by someone who is trying to make ends meet, pay their staff and keep their patrons happy. It's not a place in which you can just do whatever the fuck you want.

It's also especially bloody difficult keeping a pub running nowadays, purely from a financial aspect. Wankers like you, who rob the pubs of toilet use without compensation, just don't seem to get it - every penny counts. First, there are the rising costs of everything that a pub needs. Then there are the astronomical business rents when the pub landlord doesn't own the building or land. Each of your toilet flushes adds to the already huge water bill. Each of your arse wipes means they're closer to having to buy more loo roll. Each time you wash your hands means they're closer to having to buy more soap. I've even heard of some publicans having to fork out for plumbers after nappies and other non-flushable items clogged up their bogs!

Admittedly, blocked toilets are not proof of non-patrons like you causing problems. But it's a fair bet that proper patrons are more likely to care about the state of the toilets, considering they will probably need to use them again in the next hour or so. And just from a hygiene perspective, have you ever seen the inside of a busy Portaloo? Looks like a vomit-piss-shit bomb has gone off. I can absolutely forgive a pub owner for not wanting their toilets to reach that level of grimness and consequently having to fork out additional money for a deep clean every fucking day.

And another thing, if your uncoordinated arse has an accident in a pub, like stupidly tripping over a loose tile and cracking your head on a urinal, the law dictates that you have just as strong a compensation claim against the establishment, whether you are a patron or not. The indignation of having to shell out for a claim, from people like you who didn't even buy a drink in their pub, would be enough to drive any publican fucking mental and make them shut down the place for good. And who could blame them?

Look, if you're that desperate and have no money, at least fucking ask the bar staff beforehand. Ninety-nine times out of a hundred, bar staff will be more than happy to let a polite person use the facilities without a purchase. You don't have to be disabled, have un-potty-trained brats for offspring or have medically-diagnosed bladder problems. We're all human after all. But if you can afford it – and let's face it, you are fucking lying if you say you can't – you should still buy something as a thank you for using their services.

– [Pointless] Exercise –

When you use a pub's toilet without asking or purchasing a drink, do you feel a little weird as you walk back through the pub to get outside? A bit sheepish perhaps? Do you keep your head down and avoid eye contact with the bar staff on the way out? Well there you go, you fucking twat, right there, that's what I'm talking about. You know you're taking the piss. The next time you use a pub's toilet, even if you don't intend on drinking, just buy a pint and enjoy the fucking thing. It's the right thing to do. You never know, the booze might loosen you and your purse strings up a little bit, you tight bastard. Idiot.

Know an idiot who needs to read this chapter?

- Scan the QR code
- Click the link
- Send it their way!

Pound on the pool table

The pool table is where the magic of proper boozers happens. It's where pub-goers meet, take the piss out of new-found mates for the night, play a boozy frame of doubles, and generally have a right laugh. It's very often the central element of the pub, with people gathering to watch frames between the better players.

The pool table at a pub is taken very seriously – admittedly sometimes too seriously. It depends on the pub. Rarely can people just turn up and play pool with their mates. We might have to wait in line.

As any proper pub-goer knows, the correct way to wait in line is by putting a pound on the table, one after another in a makeshift queue. If no one is at the table and there are no other pounds in sight, then, by all means, whack your pound in and play a mate. But if people are already playing, the default rule is 'winner stays on'. End of story. We have to earn our table time by paying our pound and beating the undefeated player still on the table.

Why do you insist on not abiding by these rules? Why do you feel like you don't need to put down a pound? Have you ever fucking been to a pub, mate? Don't you dare disturb the person currently lining up their next shot, just to ask if you can play next!? Can't you see the line of coins waiting on the table? Why the fuck do you think they're there?

In addition, once you've finally worked out you need to put a pound down, why do you think you can then just play your mates when your turn comes around, without first asking if it's 'winner stays on'? It's disrespectful to not even ask the question. I don't give a shit if you "just want one game with your mates". What if the person who just won the last game also wanted to play their mates, and put their pound down to earn their time until their mate's pound was next? For you to just jump on and take over the table is pretty fucking selfish – tantamount to treason in some pubs.

The worst thing about all of this is that people like you are always so shit at playing the game itself! You play doubles with your wanky mates and your game lasts *forever*. It takes you a fucking age to sink the black. It's embarrassing. And it pisses off the rest of the pub something silly – surely you can feel the tension?! Not only have you flouted the pound on the table rules, but now you're giving the impression that you're wasting others' playing time on purpose because no one can possibly be that useless.

Look, if you want to mess around and play pool with your mates undisturbed, fuck off to a bloody pool hall. There, you can practise in peace, not show yourself up in front of a whole pub and avoid a potential beating outside the more nutty establishments.

– [Pointless] Exercise –

Turn up at a proper boozer. Put your pound on the pool table. Wait your turn. Play the previous winner. If you lose, you don't play your mate. If you win, you can play your mate. But only if their pound was next. If not, you need to keep winning until your mate's pound is next. Simple. Idiot.

Know an idiot who needs to read this chapter?

- Scan the QR code
- Click the link
- Send it their way!

When the bartender asks who's next

Queues at bars are an absolute nightmare. There's never a straight line indicating who's next. Rather it's just a bunch of thirsty fuckers all trying to catch the eye of the bartender. Great bartenders will know who is next and are always aware of who is coming and going. But we can't expect this kind of service all the time, especially when it's very busy. This is why sometimes, just because we get to the bar before another person, doesn't mean we will get served first.

The thing is, despite the disorderly nature of bar queues, everyone is fully aware of who is before them and who should be served next. And when the bartender shouts, "Who's next?", we are all expected to point them out. Courteous people will always do just that.

Other times, the bartender might just choose someone from the crowd to start serving. However this is not one of those, it's your lucky day, things. Bartenders do this to avoid wasting time - they assume you will quickly point them in the direction of whoever is actually next in line.

Predictably though, greedy pricks like you don't give a shit about common courtesy. You are more than willing to point to yourselves when the "Who's next" shout comes or accept your "luck" at being chosen first by the bartender. It's completely fucking unacceptable.

You can protest your innocence and say that you didn't realise who was next in line until the cows come home, mate. You, and everyone else in this queue, all know you're a bare-faced fucking liar. Unfortunately, you just don't care. You think only of your own gain and would never just do the right thing for the sake of it.

Invariably, you are one of the small bitches who have no qualms pushing past the waiting crowd and basically getting their tits out to get served first. Or one of the wankers who shout at the bartender while waving their money or card.

In any case, it's painfully obvious that you're a prick who considers bars and pubs as just places to get drunk, and that's it. You want to come with your mates, get your drinks as quickly as possible and get slaughtered. But you're completely missing the point. Most people consider drinking holes to be a social haven, where we share beverages with friends and meet new people – not a place to piss off anyone who isn't your mate, or who comes between you and getting pissed.

What you don't realise though, is you could use your ability to get served quicker to your benefit. Why not, in the first instance, tell the bartender who is really next when they ask and get in everyone's good graces? Remember that at some point you will be buying another drink and they will remember what you did. I'm sure you can imagine that having bartenders and fellow patrons on your side has its advantages.

It's worth remembering that people you fucked over previously will inevitably see you trying to barge in next time. Take it from me, they will make a beeline for you. It will become their personal mission to ensure you don't get served again for a good while. Minuscule shoulder barges and elbows are inevitable and you will have brought it all on yourself. A lot can happen during a drinking session – it's not worth making enemies early on over who's next.

– [Pointless] Exercise –

Put your tits away. Lower your voice and put your money back in your pocket until it's time to pay. You'll still get served in good time, don't worry. Remember that there is always some nutter out there who will not stand for your lack of honesty when it comes to pointing out who's next, which may well result in a distinct lack of alcoholic refreshment for the rest of the evening and a nice, shiny black eye. Idiot.

Know an idiot who needs to read this chapter?

- Scan the QR code
- Click the link
- Send it their way!

Ordering complicated drinks

At one point or another, everyone wants to drink at a busy spot in town. Somewhere that has plenty of people and seems like a good night out. However, as we all know, there is a payoff. That payoff is it taking far too long to get served. Unless we happen to be objectively good-looking wankers, in an establishment employing a distinct lack of self-respecting bartenders, we've got no chance of buying our round within twenty minutes of joining the mass of sweaty pricks at a busy bar. It's fucking annoying when we just want to keep our night flowing, but it's a necessary evil that we have come to accept if we want to enjoy a night at a popular place.

The majority of bar-goers understand that we are all in the same boat and therefore keep their drinks orders sensible. Everyone in the queue is dying of alcoholic thirst and the bartenders are busy as shit, having absolute kittens trying to keep everyone happy.

But not you. You just *have* to piss on everyone's good night parade and couldn't give a rollox about anyone other than yourself and your mates. "Fuck those in the queue around me", you think. "Fuck the bartenders - they'll make what I want, it's what they get paid for", you surmise. "I've waited twenty minutes, it's my turn now, my time to shine!" you exclaim internally. "I'll have five blended cocktails with five different fruit garnishes and eighteen layered shots! Ohhhh and four Guinnesses!!" you shout triumphantly.

Here is why such a drink order is far from fucking sensible in a busy bar. It's not rocket science. It's because it takes fucking ages to make!!!! It's the kind of drink order that leaves the baying crowd either calling for your head or leaving for another bar. It's also the kind of drink order that pushes our precious bartenders one step closer to quitting.

You are simply arseholes who genuinely do not give a shit about your fellow human. There's not much hope for you and you deserve to get barred for life from absolutely fucking everywhere. We all not so secretly hope you drop your drinks; we may even give you an "accidental" nudge with the old shoulder to speed up the process.

Or you just genuinely don't seem to fully comprehend what your drink orders are doing to those in your immediate vicinity. And contrary to the title of this chapter, it's not always the *complicated* drinks that are the problem.

So let's make it really bloody simple for you. If it's busy:

- Do not order hot drinks – you fucking grandad/grandma;
- Do not order any drink with more than two ingredients – I don't give a fuck what's on the menu;
- Do not order layered shots – get a Tequila or Sambuca like a normal self-loathing drunk bastard;
- Do not order anything needing a blender – what a colossal waste of good fucking drinking time;
- Never ever, ever order Bloody Marys, Long Island Ice Teas or Mojitos – these fuckers either have a bunch of ingredients or require extra steps like muddling mint leaves;
- Do not order Guinness last – it needs time to settle, you stupid prick;
- Do not ask bartenders to surprise you – know what you want to order and order the fucking thing;
- Do not try to spark up a conversation with the bartenders – I don't know if you realised, but they're fucking *busy*!!

- [Pointless] Exercise -

If you really are that much of a fucking arsehole that you have no respect for the hard task facing bartenders in a busy bar during peak hours, remember this. Forcing a bartender to make your bastard of a drink order on a busy night is equivalent to your boss dumping some urgent work on your desk on a Friday, half an hour before you are supposed to finish, making it abundantly clear that it needs to get done before the end of the day. Yes, it's your job and you get on with it. But that doesn't mean you can't be pissed off about it. And it doesn't mean your boss isn't an absolute wanker - just like you. Idiot.

Know an idiot who needs to read this chapter?

- Scan the QR code
- Click the link
- Send it their way!

Food

Empty containers

I can't believe I need to ask this question. What are people supposed to do with a container, such as a milk bottle, once it is empty? That's right – put it in the fucking bin.

The vast majority of us do just that. We finish whatever food or drink was in a given container and we throw it away. However, for some fucking reason, you still insist on putting empty containers back into the fridge or cupboard.

I mean, why?! What the fuck possesses you to do that?! They're empty! There's nothing left! Fuck all! Nada! So why are your empty containers anywhere other than in the bin!!!

There are few things more frustrating than craving a specific food or drink, going to the fridge or cupboard, then finding out the container is empty. What makes this even worse is that sometimes we only fancied the item because we saw the container earlier that day, and logically assumed there must be some left. Enough to drive anyone to the point of madness.

Sometimes you'll leave the tiniest crumb or dribble so that the container isn't strictly empty – although it might as well fucking be. And you do it on purpose so that when someone asks why you didn't just put the container in the bin, you can hide behind the shittest excuse ever that there was still some left. But surely you know that this measly amount of sustenance isn't going to satisfy anyone?

You will even claim that you're just being helpful. You'll say that you leave empty containers so that whoever does the shopping knows what they need to buy. What a fat load of bollox. How does a bunch of empty containers help? Do you really expect the shopper to pick up and shake every single container in the fridge and cupboard to see if they're empty or not? If this stupid method was truly going to work efficiently, you would need to put a Post-It or something on each container reading, “Empty”.

Which you would never do. Why? Because you're actually just a lazy fuck, masquerading as a proper, functional member of your household and society. If you were that bothered about helping with the shopping, you would simply go and bloody do some, or at least start putting a shopping list together, instead of pretending that you employ some bullshit empty container system.

The rise in people having to deal with empty container-leaving freaks like you, surely says something about the rampant laziness we are starting to see in the world. It's mind-blowing that you could find the trip to the bin so arduous, that you would simply refuse to make it. But, here we are!

- [Pointless] Exercise -

The next time you finish something from the fridge or cupboard, throw the container in the fucking bin. It really is that simple. Don't leave a tiny bit to “help with the shopping”. Finish it, then throw it away. The bin is right there, right next to you. Fucking use it. If there is no improvement, those of you who live with people who keep leaving empty containers can try the following. Every time you find an empty container, fill out a Post-It saying something like, “Milk = Empty”. Bonus points if you add,

"Idiot", at the end. Then without a word, slap the Post-It smack bang in the middle of their forehead, then walk away. You never know, the lazy prat might actually get the message after the thirty-seventh forehead slap. Idiot.

Know an idiot who needs to read this chapter?

- Scan the QR code
- Click the link
- Send it their way!

Loud eating & drinking

Everyone eats and drinks. Most people do it quietly and without bothering others. But not you, you fucking animal. You somehow make so much noise while eating, it's fucking ridiculous. How does your masticating human mouth make so much of a bloody racket?

Well, many of the decibels come simply from eating with your mouth open. Did no one ever teach you to eat with your mouth closed? Maybe you think this is one of those pointless things you were told as a kid; a common courtesy that no one really cares about. Take it from the rest of us who have to fucking listen to you eating – it's not. It's actually a vital lesson, one that means other people can stand to be around you without getting violently sick at the sound of your dirty teeth gnashing up and down, not to mention the sight of mashed up food swirling around in your mouth. That sound you make – chomp, chomp, chomp, slurrrrrrpy slurp, then back to the chomps… it's enough to send shivers down our spines.

Don't even get me started on you eating with your mouth open when on the phone. We'll be on the other end of the line trying to tell you something, and all we can hear is that horrendous chomp, chomp, chomp, but magnified ten times right into our earhole. We can literally hear your food being broken down, mate. It's fucking disgusting.

Even worse is the sound of you talking while you're eating, the advanced level of eating with your mouth open. It's a double whammy of horror. Not only do we need to listen to the grinding of your teeth, the squelching of your tongue and your lips making kissing sounds every half second, but we need to also listen to your voice. The latter is just about bearable at the best of times, let alone while you're chucking chicken wings down your throat.

What is most frustrating about all this eating with your mouth open, is that it's completely fucking unnecessary. You don't actually *need* to open your mouth while you're eating, except to take your next bite of food. If you're worried about being able to breathe, well, that's why the nose was invented, you fuckwit. So that you can breathe and have your mouth closed at the same time. Amazing isn't it? You should try it sometime.

The other element of loud eating and drinking that drives us crazy, is when you swallow. Yes, swallowing will always naturally involve a little noise – but you take the absolute piss. The volume of your gulps is like the noise a giant plughole would make while gobbling up the last dregs of water, amplified by a giant fucking microphone.

You do realise that it takes *more* effort to swallow loudly, right? Try it now, go on. Try to be loud when you swallow. It actually requires a bit of force! So why do you do it?

On the whole, the only time it is acceptable for a loud swallow is when you accidentally take too big of a mouthful or you've got a sore throat. But, judging by the noise of your eating when your mouth is open, you've mashed up your food pretty well – too fucking well if anything. And no one has ever had a sore throat their whole fucking life. So it would seem that you either just love pissing people off, or no one's ever told you how annoying your eating and drinking is. Well, consider yourself told, you prick.

– [Pointless] Exercise –

Got food in your mouth but something to say? You're not a fucking goldfish, you can hold that thought for a few seconds. Finish your mouthful first. While we're at it, here's a technique you can try for eating quietly. Put the food in your mouth, put your right hand under your chin, put your left hand on top of your head, then press your hands together. The bottom part of your jaw should move upwards and your lips should touch. Now chew without your lips separating. Much better. Idiot.

Know an idiot who needs to read this chapter?

- Scan the QR code
- Click the link
- Send it their way!

Dietary choices

People make pretty drastic dietary choices all the time and for a whole host of health, ethical or other reasons. We might choose to eat vegetarian food because we can't stand the thought of animals being slaughtered. We might choose to eat vegan because animal agriculture has such a destructive impact on the world's environment. We might choose to eat pescatarian so we're not restricted so much by a vegetarian diet.

The important thing to remember though is that one person's dietary choices are just that, one person's *choices*. No one should be forced to eat differently or made to feel bad for what they eat, based on someone else's diet. Unless they're eating weird shit like bats and dogs.

But not everyone who makes a major dietary choice seems to understand this. You, for instance, seem intent on shitting on other peoples' eating habits, making them feel guilty for eating as the majority of people do.

Look, I get it. We do need to be more aware of the repercussions of our dietary choices, for example, the devastation that is caused by animal agriculture. If everyone did eat vegan or at least vegetarian, the reduction in deforestation and methane emissions would have an enormous impact in reducing the rate of climate change and environmental destruction. And I do agree that we, as a species, need to make dietary changes because of this reason.

That being said, you are never going to get people to change by telling them off. Pushing dietary choices on people will never work, mainly because they will think, "Who the fuck are you to tell me what to do!?" What happens when you tell a teenager not to do something – something that they see all their mates doing? They do it! Adults are no different really, they're mostly stupid kids at heart. They don't want to give up stuff they like when it's not yet incumbent upon them to do so.

If you're trying to bring about dietary changes in other people, it needs to come from a place of pure, calm logic. What do people, unfortunately, care about most? Themselves. "If you and I don't make these dietary changes, the world is fucked. And if there's no world, you and I are also seriously fucked". There's your argument.

What annoys me, even more, is when you try to force dietary changes in others, for reasons that have nothing to do with logic or ethics. If you love animals and can't bear the thought of them being slaughtered, then feel free to eat vegetarian. But your love of animals is not enough to have a go at others. Not everyone cares as much about other species as you do. Unfortunate but true. In addition, we must remember that we too are animals. There *is* a food chain, of which we are a major part. We *are* omnivores and capable of digesting both meat and plants. There's also no point harping on about humans having higher consciousness and a larger capacity for compassion, meaning we should not be killing other animals for food. Especially not when, in the same breath, you also tell us that other animals have a similar emotional capacity to humans, yet also kill and eat their prey. That argument just goes round and round.

The other grievance is how much you make your dietary choices an issue when we all meet for a meal. You'll rock up to a restaurant and moan the whole time you're there about the lack of vegan options. Despite the fact that the restaurant is called Jim's fucking Steakhouse and you agreed to come knowing that. Or you'll come to a BBQ at your mate's house, then proceed to make the host and everyone else in attendance feel bad that they didn't consider your personal dietary preferences. Even though you decided you were going vegan two weeks ago and forgot to tell anyone.

So you've chosen to eat a little differently – whoopee for you. But stop imposing that choice on other people. Stop making it such a big issue. Stop creating awkward situations where some poor person is hosting a BBQ, has bought all the meat and the booze with their own money, yet all you want to do is complain about them not considering you – the one person who has chosen to eat differently. They forgot, mate. Big deal. Bring your own fucking food next time, you entitled prick.

– [Pointless] Exercise –

Remember that your dietary choice is not a religion. You're not vegan, you've decided to *eat* vegan. If you want to convince other people to follow suit, give them a logical reason and let them make their own minds up. Trying to make people feel like wankers for eating like the majority will get you nowhere. And if you say yes to attending a meal at a restaurant or someone's house, make sure your choice will be catered for. Check the menu ahead of time, let the host know or, better still, bring your own bloody food. Idiot.

Know an idiot who needs to read this chapter?

- Scan the QR code
- Click the link
- Send it their way!

Ordering at the counter

For many people, ordering some food or coffee at the counter is a very important aspect of their day. It's a fantastic opportunity to get the dopamine fix that comes from a thoroughly lovely exchange of pleasantries, niceties and reciprocal politeness. Where else are we guaranteed to be able to show off our impeccable manners to our colleagues and mates, or reach the coveted, "Want the usual?" level with a café owner? Who the fuck orders at the counter simply for the caffeine fix?

Well, the truth is, a lot of people do. But the underlying point still stands. When ordering at the counter, it is universally understood that we should be polite and give our full attention to the employee taking our order. Aside from the fact that it's just simple manners, we need to be ready for the inevitable follow up questions about milk type, sugar volume, pizza toppings, our name, temperature, and more.

However, prats like you just do not appreciate the need for being polite at the counter, let alone the potential social value of such an exchange. Judging by the way you treat them, you consider counter staff to be no better than the shit you stepped in after a particularly dirty, rabid dog fouled itself on the pavement. And there is no more representative manifestation of your lack of consideration for counter staff, than taking a phone call while you engage with them.

You might not think it's that big of a deal, but it is extremely infuriating for those taking your order. You don't listen properly to their questions and then moan like a little bitch when the order turns out wrong. Most of the time you answer their questions by snapping a one-word answer at them, employing absolutely no fucking use of pleases and thank yous.

Answering that phone also forces everyone else in the queue and the whole establishment to listen to your shit phone conversation. Mainly because you are generally the type of prick who likes to shout into their phone because they have a bloated sense of self-importance.

Sometimes, you even end up making those in the queue behind wait longer because you aren't listening to the counter staff, meaning they have to repeat their questions again and again.

Look, there are very few calls so important that they can't wait two minutes while you're at the counter. It's almost always some irrelevant discussion with a friend or a relative during which you talk absolute fucking nonsense and drive everyone mental with your shit chat.

If it really is that important a call, you probably know when it's coming. In which case, there is no reason why you can't schedule it for when you're not at the counter. And if there is no way for you to foresee the call, you can always fuck off out of the queue to take it.

But no, knobheads like you are more than happy to stay on a call that lasts the whole queue and even answer the phone at the precise moment that counter staff are taking your order.

I'm certain that you think being on a call makes you seem like a super busy, important person. But it doesn't, mate. This isn't some shitty lawyer show on Netflix with you as the high-flying, suit-wearing executive, saving the day one phone call at a time. You shouting on the phone at the counter doesn't come across as cool, it just makes you look like a complete arsehole with no manners.

If you actually are a bit of a big deal – which I'm willing to bet you are not – how about you work on your time-management skills, get yourself a personal assistant or use the fucking voicemail function. It's provided for free with every phone in the world for precisely these moments when you can't, or shouldn't, answer the pissing phone.

- [Pointless] Exercise -

The next time you're in a queue or at the counter and you get a call, try this revolutionary tactic. Answer the phone and say you'll call back in two minutes, then end the call. Everyone in the queue and the establishment will thank you for it. You might even get extra special service from the counter staff for taking them seriously and giving them your undivided attention. If you continue to be impolite to counter staff, I fully condone them employing tactics such as calling forward the next customer and refusing to acknowledge you until you're off the phone, screaming any follow-up questions at you, or – my personal favourite – pretending they're on the other end of the line. Idiot.

Know an idiot who needs to read this chapter?

- Scan the QR code
- Click the link
- Send it their way!

Chewing gum disposal

If I were to ask where you should dispose of the chewing gum you just had swirling around in your bacteria-ridden cesspit of a mouth, I think that you would say without hesitation that it should go in the bin. So why the fuck do you insist on disposing of your chewing gum in other ways?

For the most part, the only real explanation is laziness and lack of shits to give. But since when has this ever been an acceptable excuse for anything…

Just from an aesthetic point of view, have you seen the state of our everyday world? Chewing gum is absolutely fucking everywhere and it looks awful. The streets look like a dirty, pointless, never-ending game of dot-to-dot. Our transport system is riddled with it; it's on the seats, floors and poles of every single tube, train, tram and bus. It really is one of those things that once we notice it, we can never unsee it.

Many of us will have experienced the fury of stepping in fresh chewing gum on the floor. We can't immediately remove it from our shoes using our hands, unless we fancy touching something that has just been in your prickish mouth. So we walk around for the rest of the day, limping like Hopalong Cassidy, getting angrier with each step, as one foot takes a millisecond longer to advance than it should, courtesy of the sticky gum underneath.

Having said this, at least when we get gum on our shoes, we have the option to simply not touch the disease-ridden, radioactive blob with our bare skin. That's why a special place in hell becomes available each time you stick your chewing gum under tables, to the backs of chairs and even to the underside of church pews, thereby eliminating our free will to not touch it. Church pews for Christ's sake… that's not very fucking Christian of you, is it?

There's not much in this world more horrific than the split second when it dawns on us that we have basically just felt the inside of a stranger's mouth. Hard, brittle chewing gum that has been there for years is bad enough. But the soft, recent additions to the furniture are truly stomach-turning. Especially when we snatch our hand away and the chewing gum comes with it in strings… eew. And I haven't even mentioned the damage that chewing gum can do to our clothes and hair!

However, aesthetics and hygiene are perhaps the least of our worries. Improper chewing gum disposal by you and all the other chewing gum wankers is a genuine problem – it is the second most common form of litter after cigarette butts. This sheer tonnage of chewing gum litter is an issue for a few different reasons.

Chewing gum is made of synthetic plastics, rubber made from petroleum similar to that used in car tyres, and other dodgy shit that does not biodegrade. This means it cannot be broken down except into smaller pieces and will always exist. This also means you are wrong for thinking you're doing everyone a favour by swallowing your gum; it will eventually fly out of you wrapped in a cocoon of brown shit, straight into the sewage system and then God knows where.

The abundance of chewing gum and its imperishable nature, coupled with the fact that it is often mistaken for food by other animals, birds and fish in particular, means it will inevitably make its way into the food chain and never leave. Furthermore, it accumulates plenty of toxins, dangerous bacteria and other shit along the way, courtesy of its stickiness, that we definitely wouldn't want to be putting in our bodies. But, unfortunately, it's already there, and it's only getting worse. Maybe we are closer to a zombie apocalypse than we think.

Chewing gum also costs a fuck ton to clean – fifty million plus quid a year in the UK, just for the streets! It costs so much because it's so difficult and time-consuming to clean, even with industrial steam guns. It's a little bit fucking upsetting to consider what better uses that money could be put to.

There is a lot of cleaning advice online for small businesses, restaurants and schools. "Hold ice to the piece of chewing gum…", they say. "Apply vegetable oil with a paper towel or cloth…", "Pour some vinegar on it…", "Use good old soapy water…". Pull the other one, mate. We've all seen how badly some of these pieces of furniture are afflicted. Imagine how long it would take to implement the above advice for each individual bit of fucking Hubba Bubba! Especially considering that each of these techniques requires a healthy dose of elbow grease and still might end up not working. It would be nice if you could just find it within yourself, for once, to spare a thought for the poor caretakers, waiters and cleaners.

There has been a lot of chatter around what we could do to resolve this chewing gum problem. Options include banning it Singapore-style, recycling it into shoes, installing special pink chewing gum bins and turning it into art. I've got a better idea that doesn't involve airy-fairy solutions or curbing the freedom to chew: you could read this chapter again, take some responsibility for the uneducated arsehole you've become and dispose of your chewing gum in a fucking bin.

- [Pointless] Exercise -

Stop using bullshit excuses for irresponsible chewing gum disposal. Put that shit in a bin. If there's no bin, put it in the wrapper it came in or use a fucking tissue. If these aren't an option, keep it in your fucking mouth until they are. Better still, just stop chewing the stuff. At the end of the day, it costs you money and it makes you look like a camel. Idiot.

Know an idiot who needs to read this chapter?

- Scan the QR code
- Click the link
- Send it their way!

Shopping

Using the self-checkout

When self-checkouts first became a thing, it was a revelation. Being able to quickly scan our items ourselves. No slow-arse, disgruntled supermarket till operators. No queuing for ages behind trolleys piled high with twenty-three packets of rich tea biscuits and Andrex toilet rolls. In and out – no messing.

But predictably, wankers like you have decided to start taking the piss.

First of all, it's ten items or less, you knobhead!! Can't you see the signs? The self-checkout is for people who aren't buying a lot of items, so they can get out of the shop quicker and shorten the queues for everyone else. It's not for you to do your fucking weekly shop. Piss off to the tills!!

Self-checkouts exist for a quick turnaround. Those using them are expected to scan their items quickly, allowing the conveyor belt of low volume shoppers to keep chugging along. But muppets like you really take the biscuit, as well as buying too many.

The self-checkout should sound like this: "Beep, beep, beep, beep, beep – please select your payment method – *selects pay with card* – *pays with card* – thanks for shopping with fucking Asda". Finished.

Instead, this is what it sounds like with you using it:

“.........Beep.........

.........Beep.........

.........Unexpected item in bagging area.........

.........Hi, can you help me, I’m not great with technology you see, haha.........

.........Beep.........

.........Beep.........

.........Beep.........

.........Beep.........

.........Beep.........

.........Beep.........

.........Please select your payment method.........

.........*selects cash*.........

.........*rummages in pockets for change*.........

.........*counts change*.........

.........clink – one coin in.........

.........clink – next coin in.........

.........£138.41 remaining.........

.........Oh shoot, I forgot to get a bag, excuse me?.........”

And so it goes on and on and fucking on!

At the end of the day, it’s as simple as this. Do *not* use self-checkouts for loads of items. But if you are going to be a twat and do so anyway, at least be quick with the beeps, for fuck’s sake.

– [Pointless] Exercise –

Next time you’re finishing up your shopping, count your items. Ten or less? Welcome to the express lane. Eleven or more? Piss off. Also, when using the self-checkout, use your card please, you knobhead. If you absolutely must use coins, the one-pound variety is the minimum socially acceptable amount. But once you've paid, leave your change, you've wasted too much time already. Gather your items and scarper. Idiot.

Know an idiot who needs to read this chapter?

- Scan the QR code
- Click the link
- Send it their way!

Returning shopping trolleys

Plenty of people use shopping trolleys when they go shopping, especially in supermarkets. They are wonderful tools that help us carry whatever we are buying with ease. Sometimes they're shit and the wheels are squeaky, but we're all ultimately pretty bloody thankful that the shops provide them for us.

However wankers like you just aren't thankful enough. In fact, you aren't thankful at all. And you demonstrate your distinct lack of thankfulness by being a complete twat and leaving them wherever the fuck you want after you've used them.

It pisses off shoppers when the trolleys aren't where they're supposed to be, and it winds up the supermarket workers. Refusing to return your shopping trolley to the designated trolley area after use, is a show of disrespect to everyone involved.

You must be aware that someone will need to use your trolley after you - not even you could be that thick. So by not leaving it where another shopper can easily access it, you make it all too clear that you obviously don't give a shit about your fellow shopper. It shows that your general thought process is based on pure selfishness. It also demonstrates your contempt for the workers. When you roll your trolley to your car, put your shopping in the boot, then just abandon your trolley in another fucking parking space in a packed car park, while you drive off whistling, who do you think needs to collect it?

It would appear that you essentially believe you are better than other people. That the unwritten rules of common courtesy do not apply to you. That you are above doing things that make life easier for others. But God knows why - look at you!

You need to remember that people are not put on this Earth to clean up after you. Supermarket workers are human just like you, simply trying to make an honest living. You are nothing special and certainly no better than anyone else. So put the fucking trolley back in the right place, you prick!!!

- [Pointless] Exercise -

Imagine how pissed off you would be if you came to the supermarket to do some shopping, yet there were no trolleys or baskets where they should be. Imagine that everyone was a lazy wanker like you and the workers refused to collect and return them. You'd be the first one kicking up a stink to customer services, wouldn't you, you twat. So please just return your trolleys - not just to get your pound back, but in an effort to make the world a less shit place. Idiot.

Know an idiot who needs to read this chapter?

- Scan the QR code
- Click the link
- Send it their way!

Products in the wrong place

Supermarkets can be a nightmarish place. There are busy people in your way everywhere you look, all foraging for the same, important staples of modern life. It's not exactly a fun place to spend your hard-earned money - not like going shopping for clothes, video games or anything else we might enjoy. So for the majority of us, the supermarket is a place to get in and get the fuck out. But that's no excuse for being a careless bastard while you're there.

One of the laziest and most infuriating things I see you doing in supermarkets is putting unwanted products back in the wrong place. I'm talking frozen fish fingers wedged between bottles of Pepsi Max and fresh red-capped milk hidden amongst squeezy bottles of mayonnaise. These are just a couple of the most recent finds that pissed me off.

You may be thinking, "What's the big deal?".

I realise it doesn't affect your pocket because you haven't actually bought the items, and I don't really give a shit about the supermarket's cash flow. But it's not always about money, you materialistic wanker - ethics are important too. And wasting food is fucking criminal in my book.

Fish died to become the fish fingers that are now inedible after you left them out of the supermarket freezer. Captain Birdseye is turning in his grave. Cows were groped to gather the milk that is now curdling like a motherfucker after you left it unrefrigerated. The very least you could do is put these products back where they belong so others can buy them and they don't go to waste.

If you don't care about exploited animals, how about humans? People are starving out there. Many supermarkets donate their unwanted produce to charities and food banks. This means that the food you've directly contributed to wasting could have been donated to someone who really needed it. Your wastage could have saved a life, you prick.

It's also not fair on supermarket workers. They already do a job that no one really wants to do - so why would you insist on making it worse? What if you were doing their job? Would you enjoy stocking and then having to restock shelves all day? Would you enjoy getting shouted at by a prick of a boss, because they've had a walk around the shop floor and blamed you for all the wastage and misplaced items? Of course not, it would do your fucking head in, just as it does for those who actually hold these jobs. And it's all because you are a self-absorbed, lazy dickhead who just wants to get out of the shop that tiny bit quicker.

- [Pointless] Exercise -

The next time you go to a supermarket, only buy products you see in the wrong place. Oh! You don't want to do that because you're afraid you'll get ill from the spoiled food? Well, stop fucking putting it back in the wrong place then!!! Walking the extra few aisles to return unwanted items is not that difficult. Humble yourself and be grateful for the extra bit of exercise, you fat knobhead. Think of the poor animals, starving humans and exploited supermarket workers. Idiot.

Know an idiot who needs to read this chapter?

- Scan the QR code
- Click the link
- Send it their way!

Window shopping for clothes

What a colossal waste of time. I just don't see the fucking point.

You will happily spend hour upon hour just walking down the street and looking in clothes shops, without buying a fucking thing. Whyyyy?? Although, I suppose at least in this case you are getting in your daily steps. The worst variation of window shopping is when you sit indoors on your arse all day, just browsing through online stores and adding shit to a wish list.

If you aimed to compare different options before deciding what to buy, window shopping would make a lot more sense. However, you appear to have absolutely *no intention* of buying what you're looking at. So what the fuck are you even doing?

If you told me you were a fashion guru looking for inspiration and researching the latest trends for your fashion job, I'd say well done, keep at it.

However, more often than not, you just seem to be browsing clothes that you could never afford, for no obvious reason. So I can only assume that it's because you wish you *could* afford these clothes. You window shop to see what your life and get up might look like in an alternate universe in which you were rich.

Mate, that is sad. It can't be any good for you. Instead of enjoying yourself and making memories, you're out here just wishing you had enough money to buy more expensive clothes. Is that any way to live?

It's not entirely your fault. Capitalism is undoubtedly somewhat to blame for you thinking that you always need more, more, more. You believe you have to have the latest fashion to *be* someone and that you're no one without it. You are constantly bombarded with ads showing beautiful men and women in these clothes, and it makes you want to be like them.

You need to realise though, that the grass is always greener. What would change in your life if you could afford to wear the clothes you so desire? Nothing. You wouldn't be a better person, you wouldn't have a more fulfilling life, you wouldn't have more real friends than you do now – if anything, you'd only have fake ones. And even after you've bought these expensive clothes, fashion would move on, tastes would adapt, and you'd have to buy even more clothes to stay on-trend. And there would always be that next level, those even more expensive clothes, with an extra zero on the price tag, that you'd pine after. It would never end.

Well, this is your reminder that life is not about clothes. It's not about *stuff* in general. It's not about what you can and can't afford. If you're in the market for new clothes, by all means, go browse and buy what you need. But don't spend your days just looking at clothes that you *wish* you could afford. It's upsetting, watching you waste your life like that.

- [Pointless] Exercise -

The next time you're itching to do some window shopping, look inwards and think about why you want to do it. Have you been a little down recently? Are you bored? Either way, remind yourself that it's not healthy and a complete waste of time. If you're looking for a bit of escapism, take the time you would normally spend looking at shit you'll never buy, and do something useful or fun with it. Remember that when you're eventually on your death-bed, you will *not* be thinking about the clothes you were able to buy. You'll be thinking about your loved ones and the experiences you've had. Idiot.

Know an idiot who needs to read this chapter?

- Scan the QR code
- Click the link
- Send it their way!

Extra charges online

Most of us love buying shit online. It's fucking awesome - so damn easy! Whack that router on, click a few buttons, chill for a day, our shit comes to our house. Amazing.

But it's not all plain sailing.

When we go to an online store to buy a particular item, we see a price. We expect to pay this price. Because that's what online sellers like you have told us it will cost. Logical, right? If we can afford that price, and sometimes even if we can't, we add that shit to our basket and click through to the checkout.

Then you add fucking shipping. Sometimes it's very expensive, which is when many of us will delete the item from our basket in disgust. But on the whole, we mostly accept the shipping; it's a necessary evil and we just forgot that it would be added. So more often than not, we still click next.

Then you add VAT. You wanker. You could have absorbed that cost yourself, making it a little less painful for your customers. Instead, you add twenty per cent plus to our bill because you're a greedy bastard.

But we mostly accept the VAT because it's also something that we overlooked and should have known might be added to the overall cost. We click next.

Let's recap here. We want to buy your shit. We've accepted that we have to pay for shipping. We've accepted that we have to pay the VAT. We are obviously very committed customers. It's at this point that you, as an online seller, should be doing everything in your power to make our checkout an absolute doddle from here on in.

But you don't, do you? Instead, you add *ANOTHER FUCKING CHARGE*!!! This extra charge is generally a credit card fee. You fucking tight arse. You won't even pay the fee for doing a credit card transaction?!

You're really going to force your customer to pay it?! What the fuck, mate!! If you're truly making so little money from this transaction that you have to charge this fee to the customer, then your business model needs serious work. If you're not a dropshipping knobhead and you're selling the actual item, you're more than likely keeping one hundred per cent of the profit. And I bet you've put a nice little mark-up on this shit, haven't you? So what's the fucking problem, you stingy prick?

However, sometimes even with the credit card fee, we click next. We must really want this bloody item.

Then, after all the bollox you've put us through, you hit us with a 'booking fee'. What, the fuck, is a booking fee?

It can't be the credit card fee, because you've already billed us for that. So what the fuck is it? I can only assume it's for your petrol to get to the fucking post office to send the item? Or for the paper that the receipt is printed on? In any case, are you having a fucking laugh?

At this point, you've gone too far. It's daylight robbery. You're evidently assuming that customers have gotten so far through the checkout process, that they'll accept anything at this point. And good luck to those customers who power through. But fuck you, mate, I'm out. And you're out. Out of my basket. We're not all made of money, you twat.

- [Pointless] Exercise -

As an online seller, you need to remember that the people you're burdening with charge upon charge are your fucking customers. Your aim should be to give them great customer service, not piss them off and make them jump through hoops to buy your products. Stop being so stingy. You're making your money - you could easily absorb the VAT and credit card fees. And you definitely don't need to be making up your own fucking fees. Idiot.

Know an idiot who needs to read this chapter?

- Scan the QR code
- Click the link
- Send it their way!

Hygiene

Toilet roll technique

It never ceases to amaze me just how idiotic people like you can be. That you can look at a simple tool, with clues galore as to how it should be used, yet refuse to put two and two together, is beyond me. Case in point – scrunching up toilet roll to wipe your arse.

What the fuck goes through your head when you see the perforated edges between each sheet? Do you somehow assume that it's for decoration or something? Surely it must have occurred to you that they exist for a more logical reason – maybe to more easily tear and fold the sheets without ripping them, you silly prat?

It's not just the irrational nature of scrunching up your toilet roll that drives us nuts. It's also the sheer wastage; the scrunching technique requires about fifty sheets for a single bloody arse wipe. When we fold toilet roll sheets, we can get at least the same amount of arse wipes as there are sheets that we tear off. But when you scrunch them all up into a stupid fucking ball, you've only got one wipe before they're down the toilet. As a result, assuming it takes you about five or six wipes to remove all the shit from your arsehole, that equates to a whole fucking toilet roll per dump! Fuck knows what you do during an episode of diarrhoea… Maybe you just opt instead to have sixteen showers that day, because there's no way thicko scrunchers like you can possibly have amassed enough toilet roll for when a particularly dodgy kebab takes hold.

And yet, despite all your toilet roll wastage, you'll still happily shout from the bog, "Can you throw me another toilet roll?". This is very frustrating, considering you've probably just wasted a whole fucking toilet roll on one shit. What's worse, sometimes you'll even come out from the bathroom after a heavy number two and say, "We're out of toilet roll – do you mind nipping to the shops?". I do mind actually, you illogical, toilet-scrunching waster – *you* can buy the fucking bog roll this time!

– [Pointless] Exercise –

Re-potty-train yourself to fold your toilet roll sheets. Think about all the money you'll save on arse-wiping equipment. If all else fails, put a Post-It on the toilet seat to remind you that 'Scrunches get punches'. Idiot.

Know an idiot who needs to read this chapter?

- Scan the QR code
- Click the link
- Send it their way!

Replacing toilet roll

Putting a fresh toilet roll on the toilet roll holder – it's a necessary, yet simple and easy thing to do, right? Apparently not, judging by the actions of lazy fucks like you.

You are more than happy to do your shit, use the last remaining sheets of toilet roll, probably scrunching it like a pagan, then pull up your underwear and walk off, leaving a miserable piece of brown, dirty cardboard on the holder for the next person to sort out. Sometimes you will actually put a fresh roll on the holder, yet you'll still leave the cardboard somewhere in the bathroom.

Why can't you just put a fresh roll on the holder *and* put the cardboard remnants in the bin? Is this really too much to fucking ask?!

Sometimes you'll even go one wanky step further. You'll do a particularly messy shit that requires you to also start on a fresh toilet roll. Then you'll leave the now semi-fresh roll on the toilet cistern or even balancing on top of the cardboard remnants of the previous roll that remain hanging from the holder.

I mean fucking hell, mate – you've done the hard bit of delicately unravelling the fresh roll without tearing it! Can't you go the "extra mile" and just switch out the brown cardboard for the new roll on the holder?!

It sounds like a first-world problem of no consequence, but it pisses people off – it's the principle of the thing. And there are only three possible explanations. You are supremely lazy, you just can't be bothered and you assume someone else will do it. You don't care who else needs to use the toilet after you and you have a, "Fuck them, it's their problem now", attitude. Or you just want to irritate the next person because you know they like things clean. Whatever the reason, one thing is clear – you're a wanker..

Here's a true, cautionary tale where this replacing toilet roll issue got a little out of hand. Shared house, six blokes, one toilet. Already sounds like a trailer for a really shit film, doesn't it? One guy never restocked the toilet roll holder. Worse than that, he refused to even buy toilet rolls. Understandably, the other five blokes weren't too happy about this. Whenever any of them needed a shit, there was never a fresh roll on the holder. So they collectively decided to change the holder when necessary, but never put the cardboard remnants in the bin. Instead, they threw them on the floor.

Predictably, the guy who never restored a fresh roll didn't take this well. He decided that if *he* had to live in this filth, they *all* would. Inevitably the bathroom floor was soon covered in cardboard toilet roll remnants. So the other five decided to start filling the bath with them too. The thinking was that maybe disrupting his showers would put some consideration into his thick head. Alas, no. The bath was soon full too. So now, they agreed they simply wouldn't buy any more toilet rolls. Mainly because there was nowhere to put them. And that's how they all collectively reached a significant low point in their lives: showering straight after shits, knee-high in what now had to be an incredibly unhygienic, brown cardboard mush.

Let that be a warning to you, you lazy, inconsiderate, piss-taking, toilet-roll-holder-phobic dickhead.

- [Pointless] Exercise -

The next time someone has a go at you for not changing the toilet roll, please don't roll your fucking eyes. It's not nothing. Remember the cautionary tale above. It absolutely *can* lead to lost friends and broken relationships. Just restock the holder and put the cardboard remnants in the bin, you lazy fucking twat!!! Idiot.

Know an idiot who needs to read this chapter?

- Scan the QR code
- Click the link
- Send it their way!

Shit on the floor, walls, everywhere

Leaving skid marks on your underwear is bad enough. But the state in which dirty fuckers like you leave toilet cubicles is just appalling!! Some toilets are left so awful that, if it was blood on the walls instead of shit, it'd probably be considered a serial murder scene.

When we're at school and there's shit all over the toilet seat, floor and walls, we don't think twice. Most of us don't have the stomach to shit at school anyway, so we just assume it's some weird, fucked-up, dirty kid who likes to play with their shit and who isn't yet old enough to be sectioned.

But as we leave school and enter the real world, we quickly realise that all the asylums must be too full for new admissions, judging by the public toilets.

It's fucking grim, mate. I don't know what type of person you'd have to be, and frankly, I'm not sure I'd ever want to. Who the hell manages to get shit on the floor and the walls?!

To get shit on the floor, I'd imagine it means you've missed the seat. If so, how?! Are you one of those freaks who squats on top of the seat? It's called a toilet *seat* for a reason, you fucking numpty.

As for getting shit on the walls, I'm sorry, but the only way this seems possible is if you've smeared it there on purpose. I can only assume you squat and shit on the floor and then use your bare hands to rub it everywhere or dip some toilet roll into the bog after doing your business. Because it's physically very difficult to shit upwards. I mean, even if you were twerking on the wall while dealing with liquid blast diarrhoea after a rough Chinese, you'd still get most of it on the floor courtesy of gravity.

In any case, the how still doesn't explain the why. Maybe you think it's funny for some unknown reason? Do you prefer poo, as opposed to paint, as a medium for your art? Couldn't you just graffiti the subway, like a normal hooligan? Were you upset that we rarely get a white Christmas, so decided to create your own brown Christmas? Or is it some fucked up sexual thing? Mixing a wank with some shit play, two girls one cup style… actually, enough, let's stop right there, my gag reflex is coming on as I write this.

Fuck knows how or why you manage to get shit everywhere in the toilet. But please stop. Please. Pretty please. Shitting please. It's not normal to mess around with your own filth, you fucking psychopath.

- [Pointless] Exercise -

Firstly, go to a doctor and get your stomach looked at. Secondly, go and ask your parents for a refresher potty-training course, you dirty bastard. Thirdly, try to remember that it's not normal or ok to spread your shit on the walls. This isn't one of those politically correct things where you like something out of the norm and we say, "You do you, boo". No, you need to fucking stop. Sort your shit out - excuse the pun. Idiot.

Know an idiot who needs to read this chapter?

- Scan the QR code
- Click the link
- Send it their way!

Pissing on the seat

Firstly to the blokes. How many times does your partner or your mum have to tell you to put the toilet seat up before you piss? Yes, they also nag you to put it back down, but that's nothing compared to not putting it up in the first fucking place! You'd avoid so much aggro if you just did it. You'd no longer have them in your earhole, you'd no longer have to wipe the seat when you return to shit and, most importantly, I wouldn't have to waste my time writing a chapter for you, you scumbag.

It's just disgusting. We've all sat down on the bog, looking forward to a satisfying dump, and then had that awful moment of realisation that the seat is surprisingly, slipperily warm and that, yep, we've just sat on someone else's piss. Horrible. All because you are a dirty, lazy bastard.

To be fair, even if you were to always piss with the toilet seat up, it can still be easy to make a mess. Despite the fact that your penis is essentially a fucking target scope, mistakes happen; piss does go astray.

But to not wipe it down after you've mistakenly missed the hole is disgraceful. I can't for the life of me understand how you can piss all over the toilet seat, sometimes even the floor, and just walk away, fully aware that people including yourself are going to use it after. That's just plain fucking careless, mate. Shape up. It's a fair bet that you also don't contribute by washing up, cleaning or ironing. So the least you could do is wipe the fucking toilet seat down after you excrete all over it, you filthy prick.

Now to the ladies. Unfortunately, it's not just men pissing on the seat, is it eh? You like to blame the men, but sometimes, again, mistakes happen.

The problem is, you don't have any excuse whatsoever. You presumably sit down when you piss. Although, the only way you could leave piss on the seat is if you didn't actually sit down. Because if you're sitting down, the piss only has one way to go… down into the mucky depths below.

So why aren't you sitting down? We're not talking about those desperate occasions when the ladies' line is too long and you're stuck trying to discreetly piss into a men's urinal. You're in the comfort of your own home. Sit the fuck down, you dirty bitch! If the issue is spillage as you get up, then wipe it down – the seat and your vag!!

– [Pointless] Exercise –

My man, take your dick out, aim it into that big fucking hole in the middle of the toilet, then let loose. If you end up with a couple of loose droplets flying out at odd angles, no worries, there's this thing called toilet paper. Most toilets have it readily available. Pick it up, tear off a few strips and wipe the fucking seat clean. And ladies, what the hell are you doing pissing on the seat. Please, it's fucking ridiculous. Men get the piss taken out of them – pun intended – when they choose to sit for a wee. You on the other hand are one hundred per cent expected to sit. Why not enjoy the privilege?! Idiot.

Know an idiot who needs to read this chapter?

- Scan the QR code
- Click the link
- Send it their way!

Cutting nails in public

Cutting your nails in public is fucking grim. No one wants to watch a dirty, unhygienic bastard like you, cutting bits off your body.

Cutting your fingernails is bad enough. But cutting your toenails is so much worse. Hunchbacked, head between your legs, huffing and puffing, showing off your lack of flexibility… It's hardly an appealing image, is it? Also, God only knows what mould is growing underneath, especially if you're the type of person who is willing to cut your toenails in front of us! And you're just going to let that shit loose into the atmosphere, into the air we're all breathing?!

The sound of the clippers is fucking unmistakeable, we know exactly what's happening when we hear it. "Clip!" One toenail on the floor. "Clip!" Two toenails on the floor. It makes us shudder in disgust. "What!!? I'll pick them up afterwards!!", you'll protest. But you never do. And actually, what the fuck makes you think you even could? Those toenail shards fly all over the place! You are never going to find every single one!

This brings us to another reason why you shouldn't cut your nails in a public area. It's always us, your poor, traumatised spectators, who end up finding them. And do you know how we find them? By fucking stepping on them. One, it's revolting – that shit was growing on your foot. Two – it's always one of the big toenails, a great fucking whopper of a piece of keratin because you left it growing too long. Three – we always manage to step on it at a razor-sharp angle. And those big toenails are tough, weathered by years of exposure to your sweaty fucking socks.

That's a double whammy. You've made us gag and injured us at the same time. We should not be held responsible for our subsequent actions.

Cut your nails in the bathroom like a normal person, you scumbag!

- [Pointless] Exercise -

The next time you feel like you need to cut your toenails in front of other people, here's what you do. Go to the bathroom, pick up the clippers, walk into the front room, put on your shoes, then fuck off out of the house. Failing that, clip your big toenail off and jam it into the bottom of your foot. You won't learn much, but you fucking deserve it. Idiot.

Know an idiot who needs to read this chapter?

- Scan the QR code
- Click the link
- Send it their way!

Fart ownership

Farting - the act of passing shit molecules through your arsehole to fly freely on the wind, frequently accompanied by a dirty clapping sound made by your arse cheeks. A completely natural occurrence, I'm sure you would agree. But for some reason, that doesn't stop you from getting way too embarrassed about doing something that everyone does, as a consequence of being human.

I can understand a little embarrassment if you let a real, stinky one rip in public, in an enclosed space like an office or a lift. But when you're called out, why are you so appalled that someone would dare accuse you? You will vehemently deny you had anything to do with it, even when it couldn't possibly be anyone else. At the end of the day, we all had salad for lunch, mate. There's no way we threw that stinker out into the world when you brought in dodgy leftover curry, topped with boiled eggs and fish paste, for lunch.

Most people proudly claim their farts as proof of their effective digestive systems. Or they'll quickly excuse themselves when they let loose. This is how we're supposed to deal with it. Own your fart. JUST OWN IT. It's embarrassing that you're so embarrassed.

But why *are* you so mortified? Are you so incredibly worried about any potential slight on your character, that you'd rather lie? Do you think people will think less of you for letting one rip? You need to get over it. Anyone who would hold something as natural as a fart against you is not worth your time. Getting constipation and a bloated stomach, just to keep other wankers on side, is fucking pointless. Especially when you remember that *they fart as well*!

Admittedly, you should avoid too much smelly flatulence around the same people, as you might get a reputation. But only because you stink out the joint on a regular occasion, not because of the natural act of farting.

- [Pointless] Exercise -

Everyone farts. Get over it. And most people admit to their farts. These are good people. They'll laugh *with* you. But some people will take your fart as seriously as if you pulled down your underwear and let loose straight into their mouth. Well, fuck them. Own your farts. If you still can't get over farting in public, even though you know it's not going to be a stinker, and you don't want to make any accompanying squelching noises to incriminate yourself, there is a special trick. It's a simple case of lifting one butt cheek when no one's looking - try not to make it too obvious. With practice, this is also possible hands-free! Idiot.

Know an idiot who needs to read this chapter?

- Scan the QR code
- Click the link
- Send it their way!

Publicly rearranging your privates

On all sides of the gender divide, there are parts of the body that, from time to time, need to be rearranged, lest we feel incredibly uncomfortable. Penis, balls, tits, vagina – they all need a quick tidy now and then.

Whether it's their position on the body, their sensitivity or the sweatier nature of these body parts, there's no denying the occasional need to scratch, reposition, adjust and stop them from being squeezed.

Everyone understands this unfortunate requirement. No one is saying you shouldn't attend to it. However, dicks, testicles, boobs, fannies… these aren't like other body parts. You can't just touch them in public like you would your arms, legs or face. There are sexual connotations, hence the raised eyebrows you keep wondering about, you muppet. You need to start respecting the fact that these body parts are referred to as "privates" for a reason!

You will happily walk around in public, grabbing your crotch every five minutes and scratching your pubic hair so loud, we can hear the fucking lice screaming. You'll stick your hands down your pants or up your shirt, and not think twice about subsequently shaking someone's hand or holding onto poles on trains and buses without washing your hands first.

You argue that everyone has this need to rearrange themselves, so why can't we just all get over it. To that I say, fuck no. A world where it's acceptable to blatantly rearrange your privates in front of other people is simply not adequately civilised. Aside from the fact that it's proper fucking off-putting to witness, it also makes it harder to tell the difference between actual nutters and those who just desperately need a quick scratch.

Rearranging sexual body parts while in the company of others can easily be taken the wrong way – and so it should!! Touching yourself while maintaining eye contact with someone is absolutely something that should only happen in a bedroom between consensual parties. This begs the question, are you a sexual predator or just a little sweaty today? Who knows! Only *you* do! So maybe reserve the public self-adjusting shit for the actual would-be rapists?

The biggest element though is hygiene. We should all be aware that fondling our privates, right before reaching for stuff other people touch regularly, is fucking grim and a big spreader of germs. One benefit of doing the rearranging in private is that there are probably facilities with which you can wash your hands after. These facilities are simply not available in public unless you carry around hand sanitiser like a germaphobe. It stands to reason, therefore, that you must be an inconsiderate, grubby git to do it in public in the first place.

Even if you're not particularly worried about the bacterial element of rearranging your privates in public, then at least consider what other people *think* of your personal hygiene. No sane person can see you adjusting yourself in public and not think, "Eughhhhhhhhh". They'll marvel at how sweaty you must be in those delicate areas to warrant scratching in front of them. They'll be trying to guess the last time you washed. They'll wonder if you have some kind of rash or STI. Public rearranging is where the rumours start, mate. Before you know it, you've got a sexual harassment claim against you, and the whole office believes it has finally unmasked the mystery office BO perpetrator.

Look, I'm not going as far as to suggest we imitate the high courts in Italy, where men were banned from touching their genitals in public in 2008. I'm just asking you to please put decorum, hygiene and your reputation above the itch in your privates. Stop rearranging your privates in public. Find a toilet cubicle, retreat down a deserted alleyway or go the fuck home and scratch away.

- [Pointless] Exercise -

We've all been in the situation where we're dying to scratch our privates in public. The difference is, the more strong-willed among us understand that not every itch needs scratching. It *is* possible to show some self-restraint. When you're in public, just think of something else. If it's that bad, find somewhere more private. But really, unless your balls are about to get chopped off by a stray zipper, you should never need to reduce yourself to scratching your privates in public. In addition, if your privates are constantly itchy, you should probably look into some breathable fucking underwear. If you've got a rash, go to the fucking doctor. If you've got too much pubic hair, shave it the fuck off. Idiot.

Know an idiot who needs to read this chapter?

- Scan the QR code
- Click the link
- Send it their way!

older people

"Back in my day…"

What is it with old peeps like you? Why do you hate young people so much? I mean, I know your memory has gotten pretty bad as you've aged, but Christ, surely you remember that you were young once too?

When you start a sentence by saying, "Back in my day…", we all know that what follows is a bunch of crap from your narrow-minded past, followed by a tirade about what you didn't do, that young people do so wrong now.

The problem with this is that you *did* what young people do! Nothing's changed, mate. You think it has but it hasn't. You were a rude arsehole now and then, you made stupid mistakes, you took the piss at school, you didn't respect your parents sometimes as much as you should have. And the things you truly didn't do, you *would* have done if you'd inherited the same circumstances!

Are you really trying to tell me that if you had grown up with these incredible smartphones, which are basically computers in your hand, you wouldn't use them all the time? Why not? Because you're so wise to the problems of technology? Bullshit, you're just fucking scared of anything you're not used to.

Are you really trying to tell me you wouldn't try to have sex, left right and centre if you'd had Tinder back in the day? Why not? Because you were a well-mannered generation with good values that practised abstinence? Bullshit, it's because the best you had was a little black book and a Rolodex.

Are you really trying to tell me you genuinely had your shit together before your thirties? That you knew exactly what your goals were and what you wanted to do? Bullshit, no one does. You simply did the 'work, get married and have kids' thing, because that's just what people did back then.

Are you really trying to tell me that whatever the fuck you're moaning about, you'd do it better? Why, because you're just better people? Yet more bullshit.

Let's not forget how you and all the other old fogies have ravaged and fucked this shit hole of a world, creating issues such as catastrophic climate change and rampant racism. Of course you think everything was better back in the day. You didn't have to worry about your actions, you just did whatever the fuck you wanted and left your grandchildren to clean up your fucking mess.

This is why, when you start with "Back in my day…", all young people see is a wrinkly wanker who doesn't understand them, who has made life hard for them and who seemingly doesn't give a flying shit about them. Selfish gits like you continuously vote for politicians whose policies suit themselves, ignoring how they will affect a future that they won't need to endure.

The truth is, you have forgotten what it was like to be young. If your generation were growing up nowadays, you'd act the same. Simply because you'd have the same parents and the same shitty circumstances.

When the generation growing up now gets old, they'll also complain about young people in fifty years. That's just the way of the world. Old people like you have lived a long life, been beaten down many times and love a good fucking moan. Your memories have grown stale, leaving only the bits you want to remember. I'd say we should just let you have it, but it's a little bloody annoying gramps. We're in dire straits at the moment, and you have no right telling youngsters how they're so shit when you've left them to the dogs.

- [Pointless] Exercise -

Please at least try and remember what you were like as a kid. Consider the possibility, however slight in your mind, that you were not as perfect as you think. We all know you weren't, but we'd respect you more if *you* could accept it. And give young people a break. Recognise that your generation has collectively left a bit of a shit world. Take some responsibility for it. Young people have to live in what you've created, you won't be here to see how bad it gets, so count yourself lucky. Idiot.

Know an idiot who needs to read this chapter?

- Scan the QR code
- Click the link
- Send it their way!

Fear of new technology

Why are old gits like you so scared of advances in technology and learning something new?

You're not past it! I recognise that learning does genuinely get harder as you age, but you've still got a brain knocking around there somewhere, don't you?! I guarantee it works a lot better than some of the youngsters out here, yet they are still able to post their shitty videos on TikTok and easily connect to the WiFi! Alright, I'll give you that they grew up with computers, so it is easier. But you can't just keep giving up and saying, "I'm too old for this", whenever someone tries to teach you.

Listen, cut the shit. You've told us time and time again that your generation just gets on with things. Stiff upper lip and all that bollox. Where's that gone then, eh?

If you *had* to learn how to use computers, let's say for your job, you'd do it – simply because you *had* to. But because you're retired, you can't be bothered. That's the truth at the end of the day, no matter how you dress it up. But you're missing out on a whole new world here mate!!

Some of the things technology can now do are incredible. You could make your life so much easier if you just gave it a chance. You can stay or get back in touch with old friends and family. You can order food straight to your house. You don't need to pay your bills at the bank. And need I tell you about Tinder, you horny fucker?

Are you really going to lay down and let this latest spurt in technology beat you, after everything you've lived through? Your generation, growing up in the twentieth century, has seen pretty much every single major advancement in technology ever. Radio, television, refrigeration – whatever it is, you always managed to get your head around it, didn't you? You adopted these advances and now they are second nature. So why are you bottling this one?

Gramps, you can tell me as much as you want that computers are a conspiracy and the government is trying to spy on you. And even though you might actually be on to something, you ain't fooling no one. You certainly haven't got the right to make that assumption, or use it as an excuse not to get to grips with the iPad I bought 7 Christmases ago when you can't even turn the bloody thing on!!

- [Pointless] Exercise -

Call up your son, daughter, grandson, granddaughter, enlightened friend, anyone who is comfortable with computers. Ask them to teach you how to use them - the basics. Don't just dismiss this new technology the moment something happens that you don't understand. Fetch your stiff upper lip from the attic, put it on, and stop being a pussy. It's not as hard as you think. What do your TV, oven, light switch, mobile and most other appliances have in common? That's right - they have an 'on' switch. This isn't some new, freaky shit. It's an 'on' button - just like all the others you use every day. So press the bloody thing and get on with it - without the hysterics. Idiot.

Know an idiot who needs to read this chapter?

- Scan the QR code
- Click the link
- Send it their way!

"Respect your elders!"

Respect is earned. The same goes for everyone in this world. And we earn it by being a good person and someone other people look up to.

Nevertheless, for some reason, we're told we must respect our elders as par for the course – something we're just supposed to do. This "Respect your elders" phrase must have been coined because the oldies in a group of people were normally the wisest, calmest and friendliest. Probably comes from aeons ago when the elders in villages and tribes were revered.

Well, fuck that.

Old people like you are rude bastards. Always moaning about youngsters or a slight reduction in your massive pension fund, creeping on younger, good-looking men and women and never admitting you're wrong. What about any of this indicates that you deserve respect?!

You even use the phrase yourself, as a backup for when you're losing an argument in which you refuse to accept logic and assume you know it all, despite the mountain of evidence to the contrary. "Respect your elders!" you scream. Piss off, mate.

The majority of old people are great. Amazing stories, lovely people. Truly living up to the stereotype of being wise, calm and friendly. They've lived for fucking ages and they've seen a lot. And just look at those wrinkles – could fit bloody rivers through there. They deserve to be respected.

But the arsehole oldies like you need to check yourselves. Age only commands respect if it comes with the benefits and hindsight that a long, well-lived life should have provided.

Having said this, giving older people no initial respect, before finding out whether they are arseholes unworthy of it, is not on. Treating them like nobodies or basically already dead, being nice to try and get on the will, targeting them for scams and robberies - anyone who does anything like this a fucking disgrace.

At the end of the day, yes some people are bloody old. But that doesn't mean they're useless or that you can be a brash little shit to them.

- [Pointless] Exercise -

As an old person, stop telling us you deserve respect simply because you're old. You will chip away at it every time you act like a prick, just like anyone else. Instead of feeling entitled to respect you don't deserve, how about trying to impart some of that wisdom that has allowed you to live for so long - or was it just luck? Idiot.

Know an idiot who needs to read this chapter?

- Scan the QR code
- Click the link
- Send it their way!

Technology

Using your phone when with company

When you're out with a mate, whether it's for a beer, a coffee or a bloody lollipop, what are you actually out for? It's for some much-needed social interaction. It's to spend time with someone you enjoy spending time with. It's enjoyable and it's important for you and your friend's mental health.

So why do you think it's ok to whip out your fucking phone and start using it in front of them? Sometimes you even take the bloody thing out mid-conversation!!

There's no way that notification was *so* important. It's almost always going to be someone sharing another pointless video on your Instagram Direct Messages, or a notification that one of your favourite wanky Tik-Tokers has posted another heaping pile of shit for you to watch, like and comment on.

Half the time, you don't even receive a notification!! You just felt some inherent need to look at your phone and "check-in". What an easily distracted wanker you are.

Think about what taking out your phone, for no urgent reason, says to your mate. You are basically telling them that you couldn't give a flying rat's arse about them. That what they have to say does not interest you enough to hold your attention. That their time does not matter to you, as you obviously don't mind wasting it. You are telling them that they essentially don't matter.

Now, I'm sure that's not what you mean to portray to your mate – after all, they *are* your mate. You probably do care about what they have to say, otherwise, why would you bother spending *any* time with them. But the question remains if you do care, why take out your phone in front of them, expecting them to just sit quietly until you're ready to interact once again? You know deep down it's incredibly rude, so why the fuck do you do it?

Maybe you *are* genuinely slightly bored with the conversation. But taking your phone out is a complete fucking cop-out. Why don't you take it upon yourself to come up with another topic to discuss? Have you considered that maybe you're not doing enough to make the time with your friend more enjoyable? Your friend is not there simply to entertain you. It's a two-way street, you self-absorbed knobhead.

Your appalling, inattentive actions are not one hundred per cent your fault, however. Mobile phones and social media networks are designed to be as addictive as possible. And as someone who takes out their phone, even when you are having fun with your mate, you are almost certainly addicted to an extent. Especially if you do so without having received a notification. But really, there's no excuse. You should have the wherewithal to stop yourself unnecessarily reaching for your phone, and to consider how your actions are being interpreted by the person sitting across from you, who calls you a friend for some fucking unknown reason.

– [Pointless] Exercise –

Take out your phone mid-conversation with a friend. Then look up at them. I promise you they will either be looking at you in disgust or they will take out their phone too. Start respecting your friends, for fuck's sake. Idiot.

Know an idiot who needs to read this chapter?

- Scan the QR code
- Click the link
- Send it their way!

Using speakerphone

When you're on a call with someone, putting them on speakerphone can be extremely useful. Maybe you're driving and need to go hands-free, maybe you need to urgently find a bit of info on your phone while staying on the call – the possibilities are endless.

However, there is no doubt that this additional element of speakerphone convenience, in our already ridiculously convenient lives, has resulted in some god-awful habits.

Firstly, when we call you, we expect you to be dialled into the conversation. We don't expect you to be pissing about doing the laundry, cleaning the toilet or making fucking pasta. If you're busy, don't answer the bloody phone, or tell us you'll ring back when it suits you. The speakerphone wasn't invented just so you could do other shit while pretending to listen. You should still give your phone calls and by extension your family and friends, at least some semblance of your full fucking attention.

Secondly, I will never understand why, in the name of all that is holy, you think it is acceptable to put people on speakerphone without letting them know!! At the end of the day, we called you, and you alone, for a fucking reason. To talk to you. Not your mates, not your mum, or whoever the fuck else is in your vicinity.

We need to know if swearing is off the table! We need to know if we should be careful about what we say! What if we inadvertently say something about someone else while they are eavesdropping? Obviously, we shouldn't be talking about people behind their backs, but let's face it, we've all done it. Putting us on speakerphone without our knowledge has the potential to create problems for us socially without any idea how they came about!

A phone call is a private conversation between you and a specific person. It's not for other people to listen to. If I wanted to tell someone *else* something, I'd fucking call them instead!

Did you know that under German law, putting someone on speakerphone, without telling them beforehand and getting their consent, can constitute a criminal offence? The German Criminal Code protects the privacy of the non-publicly spoken word. And so it fucking should. Admittedly, Germans take their privacy ultra-seriously, but in this case, I think they have a point!

The other element to consider when using the speakerphone functionality is how people nearby feel about having to listen to your conversations. I'm sure there are thousands of Nosey fucking Nellies out there who'd love a naughty eavesdrop, but most people have no interest in your stupid, whiney little chats discussing your first-world problems. And as Nosey Nellies look very similar to normal people, you can never be sure who fancies an eavesdrop and who doesn't. So turn the speakerphone off when you're around other people and just hold the fucking phone, you lazy bastard.

- [Pointless] Exercise -

Have you ever said anything dodgy about anyone while on the phone? Yes? Well, imagine that person is nearby while you are put on speakerphone without your knowledge. Makes for a pretty sticky situation, doesn't it? Consider this the next time you're on a call around other people and can't be bothered to hold the phone anymore. While we're at it, try to remember that no self-respecting person gives two flying shits about your conversation with Aunt Sally. So turn off the speakerphone and keep your fucking phone call to yourself. Idiot.

Know an idiot who needs to read this chapter?

- Scan the QR code
- Click the link
- Send it their way!

Making shit TikTok videos

Let me say, first of all, I love videos. They can be brilliant. Brilliantly funny, brilliantly insightful, brilliantly emotional.

Take Vine for instance – as a social media video platform, it was awesome! I understood the point of it. Seven-second snippets of hilarity that don't take all day to watch. But TikTok on the other hand… what is the fucking point?

In the beginning, TikTok was called 'musical.ly', and it appears that the whole point of making a video on the platform was to lip-sync to a song while copying someone else's crappy coordinated dancing. And as much as TikTok now has more variety, with a lot of the big content creators gracing it with their funny videos and whatever else, there remains a high proportion of content on this platform that still consists of these musical.ly-esque tripe. Again, what is the fucking point?!

I initially thought I was missing something. Why would you make these videos? And why would you willingly watch others doing the same thing? Where is the talent in imitating other people who are pretending to sing a song, with an accompanying dance that anyone with the slightest sense of rhythm can copy? At first glance, it doesn't make any sense.

Wanky TikTokers like you will tell me that you are just expressing yourselves. But that's bullshit. I gradually realised that the point of making TikTok videos is the pursuit of popularity. Popularity drives everything on TikTok. You make these TikTok videos to latch onto a trend driven by fellow knobheads, hoping to get followed by a bunch of other knobheads. How can you express *yourself* if you're just copying *others*?

I also realised that the videos with the most likes, going viral on TikTok, are those where the creators themselves are good-looking. Which, especially in modern times, is all-important. The thought process is something like, "Good-looking people are cool and popular. Therefore, this no-substance video of a good-looking person, lip-syncing and dancing, must also be cool. Therefore I must copy it. Because I want to be that person. I want to be famous too". Get a fucking grip, you fame whore.

And it gets worse – a lot of the videos now are just people like you trying to look pretty while music plays in the background. Literally, you just smile, pout, push your hair about, normally in bikinis, tops off or tight gym clothes and stare into the camera. I mean, come on. What are you doing? You are obviously well aware that people only watch these videos because they think you are good-looking. So if you aren't trying to do anything specific with the videos except look good, if you aren't trying to do funny videos, if you aren't trying to provide any other value than what you look like, the only possible conclusion left is that you just want popularity. You've tapped into the 'sex, sells' adage, but normally it is used to sell *something*, not popularity itself.

I have much more respect for those who do these kinds of TikTok videos because they are hoping to get a bunch of eyes on their product. But to do these shitty videos because you're a sheep who craves popularity… That's a really sad state of affairs.

As embarrassing as it is as evidence of where we are as a human race, I suppose it's not all bad. My favourite of these videos is when muppets like you are subsequently caught red-handed creating one of these fuck awful videos – because it truly exposes how shit this stuff is. Rightly so, you are pretty damn ashamed. Because deep down, you know you look fucking stupid. "Mum, I'm trying to do a TikTok!?", you'll exclaim – as if that is a viable explanation for why you are voluntarily showing yourself up online.

I saw one where the mum then tried to beat the stupid out of her son who was slutdropping in his bedroom, on camera, at his mum's house, at 25, by himself. Now that's *entertainment*. And another one where two dads on a beach were twerking to shitty songs, copying their thirteen-year-old daughters doing TikToks a few metres away. Mortifying for the daughters. *Entertainment* for us.

- [Pointless] Exercise -

If you create lip-syncing, while dancing like a prat, copycat videos on TikTok, yet you have nothing to sell, ask yourself why you think they're worth doing. Would you do them if no one else was doing them? Would you find them entertaining then? No. You wouldn't. Also bear in mind that your future children and grandchildren will see these videos of you posing like a self-absorbed, materialistic pillock. If that doesn't make you think twice, I don't know what will. Idiot.

Know an idiot who needs to read this chapter?

- Scan the QR code
- Click the link
- Send it their way!

Buying the latest model

Have you got your phone close by? Is there anything wrong with it? No? So, when the latest model is released, why the fuck do you feel the need to instantly buy it?

If your phone is broken, I get it. If it's cracked, I get it. You do need a new one. But to buy a new phone just because there's a newer model out… what the fuck is wrong with you? It would appear that you haven't evolved from the spoilt kid who absolutely *had* to have the newest toys. If you don't need it, why are you buying it?

I'll tell you why – you have been duped by marketing and consumerism, mate.

One of the prime instigators is Apple. Their marketing is fantastic. They have made you believe that owning an Apple product is like proclaiming to the world that you are building something, that you are a creator, that you are hustling. You believe that, by using a Mac, you too are now a real entrepreneur.

The problem with this is that anyone with a pair of eyes and a little bit of self-awareness – something you clearly lack – can see that you are a lazy prick who does fuck all. You don't need to buy a new phone to feel like a hustler. You just need to do some fucking work. You are not the product of your bloody products. You are the product of what you do.

Apple's marketing is *so* good in fact, that their products are now even akin to a status symbol. If muppets like you have an iPhone 6 while all the other sheep own the latest model, you somehow feel inferior. So you believe you have no choice but to buy the latest model just to stay relevant.

This doesn't say much for you and the rest of humanity does it? Yes, this notion that you have to buy the latest model has been cultivated by capitalism and force-fed to you since birth. So that you spend more and companies can earn more. That's the whole game. But the fact that you don't have the awareness to know that this is happening to you… the fact that you allow yourself to feel inferior just because you have an older model… that's just plain sad, my friend. Have you no belief in just yourself, as a person?

What drives me crazy as well is when you buy the latest model, then say things like, "OMG, did you see Apple is now worth blah blah trillions and have this much cash? Crazy right?!" Well actually no, it's not fucking crazy. You keep buying all their shit – what did you expect? All it means is that there are enough shallow-minded people in the world like you to keep this company at the top. Surely you realise that if you all collectively decided not to buy their latest product for once, they might start struggling as a business? They may even start releasing new models that actually feature some major improvements, rather than the piss-take of a sleeker finish being worth an extra five hundred quid!

I pick on Apple only because they're one of the best at marketing and convincing you to buy the latest model. And because Apple in particular takes the royal piss while they do it. With a new model, they make you buy a new charger and a new this and a new that, after ensuring your old accessories aren't compatible anymore. And you just lap it up, like the good, little doggy you are.

I have nothing against Apple – okay maybe I do a little. But seriously though, every company wishes they could do it like them – getting people to *need* their new product. If it wasn't Apple, it would be someone else. The blame lies with materialistic prats like you for buying the products and attaching more importance to what people have, as opposed to who they are.

- [Pointless] Exercise -

The next time your favourite tech company launches a new product, just relax. Recognise that thing inside you that makes you want to buy it, then ignore it. If someone asks you if you've got the new model yet, say, "Why would I? My old one still works fine". Because let's face it, that's the truth. Start to see the people you've surrounded yourself with, for how shallow they really are. See what happens if you start wearing cheaper clothes and using cheaper tech products. You will see who likes you and spends time with you because of you, and who does so because they thought you held a certain status. Idiot.

Know an idiot who needs to read this chapter?

- Scan the QR code
- Click the link
- Send it their way!

Pointless photos

Photography is incredible nowadays, particularly when it comes to our mobile phones. The camera quality on these relatively small handheld devices is mind-blowing. And it truly is amazing that we can now take pretty much as many photos as we want, just by opening the camera app on our phones. Youngsters will never understand the photographic struggle before this digital age. It wasn't so long ago that a limited number of photos on a wind-up single-use Kodak was the norm!

But, as with many advances in technology, there are drawbacks. There are a few things dickheads like you do, specifically around the taking of pictures, that make the rest of us want to snatch your camera or phone out of your hands, throw it on the floor, stamp the fuck out of it, then hand it back with the same stupid grin you had on your face when posing.

For one thing, you seem to have this incessant need to take at least seventeen photos of *everything*, including each fucking meal you're about to eat. Let's face it, these are photos that, unless they're taken "for the gram", will never be looked at again. When are you ever going to look again at a boring photo of the Leaning Tower of Pisa, or indeed a pizza you just ate? You're not. Because there's no difference between your photo and thousands of others like it online.

"What's it to you?", I hear you ask. Well, it's of no real consequence to us that you take too many photos you'll never look at again, mate. But surely you understand that making hungry people wait to eat their food, while you snap it from every angle, will inevitably make them think of you as a fucking twat!

Another infuriating habit you photographic noobs have is commandeering whole gangways to get the perfect shot. You'll pose in front of some shitty mural or historical monument, then ask your "photographer" to retreat and get as much of the background as possible. The problem is, by taking a photo in this fashion, you are essentially forcing polite people to wait to get past because they feel bad about messing up the shot.

This is fine on a quiet street. Most people are happy to wait a few seconds for your photo in return for an enthusiastic thank you. But on a busy street, you've got no fucking business doing this. The street is busy because the people *on* it are busy, going about their daily lives, maybe even in the worst of rush hours! Yet you still think it's reasonable to force them to wait or walk in the road to get past, while you strike fifty-eight different poses! Fucking selfish.

The last annoying thing is the taking of selfies – the ease of which is, without doubt, the worst improvement brought about by the advancement in photographic technology. They just don't make any sense. Well, they make sense, but only if you're an unbelievably vain, self-centred prick. Yes, it's a good thing to love yourself, but this incessant selfie-taking takes your self-love to a bit of a weird place. And what do you do with your selfies? Yep, you post them online – which is basically like shouting, "Look at me, look at me! Please, pretty please, notice how good-looking I am!" Even if you are good-looking – which for you is seriously wishful thinking – you've got to be a right sad fucker to need such validation.

– [Pointless] Exercise –

Stop taking thousands of photos of buildings and your meals. They're pointless and fucking boring. I don't need to see your photo, because I guarantee millions of people have taken one just like it. If you need to keep capturing shit images of stuff no one cares about, at least get a bit creative and make them slightly more interesting. Maybe add your ugly mug into it making a funny face, or include an object in the picture and make it like a *'Where's Wally?'* challenge. Also, stop commandeering so much space to take photos on busy streets, you entitled prick. If you can't wait until there are fewer people and you can't find a quieter spot, do us all a favour and just don't take the fucking photo. You don't need another picture with you in it anyway – I bet there are fifty thousand other selfies on your phone, just sitting there as nothing other than a representation of all the time you've wasted adoring your ugly self. Idiot.

Know an idiot who needs to read this chapter?

- Scan the QR code
- Click the link
- Send it their way!

Letting dogs off their lead

When people go for a walk in the park, it does *not* mean they are automatically happy to be confronted by your dog. It's not a given that everyone wants to meet it, pet it, or have it sniffing around them. And letting your curious dog off its lead, in a public place, takes that choice away from people, you prat. It doesn't matter whether someone is petrified of canines, simply not in the mood, or overjoyed at the sight of yet another dog. People who love dogs will come up to your dog and interact with it of their own accord. Unless someone does so, there is no indication that they have any desire to deal with your dog in any way whatsoever.

We know you think that your dog, in particular, is lovely and super well-trained. But every owner says the same fucking thing! So please explain to me why, when people let their dogs off their lead, so many of them bound away, completely out of control, ignoring all commands?

I once saw a dog attacking and chasing children at one end of a park, while the fat owner, pretending to rush over, mildly called the dog's name as if it was doing nothing wrong. "Poppy, Poppy! Come here, girl!" Get your fucking dog under control and put it on a lead, you prick.

You'll tell me that only bad owners are an issue and they should never have been allowed to keep dogs in the first place. And I'd agree with you. But let's be real, even good owners should not let their dogs off their leads around other people in a public space. Because, at the end of the day, dogs are animals. End of story. They are driven by instincts, including fight or flight.

Yes, I know - we are animals too. However, unlike humans, dogs don't have additional controls such as the law, society or rational brains to keep them from succumbing to their instincts. Can you truly guarantee that your dog is *so* well-trained, even though it still shits itself now and then on the living room carpet, that there is no chance it would attack someone if it felt threatened? No, you can't. No one can. Because it's a fucking animal!!! Take your "Don't worry, they won't bite" bullshit and piss off, mate.

I understand that you might have grown up in a cushty area with nice people and that you've only ever been exposed to fluffy dogs with calm dispositions. But dogs can be horrible - trained and used as weapons. They can be very fucking dangerous. And the fact of the matter is, even the fluffy ones have teeth.

- [Pointless] Exercise -

Be honest - has your dog ever disobeyed you? Of course it has. Did you ever have to repeat a command? Of course you did. So what the actual fuck makes you think you should be letting it off its lead around strangers? Even the compromise of using retractable leads at full length is not good enough. I know you want to give the dog space to roam, but what's the fucking point of even having it on the lead if you're just gonna let it run up to people anyway. Idiot.

Know an idiot who needs to read this chapter?

- Scan the QR code
- Click the link
- Send it their way!

Picking up your dog's shit

Parks are for playing, running and picnicking. Pavements are for walking and stumbling home drunk. Beaches are for sunbathing and pretending we like sand. But do you know what these public spaces are not for? Letting your dog shit all over them and you just leaving the turds where they lay.

Look, dogs are a ball ache to look after – I get it. Hair everywhere, a constant need for food and affection, always looking for bigger balls to play with, shitting all over the place. Reminds me of my partner actually, but that's beside the point…

The point is yes, dogs can be a chore. But you decided to look after the thing – you have a responsibility to it now. You do not have the right to get exasperated and lazy, to the point that you neglect that responsibility. If your dog shits in the park, on the pavement, on the beach, or anywhere else, you need to sort it out.

I don't care how fucking slimy, liquified or stinky the latest particular excrement is. I don't care if there is no dog litter bin anywhere in sight. You should have thought about that before you brought your dog there. Get your hands on that shit and walk around with it in your pocket for miles if you have to.

There are plenty of reasons why it's important to pick up your dog's shit in public spaces. The obvious one is the absolute horror of stepping in dog shit. We've all done it at one point or another. It's fucking horrible, truly revolting. A day ruined. The stench stays with you everywhere you go, invading the noses of everyone within a ten-foot radius.

We shouldn't have to be mindful of every step we take when using public spaces. We deserve the peace of mind necessary to look up and admire the world around us, instead of having to look down at the floor all the fucking time to avoid the foul result of your irresponsibility.

I mean, what's the alternative? Think about it for a second. What would our public spaces look like if every single dog owner refused to pick up their dog's shit? Imagine if every dog shit that has ever been picked up was instead left to fester. The world would be a very fucking smelly place, that's for sure. And I bet you'd be the first to moan, you dog-shit-leaving wanker.

- [Pointless] Exercise -

Pick up your dog's shit. Plain and simple. I recognise it's grim. I understand that on a bad day, you might not want to pick it up. But I do not empathise with you. You chose to get a dog. It's your own fault. You have responsibilities now. Fucking deal with it. Idiot.

Know an idiot who needs to read this chapter?

- Scan the QR code
- Click the link
- Send it their way!

Treating pets as humans

So, before you go ballistic, you animal lover, I would like to stipulate that I also like animals. If someone is going to own a pet, they should look after it. Pets have the right to be fed and watered, cared for and loved.

However, you take things waaaaay too far. Treating your pets as humans is a fucking no-no.

It doesn't matter whether your pet is a dog/cat/tortoise/spider/mouse/guinea pig/bird/elephant/snake, it is still a pet. You *own* it. It is not a human. It is not capable of the same level of thought and emotional or logical intelligence. It is not a family member. It is not your peer. It cannot discuss anything with you in any way shape or form, no matter how much human language you believe it comprehends. It may well have been trained to respond to certain words, but only as sounds corresponding to concepts that it does actually comprehend, such as pain or food. You are not a mum or a dad just because you own a pet - you did not give birth to it, you prat. Yes, it *is* weird that you are just as upset about your pet dying, as the death of someone close to you. And while we're at it, please stop carrying the thing around like a baby or in your purse, you fucking weirdo.

To put the ridiculousness of the situation into some perspective, there are now grief sessions for deceased pets. Some polls have even suggested that a third of people now feel animals should have the same rights as humans.

Now, look. Any sane, socially active person can tell you that it's not normal to treat your pet as a human. I'm not going to dignify the stupidity of treating pets as humans, with an explanation as to why it is so stupid. If it's not immediately obvious, go and get your head examined.

What is interesting though, is to try and work out why you do it, you raving nutter.

A rising number of people like you find it easier to deal with animal companions, who don't judge them in any way and require nothing in return for their unconditional love other than a bowl of food and water every few hours. Is it the explosion of technology usage that has caused this increased preference for dealing with animals as opposed to humans? Too much time spent on a screen and not enough with people perhaps? Has it consequently become too difficult to talk in real-time with a real-life human, considering all the complexities and nuances involved in social interaction? Or is it just that people, in general, have become such arseholes that we are simply harder to handle?

It's probably a mixture of all of these reasons, including the last. After all, I'm not writing this book because I think humans have become a kinder, gentler, more intelligent species.

Reasons aside, it's worth remembering that you cannot replace human contact. A connection to a dog or a cat can never be as fulfilling as that built with a trusted, fellow human. Yet you still appear to think that the interaction with your pets is just as nourishing.

Or so you would have us believe. Deep down, I think you know the truth that the relationship with your pet is a plaster. Papering over the cracks of failed relationships, the subsequent fear of new social connections and laziness borne from infinite digital connections being available at your fingertips.

At the end of the day, I don't truly know the real reasons why you would treat a pet as a human. Only you can answer that. If anything, I'm just trying to do you a favour by coming up with a logical reason, other than being crazy, for your crazy behaviour, you bloody misfit. I'm simply here to say that pets are not humans. So please stop treating them as such.

- [Pointless] Exercise -

Sit your pet down and engage it in a debate about any topic. Go on, I dare you, any topic. Can it give you any insights or opinions, however badly thought through? No? Why? Because it's a fucking pet. Not a human. Idiot.

Know an idiot who needs to read this chapter?

- Scan the QR code
- Click the link
- Send it their way!

"It's more afraid of you…"

Let's get one thing straight. Insects, bugs and spiders can be fucking dangerous. Some are fast. Some can fly. Some are even poisonous. Basically, fuck nature.

So when you, a Billy Big Bollocks wanker, tell us, "It's more afraid of you, than you are of it", we are well within our rights to take umbrage. It may *well* be more afraid than we are, but that doesn't mean we shouldn't also have serious reservations!

I do not doubt that the spider on my wall is more scared of me than I am of it. I'm fucking huge in comparison - thank God. However, I am no bloody arachnid specialist. And neither are you. You have no bloody idea whether the menacing black spots on the spider's back mean it's harmless or capable of my murder!

I know you use this phrase to try and calm others down, but logical people will get even more panicky as a result. Think about it - what do many living things do when they're scared? They fucking lash out is what they do. They attack with teeth, they sting, they eject poison, you fucking name it. So instead of telling us it's more afraid of us than we are of it, and thereby forcing us to consider all the hellish ways it could potentially injure us, please just let us sit here praying it hasn't even noticed us.

Nevertheless, being scared stiff is pointless. Especially if it's fear of something that is seven hundred times smaller than us. We aren't going to get rid of the little bastards plaguing our lives by standing there shitting ourselves or jumping on the bed screaming. Caution is king, yet we still somehow have to do something about it. The one thing that is certain - telling us it's more afraid of us is never going to help.

- [Pointless] Exercise -

You fucking squish it if you're so fucking brave. Let's hope it isn't pregnant and doesn't spout a million miniature, venomous babies. Idiot.

Know an idiot who needs to read this chapter?

- Scan the QR code
- Click the link
- Send it their way!

Romance

Using chat-up lines

Chat-up lines can be fucking hilarious.

My favourites include, “If you were a vegetable you’d be a cutecumber”, “This is so us. Me doing all the talking. You sitting there looking all cute”, and “See my friend over there? He wants to know if you think I’m cute”.

The problem is, they rarely work. In fact, the only occasions on which they *are* successful are when you’ve chanced upon someone incredibly desperate, or you are good-looking enough for the chat-up line recipient to look past the initial stumbling block of you having bloody used one.

What a chat-up line advocate like you fails to realise, is what the mere usage of a chat-up line says about you. Using chat-up lines on people is a blatant admission that you’re interested in sleeping with them. The fact that you’ve openly admitted you want to sleep with them, is like waving your own red flag of sexual desperation. Which isn’t very sexy.

Using chat-up lines is a concession that you don’t have the basic social skills necessary to start and continue a normal conversation with someone you find attractive. It’s way too obvious that you are trying to hide all your insecurities and nervous desperation behind poor, rehearsed humour. Again, not very sexy.

The lack of personalisation in chat-up lines also suggests you do it all the time. But who cares - it's a numbers game, right? Wrong. Do you think potential romantic partners want to feel like you've approached loads of other people in the exact same way before you resorted to them? Do you think knowing you've used these lines on other people makes the next one feel wanted? Chew on that, you muppet.

Consider what goes through the head of someone who is approached via a chat-up line. What do you think their immediate thoughts are?

It's normally something along the lines of, "For fuck's sake, not another one. Do they truly think this will work… has it ever worked?!" Then, "They don't even want to know anything about me… they just approached me because of my looks".

What do you reckon - are people right to jump to this conclusion? Let's break it down.

Are your advances based on appearances? Of course they fucking are, almost exclusively in fact. And initially, that's fine, because without knowing the chat-up line recipient, that's pretty much all you *can* be attracted to. But do you then subsequently give any indication that you want to know more about *them*? No. Instead, all you do is then use another shitty line geared towards aesthetics.

All of this is why you'll only ever get one of two responses when using chat-up lines. Much, much more often than not, you'll get fobbed off and left looking like the prat you are. Or, if the recipient is desperate enough, you'll get some superficial response back and potentially a one night stand. The second response is rare, and is the effort really worth the reward? Depends on what you're looking for I suppose, you thirsty fuck.

- [Pointless] Exercise -

Get over your insecurities and learn some decent conversation techniques. Otherwise, you are doomed to relationships with desperados and eternally using made-up words like cutecumber. Making you what? That's right. An idiot.

Know an idiot who needs to read this chapter?

- Scan the QR code
- Click the link
- Send it their way!

Fixating on break-ups

Breaks-ups are horrible, aren't they? Especially that first one. It feels like we're never going to find anyone ever again. Like that was our one shot at happiness, and now it's gone.

We get it. We all understand. We've all been through it.

The thing is, as much as it hurts to end a relationship, it's not the end of the world. It will take time, sure, but we all know what we need to do to get over it. And it's the standard things everyone swears by, like hitting the gym, throwing ourselves into work, getting a new hobby, being more social etc.

Most people realise, after one or two harsh break-ups, that it's ok to feel sad for a time, while it's still raw – but not for too long. Otherwise, we're giving someone, who no longer cares about us, an indirect power to make us feel like shit. That's messed up. So most of us pull ourselves together sharpish, so as not to give our exes the satisfaction. We know when it's time to get on with our lives and move on to the next one.

But some emotional wrecks like you do not appear to have read the break-up memo. You're the kind of twat who loves a bit of drama, who loves to make everything about them. And a break-up is too perfect an opportunity for you to pass up.

You never stop fucking going on about it! Every conversation we have with you is about the bloody break-up. If we try to change the subject, you'll make damn sure the conversation works itself back. You'll talk about all the things that your ex likes that, in fact, *everyone* fucking likes. "My ex loved the sunset…", you'll say in between sobs. But who the fuck doesn't like sunsets, you mug.

You'll think you saw your ex at the supermarket, at the cinema, fucking everywhere. But there are only so many times you can mistakenly go up to random people and say that you made a mistake and want to try again, just because they were average height and had the same hair colour as your ex!

You'll constantly point out places around town where you did things with your ex for the first time and went on dates. You'll go on a posting spree on social media, trying to appear philosophical, but instead looking like a right tit crying out for attention. Shit like: "Sometimes you must forget what you feel and remember what you deserve", or, "It's hard to tell your mind to stop loving someone when your heart still does". Cry me a fucking river!

Don't get me wrong, I'm not talking about the heart-broken unfortunates who were with their partner for decades or whose partner has died. These are proper mourning circumstances and are more than understand-able.

I'm talking about you moping about for months on end, expecting people to feel sorry for you after a relationship that only lasted a few weeks. It's like, mate, you are not the first person to ever go through a break-up - the whole fucking world's been through something similar at one time or another. Everyone else, male and female, realised pretty quickly that they needed to shape up and get over it. Why can't you?

Break-up whores like you need to start realising that no one gives a shit after a certain amount of time. I think we need to start setting some rules on this. I vote that for any former relationship lasting less than two years, you've got one week to feel sad before it gets annoying. Between two and five years, you've got two weeks maximum. Above five years, let's call that a grey area. But even then, if it hits six months and you are still going on like a moany bitch, it's time to call it.

- [Pointless] Exercise -

Get rid of all signs of your ex to get over them quicker. Delete their number, crop them out of pictures, unfriend or unfollow them on social media. You can continue to feel sad if you really need to, but do it on your own time and don't keep bloody telling us about it. There are plenty of people with actual problems in this world. Idiot.

Know an idiot who needs to read this chapter?

- Scan the QR code
- Click the link
- Send it their way!

Always mentioning your other half

We get it, you love your other half. That is amazing, it really is. True love is hard to come by, assuming it even truly exists. Maybe your other half actually is your best friend, rather than that just being something people say.

However, we don't need to hear about your partner in every fucking conversation. Whatever the subject, you somehow find a way to shoehorn them in. Even if it adds *nothing* to the discussion. If we're talking about cars, you'll tell us that your partner can drive. If we're talking about healthy eating, you'll tell us that your partner eats food too. If we're talking about problems at work, you'll tell us that your partner has a job. If we're talking about travelling the world, you'll tell us about the time you and your partner went to Spain. Everyone's been to fucking Spain!!

On a side note – one of the weirdest elements of you talking about your other half all the time is never mentioning their name, especially at work or when meeting someone new. Why would you not mention their name? It's always "my partner" this, "my husband" that, or "my wife", "my girlfriend", "my boyfriend". *What is their fucking name?!* It's fine the first time you meet someone, but then the normal thing would be to say their name straight after and use it moving forwards. Sometimes we've even met your partner in person, and you *still* don't refer to them by name!

I get it if you want to keep your personal life private – no issues with that at all. But then why mention your partner at all? It makes people wonder whether they really exist!!

Anyway, returning to the main point, why is it that you need to keep mentioning your partner in conversation? On the surface, it would seem that you just really love your partner. But is everything honestly that rosy? Genuinely happy people, do not generally feel the need to keep going on about it. Maybe you continuously mention your other half to convince others, and yourself, that you are, in fact, happy?

Is your partner literally the only person you do anything with? Maybe you don't really have any friends, and your partner is the only person with whom you have any recent stories or shared experiences.

Is it because you want to make sure everyone knows that you are desirable? Maybe you feel unappreciated in certain situations and around certain people, so you compensate by reminding them constantly that others on this planet value you.

In any case, none of these reasons is acceptable. They all require you to do a little bit of work on yourself or your relationship. Find some friends, build more confidence in yourself and make sure your relationship is actually strong instead of pretending to the outside world. If there is another genuine reason that explains away your incessant need to mention your partner all the time, hit me up. But I don't see it.

- [Pointless] Exercise -

Remember that mentioning your partner in a conversation does not automatically make what you've said more interesting. In fact, it just makes you look desperate to make sure everyone knows you're in a relationship. Can't you see all the eyes rolling at yet another mention of your other half? Start picking and choosing your moments to talk about your partner a bit more carefully. Ask yourself if what you are going to say about them adds anything to the discussion. Does your contribution stand alone, without the need for your partner to be mentioned? And if you absolutely must mention your partner, use their bloody name. Idiot.

Know an idiot who needs to read this chapter?

- Scan the QR code
- Click the link
- Send it their way!

Boasting about sexual escapades

Everyone loves sex. Well, apart from weirdo asexuals. Most people have had it, and with several different partners. But only thirsty fuckers like you feel the need to constantly go on about your latest sexual escapades – or sexcapades if you wrongly think you're down with the kids.

Every time we meet you, you can't help but mention sex. You take every opportunity to remind everyone and their mother that you're doing the dirty. Even when that opportunity doesn't *lend* itself to the mention of sex! You'll start off telling an average-at-best story about something relatively mundane, and all of a sudden, boom, you've mentioned it. Something like, "I was incredibly hungry the other day – my stomach was growling! So, while I was banging this girl, I decided to have potatoes for dinner as I hadn't eaten them in ages!!" I agree you gotta get your starch in, mate – but what the fuck has that got to do with sex!

Admittedly, we all talked about sex a lot when we were younger. Notches on the bedpost were a status symbol, proof that we were experienced even if we weren't, evidence that we weren't one of the undesirable virgins. Sex was fun, new and constantly on everyone's minds. We all remember the countless, funny-at-the-time games of 'Never Have I Ever' which inevitably devolved into sexual tales of woe or conquest. Kings and Queens were crowned via sexual prestige during our late teenage years and early twenties.

However, after the age of around twenty-five, that shit wears off I'm afraid. But you refuse to grow up, stuck in some sex-obsessed time loop.

What you do not realise is that, as you get older, having sex is no longer some mystical, commendable, celebratory thing. We've all had it. Plenty of times. With plenty of people. Most of us know what we like, who we like it with and we're comfortable with it.

We're all a little more clued up. We know that quantity of sexual partners means precisely fuck all when it comes to performance or quality.

Being overly graphic and crass when talking about sex is also no longer normal when you're older. But that doesn't stop you from acting like a poor man's Jay from '*The Inbetweeners*'. Your mates might well have laughed when you were younger because they were trying to fit in and were too insecure and inexperienced to know whether it was weird or not. Everyone was figuring themselves out. But that's finished now, you prat. Most people know themselves well enough by now and are secure enough in their sexuality to not have to laugh at your shit.

You, as a fully-formed adult, inserting the fact that you've recently had sex into every story and conversation, simply to boast that you've had it, only serves to put your insecurity on full display. Why, is anyone's guess.

Maybe you're just bad at sex and want people to assume otherwise. Maybe you want your mates to believe you're getting it on left, right and centre, when in truth you're masturbating like a wanker - pun intended - in your hovel. Or maybe you're actually having *that* much sex, that it's the only thing you could possibly talk about, as you don't have time for anything else.

In any case, no one cares, mate. Boasting about your sexual escapades just makes you seem like a weird, dirty, old git, stuck in that immature stage of trying to impress through sex. Sex is for you to enjoy with whoever you want, providing they consent - no one else needs to know. Maturity is discretion.

Don't get me wrong, sexcapades can still be fun to talk about when older, especially the funniest anecdotes from our past. By all means, feel free to tell a story about your latest hook up. Reminisce all about the standout sexual moments my friend. I'm always up for hearing about you slipping on a loose piece of toilet roll in a Wetherspoons cubicle and breaking your dick, or getting walked in on by a now traumatised mate with a randomer on the train to Slough.

The difference is that these stories are being told for a communal purpose. Whether they're funny, brutal or embarrassing, they are for everyone's benefit. They're not purely a means for bragging and they're not told all the fucking time.

If you don't understand why you still have this need for people to know that you're having sex, that is a question you should be asking yourself sooner rather than later. Only you can answer it. But people are not fucking stupid – you best believe they are already speculating as to why you're so insecure. Girth? Length? Needs Viagra? Too tight? Too dry? Too wet?

– [Pointless] Exercise –

Be brutally honest with yourself. If you're compensating for your unhappiness through sex, work on the reasons why instead of spouting sexual bullshit all day to cover it up. If you just haven't matured past the stage of constant sex on the brain, it's time to fucking grow up. Trust me, you're coming across as a real pillock. Failing that, try counting how many times a day you feel the urge to mention the fact that you're sexually active. Then masturbate all the way to climax that number of times. Think of it as a penance. For a serious sexual chatterbox like you, this should be enough to shut you up – for a few hours at least. Idiot.

Know an idiot who needs to read this chapter?

- Scan the QR code
- Click the link
- Send it their way!

Music

Concert problems

Concerts and gigs are awesome. Seeing your favourite artists singing your favourite songs, being part of a huge, energetic crowd, watching talented musicians churn out amazing melodies, the singer pausing mid-song to let the crowd take over in unison, the whole band coming back out for an encore… what's not to love?

Well, for one, you feel the need to record the whole fucking thing with your phone! Blocking the view and destroying the experience for other concert-goers in the meantime. And for what?!

When you post your concert videos on social media, no one cares. I know you have this desperate desire to show people that you have an interesting life, but trust me, no one gives a shit. Your stories and posts inevitably get swiped away, as fast as people would secretly love to snatch your phone from in front of their faces, throw it on the floor and stamp it to oblivion.

If these videos aren't even for social media, what the fuck *are* they for? Are you really telling me you go back and watch the fifty-seven clips you made at one bloody concert? Maybe so – but once at most, surely? Are they worth messing up the viewing experience of those around you? I can accept a ten-second video that reminds you of the memories you made that night. But anything longer truly is pointless.

It's not just the surrounding attendees that hate this behaviour. The artists themselves have started asking the crowd to put away their phones and live in the moment. Yet you do not flinch. You just don't care. Your selfish need to take worthless videos and document every pissing second is obviously more important to you than the real-time enjoyment of fellow, paying concert-goers.

Another problem at gigs – too much shade thrown at taller people. This is ironic considering they are normally the shade-throwers.

You do realise that it's not a tall person's fault that they're tall, right? There's very little they can do to avoid restricting your view in a packed concert – but that doesn't stop you berating them. One specific incident of height-bashing sticks in my mind – when one prick of a midget screamed at a taller specimen to get out of the way while – get this – they're both in *assigned seating*!? What the fuck do you want the tall person to do? They have nowhere to go! Do you want some kind of maximum height limit enforced at concerts? Instead, how about we put limits on how much of a wanker you can be before you're put on permanent house arrest so no one has to fucking deal with you?

Interestingly, height doesn't bother you so much at festivals, where you plead with tall people to put you on their shoulders – a combination that restricts the view of so many more people, might I add. You're more than happy to suck up to tall people when it might enhance your experience, you selfish twat.

How strange that you think you are more within your rights to have a go at a tall person who is unwittingly restricting your view, than scolding someone for holding a phone right in front of your face. Even though the former can't help it and the latter is a privileged prick.

- [Pointless] Exercise -

Get your bloody phone out of our faces while we're making *real* memories. Try being present and enjoying what's in front of you - not what's on your screen. While we're at it, it's time for you to rethink having a go at tall people at concerts. They have feelings too. If you're not careful, they'll stop helping you retrieve your favourite top-shelf goods at the supermarket. And where would that leave you? A flailing, angry Oompa-Loompa eating Asda's own. Idiot.

Know an idiot who needs to read this chapter?

- Scan the QR code
- Click the link
- Send it their way!

Singing along to every song

Who doesn't enjoy a cheeky sing along from time to time? Most people will recognise a track from its initial bars and they're like, "Boom, this is my jam", and they go for it. It's great to see – people loving particular songs and singing them the whole way through. There's nothing wrong with that at all.

However, you go too far. You sing along to every single fucking song that comes on, whether it's one of your favourite songs or not. You treat every day like a fucking karaoke session. I don't get it. It's like you enjoy the sound of your own voice more than the voice of the singers themselves. You must think you have one hell of a voice. But you really, really, really don't, you deluded bastard. There's a reason why singers get paid to sing and you, well, we'd pay you *not* to.

It's a quiet, absent-minded singing you do that drones on for hours on end. But it's not quiet *enough* and it underpins every note. Your voice becomes like a drill to our brains. We end up hoping beyond all hope that you've never heard the next track so we actually get to listen to it without your monotonous drivel.

Alas, it turns out it doesn't even matter if you've heard the next song. You'll still "sing" it whether you know all the lyrics or not. WHYYY!!! You don't know the words, so why the fuck are you singing?! And what are you singing if you don't know the words?! I'll tell you what it is – way too much fucking mumbling of, "fernum dernum mmm mernum bernum sternum dad dum chernum". With a little bit of shitty humming thrown in.

I don't understand why you do it. Are you trying to impress people with your lyrical knowledge? Well, I've got news for you, mate. This isn't the way. We all *know* when you don't know the lyrics. It's pretty fucking obvious with all those non-words coming out of your mouth.

You need to bear in mind that, sometimes, other people just want to listen to the track. No one will be disappointed if you don't sing along. People rarely put on their favourite tracks just so they can listen to you butchering them.

- [Pointless] Exercise -

I recognise some people might know some of the lyrics to lots and lots of songs. But no one can know every single word to every single song. It's impossible. So, if you really can't stop yourself from singing along, instead of ruining every tune using words that don't exist, how about you only sing along to the bits you bloody know? At least then we get some well-deserved respite from your incessant, awful, mumbling voice. And if people raise the volume of the music while you're singing along, it's rarely because they want you to sing louder. It's more than likely a hint that your singing needs drowning out. Please take the fucking hint. Idiot.

Know an idiot who needs to read this chapter?

- Scan the QR code
- Click the link
- Send it their way!

Changing someone's music

When you're in someone's car or at their house party, you should *never* change the music. It's *their* car, *their* house. You can ask, sure. But you should never take it upon yourself. Doing so shows a total lack of respect and a distinct lack of manners.

Who the fuck do you think you are? This isn't some shitty silent disco, where only *your* ears are affected. What gives you the right to change the music to cater to your own tastes when it means you're changing it for everyone in the vicinity?

I understand your frustration. You're not enjoying the tunes. You think your music taste is superior and believe you'd do a better job as DJ.

And you may well have a better understanding of what people want to hear. But that's completely irrelevant. At the end of the day, you're being given a lift, or you're at your mate's house party that they're kindly hosting. You do *not* just go and change their music on a whim. And if you ask and they say no, you accept it.

Changing someone's music without permission is bad enough when you change it to something that people actually like. It's so much worse when you're a prat who can't read a crowd. Turning off a Motown epic to put on the most obscure, shitty, indie song or worse yet, death metal, is enough to completely destroy a party. All because you're a selfish wanker with no boundaries.

Music tastes vary, you muppet!!! Music at a party needs to find a middle ground acceptable to the masses. If you don't like what you're hearing, fucking leave or get out of the car and walk home.

Listen. Even if you think everyone is hating the music, even if you have the perfect bangers in mind for the crowd, do not change the music. You could be wrong and you haven't asked the permission of the person whose car or house you're in. Make no mistake, if you change the music without asking in *my* house, you're getting thrown out. Do it in my car, you're walking home on the hard shoulder.

- [Pointless] Exercise -

Next time you're at a party and want to change the music - don't take it upon yourself. Humble yourself and ask your mate if you can. If they say no, fucking accept it. If they wanted you to DJ, they would have asked you beforehand. And if you ever feel a desire to switch genres to indie or death metal at a party, piss off home and rethink your life choices. Idiot.

Know an idiot who needs to read this chapter?

- Scan the QR code
- Click the link
- Send it their way!

Not letting songs finish

Why can't you fucking let a song play the whole way through?!!

We'll be chilling with mates, tunes on, chatting about music. You'll say you've got a new banger. We'll say whack it on. And it's actually good! The rest of us are enjoying it. Then out of fucking nowhere, you'll stop it after the first chorus to put on another song. We all complain and ask you to let it finish. But then you do it again. And again. And again.

WHY???

You act like a radio station DJ in disguise. But unlike radio DJs, you don't need to cut songs short just so you have time to run some shitty ads. You're chilling with mates, not playing music to strangers whose attention you are trying to monetise while asking them to compare insurance at the behest of meerkats and fat opera singers. Radio is dead for a reason, you twat!

It's even worse when everyone recognises the song you've put on and we know the lyrics. Mid-second verse, we're all belting it out, spitting rhymes all over the gaff – then you cut us off!! People have killed for less…

It's like you're in some kind of rush to get through all your recent discoveries, so you can prove your credentials as a music taste-maker. But how are you supposed to prove these so-called credentials, if you don't let us listen to the whole thing?! Relax, mate!!

I get that, from time to time, a song being played will remind you of another banger, and you want to put it on before you forget. But that's not a good enough excuse to prevent the current tune from doing its thing. You are not a goldfish or child with a limited attention span. Remember the song you want to play and put it on when the previous one has finished – it's not that fucking difficult.

- [Pointless] Exercise -

Next time you're listening to music with mates, be patient. You're not an uncontrollably excitable dog with no self-control. So let the bloody song play to the end. You might even notice something new or have a revelation about a certain lyric. Failing this, go back to listening to the radio for a couple of days. I guarantee you'll start tearing your hair out at the DJs' seeming inability to play a song in its entirety. Hopefully, you'll realise the process that you have been acting just like a shit, radio station DJ. If that doesn't calm that trigger finger of yours, your stereo privileges will have to be revoked. Idiot.

Know an idiot who needs to read this chapter?

- Scan the QR code
- Click the link
- Send it their way!

Playing music out loud in public

There are two instances of this that I want to discuss with you, you prick.

The first is when you play music out loud on public transport, mainly trains or buses. Why can't you understand that other people around you have not asked to listen to your shit? We aren't attending one of your dead house parties. We have absolutely no obligation to listen to your music or whatever else you're listening to. So what gives you the right to force it upon us?

One retort I have received countless times after raising this exact point with wankers like you is, "Why don't you just put on earphones??". Hold on a minute, mate. You're aware of their existence? How about *you* put on *your* fucking earphones then?!! Who the fuck do you think you are?! You're the one who's decided to listen to something out loud, you twathead. And why would you assume other people have earphones on their person if they're not currently listening to anything? The onus is not on everyone else to mitigate your actions, it's on you to ensure that whatever you're doing doesn't affect other people.

The second instance is when you ride by on a bicycle with the equivalent of a boombox on your back, blaring out music. Admittedly not as painful as public transport, because we only have to listen to your shit momentarily as you ride past. But in this case, it's the sheer arrogance of what you're doing.

It's like you think you're doing the world a favour. Maybe you believe you're admirably spreading a little joy. Yes, some will bang their heads for the five seconds it takes for you to pass by. But everyone has different tastes in music, mate. For every one pedestrian who enjoys it, there are a hundred who just want you to shut the fuck up so they can hear their own playlist, podcast or audiobook. I'd love to see you blasting the same music while *walking* through a dodgy estate instead of cycling – you wouldn't have the bottle.

– [Pointless] Exercise –

There's not much more I can say other than don't play your music out loud in public. You don't need to nowadays, we have these things called earphones now. Some people even have headphones! If you can afford the music-playing device, you can afford the tech that keeps your music to yourself. You can even get some shit ones in Poundland – they only cost a pound would you believe! If you absolutely cannot stop being an out-loud music-playing prick, then please, play some music I like. Put some funk & soul on or something. At the very least I can then bob my head along while I go about hating your guts. Idiot.

Know an idiot who needs to read this chapter?

- Scan the QR code
- Click the link
- Send it their way!

Ripped jeans

The truth is, they are and look fucking stupid. It's not just because it's one of those many trends that should be reserved solely for young people. It doesn't even matter whether we're fat, thin, ugly, or good-looking. They look completely ridiculous on everyone.

I get that you want to be at the cutting edge - shit pun intended - of fashion and everyone is entitled to their opinion. I mean, let's face it, we've all followed a fashion trend, or attempted to, at some point in our lives. But fuck me, ripped jeans? Jeans that have been ripped, on purpose?!

I can just about accept that a few little slits might give off a kind of edgy, cool vibe - to an extent. But when you have massive holes in your jeans and bits hanging off all over the place, it just looks like your legs got kidnapped and they tried their best to escape several times through a dense forest of nothing but holly, cacti and thorns. It doesn't look vintage or authentic, as is claimed by your favourite wanky fashion brands on the regular. It just looks like you simply need a new pair of jeans. Which is weird, because you just fucking bought some!

It was slightly more acceptable in the 1970s, as a rebellious, anti-establishment, punk and grunge outburst against society. For those who wore them around this time, it wasn't about fashion; they wore the jeans to exhaustion, despite damage all over the place, instead of buying new pairs, as a fat, middle finger to capitalism and consumerism. But now, there is no political statement being made. Currently, it's just sheep like you, following a flock of other sheep, who wear these stupid fucking ripped jeans because they mistakenly think it looks good.

The impracticality of these jeans is just too much to ignore. There's a good bloody reason for wearing long-legged garments. They protect us from things like getting stung by nettles, cold weather and the most inexcusable, oddly-shaped cancer-inducing sunburn known to man. Nevertheless, you still make the incredible decision to wear ripped jeans, which are essentially long-legged garments that offer none of the long-legged garment benefits. What is the fucking point?!

In addition, denim is a tough material, meaning clothes made from it should last longer. However, putting rips in them irrevocably reduces their durability and lifetime value, meaning they'll be going in the bloody bin where they belong sooner or later anyway! This waste is not great for the environment either, as they then go to landfill much quicker and you will need to buy new ripped jeans much sooner, then they will go to landfill before the year is out and you will need to buy yet more ripped jeans… you get the vicious, cyclical picture.

Staying on the theme of environmental impact, a crazy amount of fresh water is required to feed the gigantic washing machines that create the stonewashed look you so crave. Wasted, probably non-renewable, energy is needed to operate the lasers that burn through the denim and create the rips. And there is even an impact on health – grossly underpaid workers, who create the rip patterns by hand for the most expensive brands, contracting silicosis through sandblasting. But hey, it's all in the name of fashion, so it's ok, right? Wrong.

While we're at it, let's discuss the financial aspect. Let's suppose ripped jeans and normal jeans cost exactly the same. You would be getting less fabric for your money, which is already a bad enough deal. But in reality, as a result of the long manufacturing process involved in making the bloody holes, you actually end up paying significantly more for the ripped jeans. So you're paying *more* for *less*! If you're that desperate to look like a twat, at least pretend to be frugal by buying a normal pair and making the pointless holes yourself.

Finally, has it never occurred to you that you are paying to look like you have no money or are homeless? When did it become fashionable to fork out money to wear butchered clothes that imitate what poorer people are *forced* to wear? Furthermore, before jeans exploded in popularity, workers typically wore them because they incorporated tough fabric and were durable, meaning they were deemed more suitable to a working environment and workers didn't have to buy new pairs all the time. Yet *you* are voluntarily buying damaged clothes, that won't last very long, all because of a fucking fashion trend. Don't you see the irony, you prat?

- [Pointless] Exercise -

Wear ripped jeans the next time you leave your house. Go about your day. Get yourself home safely. Take them off. Throw them in the bin. Go to your wardrobe and drawers. Take out all your remaining ripped jeans. Throw them in the bin. Pick up the bin. Put it in your car. Drive to the dump. Chuck the bin in the biggest skip you can find. Idiot.

Know an idiot who needs to read this chapter?

- Scan the QR code
- Click the link
- Send it their way!

Sagging trousers

Why do you wear your trousers down by your arsehole? Surely you're not *that* proud of your underwear? I get that you've seen celebrities, pop stars and other "cool" people doing it, and you want to copy them like the sheep you are. I know that sometimes you even do it because you think it makes you look like a gangster.

But here's the simple truth - you look like a right twat. I mean, walking around with an attitude, as if you own the place, while your arse is hanging out, just doesn't compute… mainly because your arse is hanging out, you fucking weirdo. And, as any truly tough person will testify, trying to look hard is the most blatant sign that you're not. If you're hard, you don't feel the need to broadcast it. You just know it.

Sagging trousers are also so much worse than just a stupid look. I bet you have no idea where they originate from.

The history of sagging trousers is grim, morbid and has two aspects.

First, at one point in time, too many prisoners in the United States were committing suicide. So a ban was put in place, prohibiting the use of belts and shoestrings. Inevitably, with nothing to hold them up, prisoners' trousers started to fall down.

Second, prisoners started using this look as a universal sign that they are sexually available to other prisoners. Probably in order to get in with a tough crowd and make prison less painful - at least on the face.

So well done you, for glorifying suicide and sexual exploitation.

One other issue - sagging trousers is linked with erectile dysfunction and hip & back problems. So the question is, do you want to appear cool and tough to all the other clueless, sexually exploitable wankers, or do you want a working penis and not to walk like an eighty-year-old before your time? The choice is yours.

- [Pointless] Exercise -

Wear a belt. And stop peacocking your flat arse. You're not in prison with a need to survive. Idiot.

Know an idiot who needs to read this chapter?

- Scan the QR code
- Click the link
- Send it their way!

Jack-ups, budgies, ankle swingers

No matter what you call them, they should never, ever have ever been a thing.

Jack-ups, for those who are blissfully unaware, are basically trousers that are purposefully too short to show off your ankles. I thought three-quarter length shorts were stupid, but, fuck me, here we are.

I'm sure most of our first memories of jack-ups are from school. When a kid had outgrown their trousers and everyone could see their legs… that kid would never live it down. The bullying was totally unwarranted, as the jack-ups existed mainly because the kid couldn't afford new trousers. It did look bloody stupid though.

But then, for some ungodly reason, it became a fashion trend. To show off your ankles, even though you're wearing trousers. WHY?! As an adult, presumably with your own income, you can buy yourself new trousers - you have that freedom! Why would you use this freedom, that your forefathers and foremothers fought so hard for, to voluntarily look like you've outgrown your trousers when you stopped growing many years ago?

What's the appeal? What are you trying to achieve? You love to assure us there is a thought process and meaning behind every fashion trend - so what the hell is it in this case? Traditionally, we wear shorts when it's hot and trousers when it's less so, or when we're going to work because no colleague should ever have to see those knobbly knees. But jack-ups are a sort of hybrid, pointless invention that does nothing for you!! They're not short enough to help with the heat! They're not long enough to keep you warm! By wearing them, you're essentially admitting to simply following a brainless fashion trend, like the thicko you are.

What's also ridiculous, is that the cost of a normal length pair of trousers is exactly the same, if not less than jack-ups. You are paying more for less, just so you can look like a bigger knobhead.

The other unforeseen issue with jack-ups is that it forces the people around you to pay more attention to your sock situation. It's something we never asked to give a shit about – but you've forced our hand. So, if you absolutely *have* to wear jacked-up trousers, at least wear some decent fucking socks with them. If you're going to go colourful, make sure it matches your personality will ya! There's nothing more jarring than bright, radioactive socks on the feet of a dull bastard like you. And don't be a posh prick who, for some reason, refuses to even wear socks. We don't want or need, the sweaty state of your insoles on our minds.

Look, I am by no means a fashion guru, but surely we can all universally agree that jack-ups look fucking stupid. Make a decision: shorts, trousers or nude, and stick with it.

– [Pointless] Exercise –

Go get your jack-ups. Cut them to shorts-length. Or better still, throw them in the bin. You're an adult, not a child. Stop trying so desperately, and actually dispensing with money, to look like someone who's outgrown their clothes. Idiot.

Know an idiot who needs to read this chapter?

- Scan the QR code
- Click the link
- Send it their way!

Sunglasses indoors

I mean, let's face it. You have to be a special kind of twat to want to wear sunglasses indoors.

Let's rewind a little.

I have nothing against sunglasses in particular. In fact, I find them very useful. They're great for getting some shut-eye while pretending to listen to our current partner's shit stories. They're great for driving on a sunny day when our car's visors have been destroyed by our ex. And of course, they're absolutely perfect for discreetly checking out our next ex.

But, at the end of the day, the main, practical purpose of sunglasses is to protect our eyes from the sun. And where is the sun? That's right - outside.

Which begs the question, unless you get migraines, are sensitive to light, have some kind of eye deformity or are blind, why would anyone wear sunglasses indoors? This is where you, the special kind of twat, come in.

You think it makes you look good, don't you? Cool, even. But fuck knows why. Maybe you've seen celebrities do it, so you automatically think it must be cool. Maybe it's nothing other than you trying to be "rebellious", by using an object for something other than its practical purpose. Whoop-de-fucking-do.

You also appear to be under the misguided impression that it makes you look hard. And admittedly, someone walking into a room with sunglasses on and no one being able to see their eyes - I can see why you think people might find that a little threatening. But just consider this for a second. It's not just the sunglasses that make for an imposing figure - it's the muscles, height and demeanour. Some stick-thin dweeb like you is never going to scare anyone by walking into a room with sunglasses on, I don't care how expensive your fucking Ray-Bans are!

I'm sure there are plenty of other similarly wanky explanations for why you wear sunglasses indoors. But whatever they are, there is one thing I'd wager they all have in common. They're all fucking stupid. Much like you.

- [Pointless] Exercise -

The next time you step inside and consider keeping your sunglasses on, remember that you are not a rapper with a brand to protect, you are not a shit poker player with a twitchy eye for a tell, nor are you an inexplicably idolised A-lister. Then take the fucking things off and put them in your bloody pocket. Idiot.

Know an idiot who needs to read this chapter?

- Scan the QR code
- Click the link
- Send it their way!

Plugs & droopy earlobes

To parody the song, "These plugs ain't made for sleeping..." As mental as it sounds, the plugs I'm talking about exist to literally plug a hole in an earlobe. A hole, might I add, that has been created *on purpose* by stretching a piercing over time. Some of these plugs even allow people to actually see through the ear, something known as a 'flesh tunnel'. I mean, surely that phrase itself should be a serious fucking red flag!!

Yet, weirdos like you genuinely believe that having huge holes in your ears and plugging them up looks good. You'll tell us they serve as an artistic accessory to give off a certain edgy or spiritual vibe. You'll tell us it's all about your individual style, your personal aesthetic preference and trying to stand out - although surely there are better methods? Personally, I'd lay money that you are simply copying other muppets or imitating a shit Linkin Park music video.

However, these plugs are not a modern phenomenon. Earlobe stretching has been going on for thousands of years for various reasons. It has been used by various groups to indicate that people belong to a certain group or tribe, as a right of passage and even to infer special qualities, such as nobility, social status, wisdom and having a connection with the Gods.

Nevertheless, if someone from the present lived under a rock, and knew nothing other than the ancient history of earlobe stretching and plug use, they could be forgiven for thinking that evolution and the advent of civilisation had surely eradicated such stupidity from the modern world. Sadly not...

Tribal use of plugs remains strong. Especially among the growing tribe of prats like you who think it's clever to follow fashion trends for no bloody reason, other than wanting to appear trendy. Regardless of the permanent earlobe stretching and irreparable damage it causes.

Despite what a numpty plug-lover like you would say, the scientific consensus is that earlobes will never recover once stretched past six millimetres. The boom in earlobe stretching in recent times has even resulted in the rise of niche, expensive earlobe repair surgery, to return decimated ears to their original state. It can't be that fucking awesome if you keep trying to reverse the effects!!

Even after surgery, there will be scars – and there are no guarantees that your earlobes will ever regain the strength to hold an earring, let alone another plug. You're also at high risk of infection, skin blowouts where the excess pressure causes flesh to be squeezed from the inside of the earlobe to the outside and smelling like the Grim Reaper. Unfortunately, the buildup of dead skin cells inside your ear is inevitable, mate.

Furthermore, to mitigate the damage from plugs, you need the proper equipment. Alcohol to sterilise the earlobe, lubricant, tapers and different size plugs as you graduate in gauge size. You also need to massage and clean the area twice a day.

All the above, just to look like a prick, whose weird, long ears are their personality…

One other repercussion of droopy, plugged-up, smelly earlobes is a distinct lack of job opportunities. You might call this discrimination. After all, a person with droopy, plugged-up, smelly earlobes is just as capable of completing simple tasks as someone with normal ears. Agreed – but I'm not so sure that this discrimination argument takes into account the bigger picture.

If you decide to mutilate your body in some way that isn't objectively considered an improvement, you have to be prepared to live with the consequences. What if your job would involve having to go and meet prospective clients? Your prospective boss has to weigh the company's revenue and the security of their other employees' salaries, against the risk that those clients might be repulsed by your earlobes and choose to work with a rival firm instead. What if people were to steer clear of the café you want to work at because seeing your ears might make them so nauseated, they are unable to keep down their carrot cake and coffee? I would say that there are also definitely some professions where stretched earlobes and plugs are an absolute no-no. Take teaching for example. Teachers are supposed to be role models to their impressionable students. Children should probably not be exposed early on to the idea, from their role models, that mutilating their body, in ways that are more or less permanent, is ok.

At the end of the day, they're your ears. Do what you want with them. But don't come crying to me when you end up with no job and looking like Dumbo the elephant or a less-intelligent basset hound. Less-intelligent, because you actually chose those ears.

- [Pointless] Exercise -

If your earlobe plug size has already gone past the six-millimetre mark, it's probably already too late for you. You're never going to be normal again. How about you pitch schools on paying you to go in and show the kids your droopy earlobes as a warning against the stupidity of plugs? Or work as a personal human umbrella stand, who follows their employer wherever they go in case it rains? Just a couple of ideas that might offset your lack of employment opportunities and contribute to your upcoming surgery costs. Idiot.

Know an idiot who needs to read this chapter?

- Scan the QR code
- Click the link
- Send it their way!

Book club questions

1. On a scale of 1–10, how strong is your faith in humanity after reading?
2. Which of these idiotic rants riles you the most?
3. Be honest! Which of these idiotic things do you do?
4. What idiotic rants are missing from this book?
5. Were there any idiotic rants you fundamentally disagreed with? Why?
6. Which idiotic exercises are you genuinely going to attempt?
7. What thoughts and lessons did you take away from '127 Reasons Why You Are An Idiot'?
8. Which idiot from your personal life comes to mind most frequently as you read? Would you give them this book to read?
9. While reading, were there any specific points at which you felt like screaming, "YEEEEEESSS! EX-ACTLY!"?
10. While reading, were there any specific points at which you thought, "Oh fuck, that's me…"?
11. Do you personally feel that manners and common courtesy are being gradually disregarded in so-ciety? Did this book change your mind?
12. If you could ask Yann anything, what would it be?

13. If you could give the book a new title, what would it be?

14. Did you agree with the introduction?

15. Will this book change the way you act around other people?

Email your answers to Yann at yann@yannsomou.com or hit him up on Twitter @YannSomou!

Acknowledgements

Again, from the bottom of my heart, I would like to thank each and every one of you who has ever done anything idiotic. Without you, this book would not have been possible; there would be no idiots in the world and therefore no one who I could call out for being stupid.

Thank you to Sam and Niall for reading various drafts and helping edit out the shit bits. Thanks to them, some chapters will never see the light of day - this is a good thing. However, if you do find any spelling or grammar mistakes within these pages, I refer you to them.

And finally, thank you to all my friends and family for not berating me as I constantly point out, "There's a chapter for that, you know". Unfortunately, this is now a habit that might never die.

Author Note

As you can probably tell, there's a tincy bit of anger in this book. This is due in no small part to conceiving the idea and starting to write during the shittiest of years, 2020, while COVID-19 kept us all locked up in our homes.

I therefore consider this finished product a homage - or a fuck you - to one of the worst periods in our collective living memory.

And for all the ranting, jokes and swearing, I'm not a complete wanker: thank you so much for reading - it means a lot.

As you may or may not know, reviews are the lifeblood of any book - especially those sold online. If you enjoyed it, despite repeatedly being called an idiot, it would be amazing if you could leave a review on whichever platform you spent your hard-earned money.

– Yann

Scan below to Review

Printed in Great Britain
by Amazon

34539129R00205